SWEET SUFFERING
WOMAN AS VICTIM

SWEET SUFFERING
WOMAN AS VICTIM

NATALIE SHAINESS, M.D.

THE BOBBS-MERRILL COMPANY, INC.
Indianapolis/New York

For permission to quote from *Mrs. Warren's Profession*, *Candida*, and *Saint Joan*, acknowledgment is made to The Society of Authors on behalf of the Bernard Shaw Estate.

"Scarlet Ribbons," copyright © 1949 by Mills Music, Inc. Copyright renewed. Used with permission. All Rights Reserved.

Patient names and identities have been disguised in the case histories presented in this book.

Published by The Bobbs-Merrill Co., Inc.
Indianapolis/New York
Manufactured in the United States of America
First Printing
Designed by Jacques Chazaud

Library of Congress Cataloging in Publication Data

Shainess, Natalie.
  Sweet suffering.

  1. Masochism. 2. Women—Mental health. I. Title.
RC553.M36S53 1984   616.85'835   83-18762
ISBN 0-672-52766-9

This book is dedicated to two of my teachers—outstanding psychiatrists and psychoanalysts—who shaped my life's efforts. Though I did not appreciate their legacy to me immediately, as time went on I came to realize their great value and skill.

To Frieda Fromm-Reichmann, I am indebted for her relentless search for truth, wherever it might be found. Known for her work with schizophrenics, she also understood family dynamics and the nuances of interaction between husband and wife. Her sensitivity was profound.

I am particularly indebted to Harry Stack Sullivan for his recognition of hypocrisy at the social level. He was ever on the alert for expressions of anxiety in communication, believing, in contrast to standard psychoanalytic approach, that they must be answered not by "interpretations" but with an appropriate response from another person, albeit a professional person.

I want also to acknowledge the contribution of my analyst, Clara Thompson, whose refusal to totally accept Freud's metapsychology of women helped me follow her in exploring the role of culture in shaping the lives of women.

Another Clara was indeed important to me—my mother. A self-educated artist, gifted with a broad understanding of social issues, she exemplified for me the tradition of Henri Matisse, who said, "The artist must be at pains to retain his radical freedom of perception, which is at odds with custom and convention." Daily, in both my office and home, my life is enhanced by her art work.

Finally, I am indebted to my patients, who helped me grow in the experience of our interactions—both professionally and personally.

Contents

SWEET SUFFERING
WOMAN AS VICTIM

1

Setting Up the System of Self-Punishment

Some years ago a patient of mine, during her first analytic session, recounted a fairy tale she had carried with her since childhood, one that seemed to have special significance for her. The tale she told me was this.

Once upon a time there was a handsome prince whose ship was wrecked at sea. Everyone aboard perished except the prince, who was rescued by a little mermaid and taken to safety on an island. When a second ship appeared and carried the prince off to his homeland, the mermaid, who had fallen desperately in love with him, vowed that she would follow and claim him. Seeking advice on how to accomplish this, she traveled through treacherous seas to the lair of the sea witch. "You will come to grief if you attempt this," the witch warned, but seeing that the mermaid would not be deterred, she agreed to grant her her wish. She gave the mermaid a potion to drink that caused her tail to wither and be replaced by legs. The mermaid was now as beautiful as any mortal on earth, but every step she took was agonizingly painful. The mermaid was glad to bear this suffering, however, and set out for the land of her prince. Alas, as she arrived, the prince's marriage to another was already in progress, and the little mermaid, witnessing this, fell into a fatal swoon. Upon her death, the other mermaids lamented that she had not even gained an immortal soul. She could only have possessed that had she won the love of a human.

This story is a nearly perfect parable of masochism, for it expresses the self-punishment, the submission to another, and the sense of suffering as a way of life that lie at the heart of masochistic behavior. The young woman who told it to me identified strongly with the little mermaid for reasons that soon became obvious. Her mother had been pressured into marriage with a man she did not love; the daughter was conceived on a wedding night that her mother experienced as nightmarish. The mother and child's relationship developed into a difficult one: It did not involve any physical cruelty, but the child was very fearful of her mother's power over her. She told me how she had once been punished by being put under the kitchen table—her mother commanding her to remain there until she returned. The mother then went off and did not return for three hours. When she finally came back into the kitchen, apologetic and chagrined by her forgetfulness, the child was still crouched beneath the table. It had not occurred to her, the young woman told me, to come out from under the table as the hours went by. Her absolute submission told me how greatly she feared her mother.

This same mother began too early to try to make a ballet dancer of her daughter. The little girl's still-soft bones responded poorly to the strain, and she was left with a legacy of terrible foot trouble. Certainly this very specific parallel with the little mermaid was one reason the young woman had been so drawn to the fairy tale. But she also responded to it on a metaphorical level. Largely because of the troubled relationship with her mother, every psychological step she took was difficult for her as well.

By telling me the fairy tale, this patient presented her own problem in an imaginative and succinct fashion. But she could have been speaking for countless other women as well, women who, like the mermaid, believe that life and love are hinged on suffering. Descartes' declaration, "I think, therefore I am," made the act of thinking the definitive characteristic of human existence. The masochist, who might say, "I suffer, therefore I am," puts pain in the pivotal position. And it is the masochist herself who perpetuates the pattern of suffering in her life, primarily by processes of communication that alert other people to her submissiveness and her fear of their power over her.

Observing this, many people (including Freud) mistakenly conclude that masochists take pleasure in their suffering. But this is not so. They simply do not know any other way to live. They have not considered and then set aside alternative methods of coping. They do not, as a rule, even realize that there *are* any alternatives. They have developed an all-pervasive defensive style that is based on suffering, and it has become the only way they know how to experience life. They are like the princess in another fairy tale who could feel the pea that lay beneath twenty mattresses: exquisitely sensitive, they are easily wounded. And because they follow the same destructive patterns over and over again, we make the mistake of thinking their pain is pleasurable.

While men also suffer from the masochistic syndrome, it is much more common among women, for reasons I will develop at greater length in Chapter 3. But, briefly, it is because women in our society bear such liabilities as inferior social and economic status, lesser biological strength, and reproductive handicaps that masochism is a special problem for them. In nearly four decades of practice as a psychiatrist and psychoanalyst, I have all too frequently encountered masochism in women and only occasionally in men. Both women and men may have early experiences that dispose them to masochistic behavior, but the cultural elements that continually reinforce masochistic behavior in women are largely absent for men. Women, in this sense, experience a real double whammy. Many emerge from their childhoods with a damaged sense of self. Then the culture in which they live ratifies that distorted image rather than helping them to repair the damage. And the odds are longer for women in the struggle to overcome masochism. To eradicate something as stubborn, compulsive, and destructive as masochism, people need all the help they can get. Our society, in its attitudes and judgments, gives women precious little of that.

One would think, in the wake of the women's movement and its attendant societal changes, that this might not be so today. Certainly women have gained greater freedom to control their reproductive destinies and greater opportunities for more varied kinds of fulfillment. Progress *has* been made. Yet in my practice and in my observations at large, I have noted no corresponding drop in the number of masochistic people I encounter. In fact, in today's atmosphere of greater promise and higher expectation, masochism may be a more destructive problem than ever. For as many women find doors opening, they also find their own masochism pulling the rug out from under them, rendering their new chances useless. And that can make experience bitter indeed.

The emphasis today on assertiveness training is very telling, I think. Why do all these liberated women need to be trained to stand up for themselves? Assertiveness, which is the ability to express honest feelings comfortably, the ability to be direct and straightforward, the ability to exercise personal rights without denying the rights of others and without experiencing undue anxiety and guilt, ought to come naturally. Why is it women must be *taught* these simple human prerogatives?

The reason is that masochism undermines women by eroding their capacity to stand up for themselves. But the assertiveness trainers do not acknowledge, or perhaps even realize, that masochism is what they are dealing with. They have stayed on the surface, teaching women strategies to be employed primarily in their professional lives. They have not addressed the underlying problem that all the tactical expertise in the world will not eliminate (although tactics are very helpful once the underlying problem is understood). Masochistic women suffer from anxieties that make it difficult, if not impossible, for them to translate assertiveness strategies into effective behavior in their personal lives.

Assertiveness and autonomy go together. But someone who has learned her assertiveness in a course is not necessarily autonomous. She is still basing her actions on those of someone else. She may have no comprehensive understanding of the psychological sources of her behavior. But someone who has addressed her central problem and overcome her masochistic tendencies can achieve true autonomy—operating under her own steam, making her own decisions, feeling a sense of confidence in her own actions as she moves through life essentially unafraid of criticism or attack. Because she is able to stand up for herself appropriately, she no longer feels hate or contempt for herself.

My concept of masochism has two facets: one is the set of feelings the masochist possesses; the other is the process by which she communicates these feelings to others, her masochistic style, if you will, a style that makes life perpetually difficult for her. The masochistic person's feelings, like the rest of her emotional framework, have their roots in early childhood. In Chapter 3 I discuss this in detail, but it is important to note here the common denominator in these experiences: All of them involve abuses of power in the relationship between parent and child, abuses that leave the masochistic person fearful of others, filled with self-doubt, and utterly unable to resist, refuse, offend, or insist on limits. The masochist's feeling of guilt is all-pervasive, her stream of apologies constant, her capacity for self-punishment and self-denial seemingly endless. She does not dare to question, too quickly takes things at face value, too readily accepts someone else's premise. She is dependent upon the wishes, whims, and judgments of any authority figure. If you were to ask a masochist to define her own best interests, she would not know where to begin.

Lucille, a patient of mine, works in a public relations firm and was part of a group assigned to develop a publicity campaign for an important new client. Her proposals were marked by the brilliance characteristic of her work, and they became the focal point of the campaign. In a meeting between the group and the client, Lucille was asked to justify the tactics her firm was proposing, and she did so competently and smoothly until suddenly the client asked a rather technical question about some radio spots that were planned.

"I don't know," Lucille recalled saying. "I'm sorry, but it just never occurred to me that this was important. I guess I wasn't as thorough as I should have been. I'm sorry . . ."

Another member of the group jumped in to take over, and the difficult moment passed. But a few weeks later, when an executive was named for this account, Lucille was passed over and another woman, whose contribution to the project had been far less substantial, was designated. Lucille's response to this was to tell me that while she was unhappy, she was also relieved. "I don't think I have the drive or the personality for an executive position," she said.

Anne is married to a well-known writer and has two teenaged children. She had been a junior editor in a large publishing house, a job she gave up at the time of her marriage, a union marked from the beginning by her husband's short-lived affairs with other women. After each affair, he always returned to Anne, contrite, loving, and passionate in his promises to reform. On a number of other occasions, however, he slapped Anne, once punching her so hard that she had to have a dentist repair the damage to her teeth.

Early in the marriage, Anne had gone to her mother to complain of her husband's infidelities. Her mother had been sympathetic, but she also reminded Anne of her marriage contract—for better or worse—and she cautioned her about separating as that would throw Anne into a world where she had little status and only a limited ability to support herself. Today, Anne herself says, "When the kids were small it didn't seem fair to them to leave and bring them up by myself. Now that so much time has passed, I don't think I'd have a very good chance of making a living or much of a life for myself. Being George's wife does put me in contact with lots of interesting people, and I guess I have to accept the fact that a creative person like him is under tremendous pressure. He has to vent his frustration somewhere. Part of my job as a wife is to help him through difficult times."

Daniel, a big, strong young man who had been an athlete in college, told me of finally getting his own apartment. He bought an old upright piano and arranged to have it moved into his apartment on the third floor. The piano proved to be too large for the elevator and had to be brought up the stairs, which took a turn partway up. The piano movers, two burly men, were being paid well for their work. But as they negotiated the stairs, they began to curse—at the piano, at the steps, and at Daniel himself for living on the third floor—and made plain their expectations of a good tip at the end of the job. Listening to them, Daniel grew anxious, and guilty. When, sweating heavily and still cursing, they finally got the piano into the apartment, he offered them beer and, because they were angry and he was frightened, gave them double the tip he had planned on.

Alice's husband asked her for a divorce after two years of marriage, complaining that he found life with her stifling. Alice, who felt the marriage had been a reasonably happy one, protested, but her husband went ahead with the divorce. Although she felt her contemporaries were shunning her as a divorced woman, Alice forced herself to attend any social occasion she could. Telling me about a large cocktail party, she reported that she stood alone for a long time, apart from the rest of the crowd, unable to initiate an exchange with anyone. Eventually, a young man approached her and stood nearby, apparently trying to think of a way to capture her attention. Alice turned to him and said, "It's difficult when you don't know people at a party like this. I don't know why I bothered to come." The man frowned and walked away, his original interest erased by her sour remark.

Myra is a middle-aged woman, separated from her husband, who one evening accepted a fellow student's offer to drive her home after class at a local college. When they pulled up at her apartment building, Myra said, "I'd ask you in for coffee, but I'm tired and I have to be at work early tomorrow." Her classmate said he would like to come in and would not stay long, but Myra demurred. He then asked if he could come in just to use the bathroom before heading home. Myra hesitated but decided she was obliged at least to extend him that courtesy. After using the bathroom, he demanded a kiss from her and, when she resisted, threw her down and raped her. She called me in the middle of the night, crying hysterically, and, although terribly upset, she refused to call the police or visit a hospital, as I urged her to do. As a matter of fact, she had already bathed and removed the evidence of the assault. The man, she said, had told her that since she was separated from her husband, the police would never believe her—and he would deny that it had been rape.

As these examples indicate, masochism can provoke a relatively minor social gaffe or lead to a life-threatening situation. It can erupt in any setting, any time anxiety triggers the masochistic person to respond to a perceived, or inner, threat that has no basis in outer reality.

Anxiety is based on experiences in childhood with significant adults, figures who are now phantoms that insinuate themselves into people we encounter in our adult lives. Masochists constantly respond to the present as if it were happening in the past, participating in a kind of shadow play in which people are not who they seem to be. What was an appropriate response for a child vis-à-vis a threatening parent is inappropriate when it occurs, for instance, between employee and boss, doctor and patient, husband and wife. What may have been necessary, and useful, adaptive behavior for a child can become a terrible liability when it continues in the adult.

The masochist is quick to apologize because she assumes she is always in the wrong. A patient of mine put it this way: "I know I haven't done anything bad, but I am constantly expecting an accusation." Another said: "If anything goes wrong, I immediately think it has to do with me." The masochist chooses self-punishment in the belief that it will ward off a worse fate. She is unable to say no because she desires other people's approval, indeed desperately needs it, and cannot risk offending them. She is fearful of authority, a quality with which she is likely to endow just about anyone: a waiter in a restaurant or a clerk in a store. She has no sense of her own rights, or her own worth, nor any ability to develop her own point of view. For all of these, she is dependent on other people. And in her acceptance of the pain that is generated by these deficits, she is completely passive. She accepts the suffering as her due.

The communication process, the use of self-damaging words, is the key to this system of self-punishment, the mechanism by which the masochist signals her feelings to other people and thus sets in motion a kind of cybernetic feedback that guarantees that the pain will continue. At its simplest level, the masochistic communication, or message, is very often simply saying the wrong thing: "I'm sorry but it just never occurred to me that this was important. I guess I wasn't as thorough as I should have been. I'm sorry." Or, "It's difficult when you don't know people at a party like this. I don't know why I bothered to come."

Several summers ago when I was in Salzburg, Austria, to attend meetings of the World Federation for Mental Health, the organizers of the conference arranged for all of us to attend a Mozart concert in the contemporary Festival Concert Hall. During the intermission, as I walked around the auditorium, admiring the hall's design, I found myself standing next to a young woman who was by herself.

"I'm holding up the wall," she said, looking at me.

"I beg your pardon?" I replied, uncertain that I had heard her correctly.

"I'm holding up the wall," she repeated.

"Oh?" I noted that her manner was as strained as her statement was peculiar. Then I excused myself and moved on.

This was a quintessential masochistic communication. It contained an open declaration of vulnerability and helplessness and a plea for pity: I'm holding up the wall . . . I'm a wallflower . . . I'm embarrassed . . . I'm alone . . . who would want to talk to me? It indicated the young woman's feelings of inverted grandiosity: She felt herself to be the center of negative attention; she felt all eyes were on her, critically witnessing her humiliating aloneness. It was strictly defensive: She advised me of her weakness and sought pity in order to ward off the criticism and contempt she expected. And it was unproductive: Her remark did not engage me; it caused me to walk away and leave her alone again. I did not want to make this a busman's holiday by responding therapeutically, and she had made me certain that I would not enjoy talking with her.

This woman, preoccupied as she was with her inner defenses, had no clear sense of outer reality. If she had, she could have spoken to me about the music, the concert hall, the conference, Salzburg itself, or even Viennese pastries—any number of things that might have drawn me into conversation with her. Instead, she was doomed to act out a self-fulfilling prophecy. She was alone and felt guilty for being so, perceiving her aloneness as a reflection of her low worth. She believed that other people would see it that way also. Out of that belief, and the anticipation of criticism, she rushed to defend herself by offering a statement of her aloneness—I'm holding up the wall—which only served to make it more apparent. Her defense, because of its inappropriateness, made real the very thing she feared. And what if I had been a predatory man with a sixth sense about masochistic women? I might have picked up her self-consciousness about being alone and invited her out after the concert with less than benign motives. The potential damage could have been much worse than simply being alone once more, holding up the wall.

When wolves fight and one recognizes that it is nearing defeat, it signals its submission by baring its throat to the opponent. Often, this gesture of capitulation is victory enough for the winner, and the loser is permitted to slink away. In human exchanges, bowing the head, symbolically offering the jugular for the kill, often does not get one off the hook so easily. The masochist thinks that a declaration of weakness will divert punishment but, in reality, it usually has the opposite effect. The declaration tends to promote victimization rather than prevent it. The more someone communicates fear, guilt, weakness, and helplessness, the worse her situation becomes.

This is how the masochist perpetuates her pain, and that is why I see the communication process as such a critical part of masochism. It is the fuel that feeds behavioral fires. In exchanges with other people, the masochist does not express herself; she tries, rather, to anticipate what will please or placate them. She never asks herself, What do I want to say? She always asks, What do they want to hear? She never asks someone else, What do you have in mind? Instead, she supplies her own answer in advance because she is afraid of what the other person will say. She readily articulates her impotent position: I'm weak . . . I'm not worth much . . . please don't hurt me. But this announcement, the linchpin of her anticipatory defense system, does not protect her. It leads her into further trouble, whether a social slight, a lost promotion, or, the ultimate danger, a lost life. Advertising one's vulnerability is *not* a good defense strategy.

Masochism is kept alive by a process of feedback. A woman who is acting masochistically collects wounds. The more wounds she collects, the lower her self-esteem falls. As her image of herself worsens, and her regard for herself decreases, she behaves more masochistically—and collects more wounds.

All of this I saw in the young woman "holding up the wall" in Salzburg. Perhaps it seems that I have read a great deal into her five simple words. You may think I have asked one remark to bear a great deal of weight. I am reminded, however, of something Ray Birdwhistle, the anthropologist and communications theorist, once said to me, referring to a tribe he had studied. "If you know the Kwakiutl people," he said, "you only have to see one funeral to know it's a Kwakiutl funeral." So it is with the masochistic communication. One short sentence can truly speak volumes to the expert. Just as a naturalist can identify a tree by its bark or by seeing only one of its leaves, so I was able to identify the young woman at the concert.

That experience in Salzburg provided an illuminating moment for me, a moment in which much of my professional thinking of the preceding years crystallized, a moment in which I decided to write this book. I hope that it may provide a similar kind of illumination for its readers. I did not set out to write a self-help book. Masochism is too complex and obstinate to lend itself to easy panaceas and glib general formulas. I wanted, rather, to raise the reader's consciousness about masochism, to make this widespread and devastating phenomenon understood.

You may recognize yourself in the pages that follow. You may, as you read, identify a problem of your own because no woman in our culture can be completely free of masochism. The conditioning that helps to produce it is almost in the air we breathe, and none of us escapes it entirely. But masochism *can* be overcome. In some ways an analogy can be drawn between masochism and color blindness. Just as someone who has grown up color-blind cannot recognize what is red and what is blue and what is green because she has never been able to distinguish and perceive those colors, so the masochist cannot identify nonpainful alternatives to her behavior because she has never experienced them. Early in life she was programmed, in effect, to have access to only a certain portion of the behavior spectrum, that part that would cause her suffering. The rest of the spectrum, the other choices, were effectively blocked from her. But while color blindness is an inherent defect, masochism is not. It is learned behavior that can be altered and, in some instances, eliminated altogether.

2

Are You Masochistic?

Many of us have no trouble analyzing other people's behavior. Someone else's self-destructive tendencies are easy to spot. Reading the first chapter, you may already have identified friends or acquaintances who appear to fit the masochistic mold. But when it comes to self-examination, our clarity often deserts us. As I've said, however, no woman in our culture escapes masochism altogether; societal attitudes guarantee this. Intelligence, education, career standing, social position—none of these can immunize us. And it is vital for us to sharpen our awareness of our own masochism, for certainly awareness is the first step toward freedom from this grave handicap.

The questionnaire that follows is not a test that you will pass or fail. It is designed as an aid to awareness, a means of provoking new perceptions, new knowledge about yourself. Your answers may afford you clues to anxieties and dependencies you have not recognized before. It is never productive to close your eyes to things. Freud noted that people suffer from repression, that they expel from their consciousness those feelings, ideas, memories that are painful or disagreeable to them. The goal of psychoanalysis, of course, is to undo that repression, to make conscious that which is unconscious. "Know thyself" is a dictum that goes hand in hand with any sort of growth or enlightenment.

QUESTIONNAIRE

1.   If someone bumps into you on the street, do you find yourself apologizing?

2.   If you drop something, do you find yourself saying "I'm sorry" even though there is no one to hear you?

3.   Do you find yourself saying "thank you" frequently, even unnecessarily?

4.   Do you go into lengthy explanations for being as little as five minutes late?

5.   When playing tennis, do you say "I'm sorry" after every flubbed ball?

6.   In an important discussion or argument, do you back down readily?

7.   Do you tend to postpone asking for things that are important to you until it is too late?

8.   At school or work, do you usually let others go through the door first?

9.   In a restaurant, are you afraid to ask for a glass of water because it might annoy or trouble the waiter?

10.   Do you usually choose the cheapest dish on a menu rather than the one you would like to have even though you can afford the latter?

11.   Are you afraid to send back a dish that has something wrong with it or is cold?

12.   Do you overtip, not to impress other people but for fear of offending the waiter?

13.   Are you meticulous about sending out birthday cards and gifts?

14.   Do you spend an inordinate amount of time buying presents for others and worry that they will not be "right" or good enough?

15.   Are you always lending people money?

16.   Do you shrug off compliments instead of accepting them graciously?

17. In group endeavors, either at work or socially, do you tend to follow someone else's lead?

18. At a large social gathering, do you try to remain inconspicuous?

19. Do people tend to ignore you when you talk?

20. On a date, are you afraid to express your preference about the evening's entertainment or choice of restaurant even though you may be going Dutch?

21. If you want to ask the boss for a raise, are you afraid you will not approach him or her properly or that, when the moment comes, you will not know what to say?

22. Are you afraid to offer an idea you have at work for fear it will be considered foolish?

23. Are you afraid to call someone you don't know on the phone—making a business call, for example, or in applying for a job?

24. Are you afraid to say no when you are asked to perform an unpleasant job that it is inappropriate for you to do?

25. Do you have difficulty talking to the landlord, or insisting that the doctor tell you what is wrong so that you understand it, or reporting an accident to the police?

26. If you have an argument with your boyfriend or husband, do you prefer to let it go instead of later discussing the cause and trying to reach some understanding or agreement?

27. If your husband or lover wants sex and you don't, do you give in rather than "make a fuss" over it?

28. Are you afraid to initiate sex with your husband or lover?

29. Do you fantasize being tied up, raped, or in some way overwhelmed in order to be more sexually responsive?

30. During sex, have you ever felt more aroused when you have accidentally been hurt, or have you ever arranged to be hurt, even in a small way?

31. Are you afraid to end an unhappy, destructive relationship because you can't face being alone or fear you will never have anyone else?

32. When your children have been naughty, do you tell them to wait until their father comes home rather than mete out punishment or correction yourself?

33. Do you feel your children are not respectful of you?

34. Are you very sensitive to pain?

35. Have you had more than your share of accidents or broken bones for someone your age?

36. Do you anticipate situations in which you will be hurt, emotionally or physically?

37. Do you imagine or daydream about situations in which you gain something by being injured?

38. Do you tend to have "accidents" when you're upset or angry—breaking dishes or dropping things, tripping or falling?

39. Do you enjoy "a good cry" at tear-jerking movies?

40. Do things always seem to go wrong for you?

41. If you were on a dark, deserted street, would you feel obliged to stop and answer a man who (a) asked for directions, (b) asked for a match, (c) asked for a quarter?

42. In your dreams do you find yourself (a) falling into black holes, (b) paralyzed and unable to walk, (c) unable to scream for help, (d) pursued by cops or robbers, (e) nude?

43. As a child were you very much afraid of one or both your parents?

44. Do you think you're excessively apologetic?

If you answered yes to fifteen of the preceding questions, it is likely that you are somewhat masochistic. If you gave affirmative answers to substantially more than fifteen questions, you are likely to be seriously masochistic. Later in the book I will discuss the sort of help you might seek.

The questionnaire makes obvious the primary symptoms of masochistic behavior: desire for approval, fear of offending, self-doubt, fear of authority, fear of abandonment, feelings of humiliation and guilt, self-punishment, nightmares of helpless-

ness and flight, and a sense of being the center of critical attention. These are the forces that manifest themselves in the
masochistic woman and shape the way she communicates with
the world.

The questionnaire also, I think, prompts in women another
set of questions: Why am I always apologizing? Why am I impelled to do things that hurt me? Why do I feel guilty about little
nothings? Why is the boss always right, especially when the boss is
a man? Why do I defer so often to my husband or lover? Why
must I go into lengthy explanations for even minor matters? Why
do I follow orders abjectly? Why can't I say no?

Answers to these questions can only be found by exploring the
roots of masochism—in the pysche, in history, and in our
present-day culture.

3

The Roots of Masochism

At one time masochism was considered a purely sexual phenomenon. Richard von Krafft-Ebing coined the word to describe a syndrome he found in the work of Leopold von Sacher-Masoch, a nineteenth-century German writer whose tales, based upon his own life, were replete with men desiring to be sexually punished. Masochism, wrote Krafft-Ebing, was a state in which "the sexual instinct is directed to ideas of subjugation and abuse by the opposite sex." Today masochism is recognized as a much more complex constellation of tendencies than that narrow definition implies. At this point it might be helpful to review some of the psychiatric thinking about it from Freud onward.

Some of Freud's basic observations about masochism were sound. He recognized that it was not a purely sexual disorder and called it "moral masochism" since it related to problems of the superego and to guilt. He also correctly concluded that maintenance of suffering was of crucial importance. "The true masochist," he wrote, "always holds out his cheek wherever he sees a chance of receiving a blow." But the rest of Freud's interpretation was skewed by his theories about instinctual behavior and the pleasure principle, by the society in which he lived, and by his general notions about the psychology of women.

Freud believed that since a woman lacked a penis she was born defective, and, when she noted this lack, she conceived of herself as wounded. This feeling of castration was not only physical but psychological. Women were born innately passive, narcissistic, more prone to jealousy than men, and with weaker consciences. To assuage women's "penis envy" and to compensate them for this exceedingly negative view of their sex, Freud equated the production of a child with the acquisition of a penis. In other words, a woman could be restored to psychological balance by motherhood, most especially if she gave birth to male children. Feminine development, in Freud's view, was a pitiable affair. And because all psychoanalytic theory was based on the maturation of libidinal stages, all of which were instinctual, he never took into account the cultural influences that strongly affected women in late Victorian, patriarchal Vienna.

"Anatomy is destiny," Freud said, and in his view masochism was a key part of female destiny. The female suffers first from a sense of being defective. Then she suffers guilt because of her Oedipal wishes in regard to her father. Finally, she suffers pain in the course of fulfilling her reproductive destiny. There could be male masochists, Freud allowed, but he noted that their fantasies invariably placed them in characteristically feminine situations. The pleasure principle—Freud's notion that the avoidance of pain is the overriding aim of human behavior—led him to conclude that the masochist must enjoy the suffering that is her lot

There are inevitable points of pain in a woman's reproductive life. Defloration can be painful; childbirth inevitably produces pain. But to assume, as Freud did, that because women suffer these pains they must also want or need to suffer psychologically, and to enjoy their suffering, is a sad and dangerous inaccuracy. The notion of pleasure-in-pain is one, unfortunately, that still enjoys life, both in the analytic community and outside of it. "She must enjoy it or she wouldn't keep doing it." We have all heard that sort of comment about someone whose behavior is patently self-destructive.

Karen Horney rejected Freud's idea that certain personality traits in women are the result of bio-instinctual substrata. "Psychoanalysis is the creation of a male genius," Horney wrote, "and almost all those who have developed his ideas are men. It is only right and reasonable that they should evolve more easily a masculine psychology and understand more of the development of men than women." Then Horney went on to emphasize the role that cultural conditioning plays in female masochism, an idea that Freud's view of humankind prevented him from seeing. Society views women as weak and helpless, Horney pointed out. It encourages them to be emotionally and economically dependent; it restricts their functioning to the sphere of family life; it blocks their outlets for expansiveness and sexuality. A personality influenced by these factors, Horney noted, will most likely suffer from low self-esteem and feelings of powerlessness, and such a personality may tend to provoke further punishment and suffering, viewing these as her due.

Clara Thompson, Horney's contemporary, was the first to abandon completely the pleasure-in-pain hypothesis and to argue strongly that penis envy is a culturally determined trait not a bio-instinctual one. It is not the penis itself that a girl envies, Thompson pointed out, but the rights and privileges conferred by the culture upon those who have a penis.

Irving Bieber, my contemporary, places problems of power at the center of masochistic behavior. A child's first acquaintance with power occurs in the family, and it is there that a child, who is initially weak and helpless, develops the fear of power in others. There are many ways, aside from physical aggression, that parental power may be abused, Bieber asserts. Parents can exploit children in order to further their own goals, or compete with them or constrict them, and any such behavior can make a child fearful of authority. That fear, says Bieber, is the trigger in any masochistic exchange. He sees masochism as a defense mechanism that seeks to prevent or extinguish hostile aggression in others; its operating principle is that self-inflicted injury can ward off even more dangerous threats.

Psychoanalyst Ruth Jean Eisenbud has summarized the masochistic process in a dramatic outline she calls "The Drama of Masochism (a continuous performance)." First she sets The Scene: The protagonist has an "unsatisfied basic need," thwarted in childhood with a resulting, and traumatic, loss of efficacy. The ego depends for that need's satisfaction on an external and denying force, as in childhood. "There is the atmosphere of a charade," Eisenbud says. Next she outlines The Struggle: The ego strives to win over the denying force, focusing on winning rather than satisfying the need, clinging to the unrealistic hope that its antagonist will agree to lose. Then there is The Defeat: The ego suffers pain at frustration of the need, shame at having lost after trying so hard. It gives up the struggle and lapses into despair. Finally, there is The Outcome: Despair is reduced by secondary gains; a protest of persecution and pain to outside judges of morality supports the unrealistic hope; denial of reality and restoration of unrealistic hope allow the resumption of the struggle. Eisenbud's perceptions should in no way be diminished by the humor with which she presents them, for she catches vividly the debilitating, self-perpetuating nature of masochism.

The psychological origins of masochism, most would agree, are established in the first days of life, and these early roots go very deep. By the end of the child's first year, the groundwork of personality is firmly laid. Other phases of life certainly make contributions to personality, but the early infant experience is particularly significant. A child's first experience of the inequity of power comes in its relationship with its mother, or the primary mothering person. An infant is small and helpless, a mother large and powerful. The way a mother exercises her power through the care of the child will, in large measure, determine her child's psychological health or lack of it. If the mother uses her power for the infant's good, anticipating its need, subordinating her own, the child will probably emerge from its first six to eight months of life with what Erik Erikson called "basic trust," a view of the world and its inhabitants as benevolent and nonthreatening. If the mother, on the other hand, is inattentive or exhibits overconcern or cruelty of any sort, the child can suffer all kinds of personality warp or deflection from what she or he might have been. Masochism is one form of personality warp.

The importance of the early infant experience has been underscored by the work of several professionals. The great American psychiatrist Harry Stack Sullivan recognized what he called a kind of empathy between mother and child, a sort of emotional contagion that is transmitted in large measure during the feeding experience, whether that is breast or bottle. If a mother is feeling happy and satisfied or irritable, anxious, dissatisfied, or angry, the infant will by affected by those states, Sullivan said. A satisfied, nurturing mother will produce an infant who grows up trustful of other human beings and not unduly fearful of the powers of others.

The work of Harry Harlow, familiar perhaps to many readers, made important additions to our ideas about early infancy. Harlow did research with baby monkeys, rigging three different kinds of frames for them to respond to: a hard wire frame that held a bottle; a frame covered with soft material but without a bottle; and a frame that offered both softness and food. He found that the hard frame made the monkeys anxious; even though there was a bottle present, they did not like to feed there. The monkeys placed on the soft frame exhibited greater ease, even though there was no food present. The monkeys placed on the frame that was soft and also held a bottle did best of all. This experiment established that the comfort of holding and softness matter as much to the infant as feeding.

Harlow's findings were reinforced by the work René Spitz did with infants in orphanages. Spitz found that these infants, who were fed but had no human contact, not only lacked emotional responses but actually did not grow properly, were greatly underweight, were much more vulnerable to disease than infants in normal surroundings, and occasionally died of neglect.

Englishman John Bowlby studied children with tuberculosis who were removed from their home settings to a hospital at the discovery of their disease. He found that the rupture of their ties to significant adults caused them to fall into severe depressions.

All of these studies and experiments give us valuable information about the genesis of psychological problems. If the ability to trust is impaired, the sense of powerlessness and vulnerability is exacerbated, and some of the seeds of masochism are sown.

Another Harlow experiment has particular relevance for the mothering experience in our culture today. He found that when he raised female monkeys in isolation, they refused to mate with males. When they were forcibly mated, became pregnant, and eventually became mothers, they were child-abusers. Harlow recorded their reactions on film, and I found watching these films an extremely disturbing experience. The mothers ignore their infants, refuse to carry or nurse them, and fling their pathetic little offspring across the cage, slamming them against the cage walls, sometimes even killing them. Harlow had to step in and rescue the babies or they might all have been killed. The results of this experiment, it seems to me, contain a warning: The more technical our society becomes, the less natural we become as mothers, the greater the potential harm there is for our children to suffer.

Our society, because it places such a low value on mothering, has done little to help women caught in the conflict between motherhood and work. Ideally, a woman should be able to stay home for the first year of her child's life. Attending to her child's welfare should be her first priority. At the end of that time, having given her child a solid foundation of love and attention, she ought to be able to return to a job that has been guaranteed to be available to her. But that sort of arrangement is rare; it is common for mothers today to turn to alternative caretakers very early in their children's lives. It is not that these mothers do not love their children; it is that they feel, rightly, entitled to other satisfactions as well.

Women in our culture are led to understand that mothering is a natural, ongoing, and rewarding process. In nature that is so, but in civilized society the experience is more complex. A woman may not always understand that a conflict exists between her needs and those of her infant's. She often doesn't realize that she may be irritated each time those two sets of needs come into conflict. And she may not recognize that, because she resents the infant's demands, she begins, one way or another, to punish the child. This punishment can take many forms: She may delay attending to the infant's cries, thus putting its needs second to her own; she may get angry; she may scream at or even slap the child. Any of these punishments, from the mildest to the most severe, because they are repetitive, continuing actions, prepares the ground for masochism.

Toward the end of the first year of life, the child, now beginning to be a person, starts to assert her own will. This capacity involves choice: Should the infant please herself or should she please her mother? For example, when being toilet trained, should she wait to have a bowel movement on the potty or give in to the sensation and have a movement at once? Clashes between mother and child now become common as the child becomes increasingly self-assertive or submissive, depending to a great degree on how the mother deals with the imposition of *her* will as she expresses it through discipline.

As a child acquires language, two other developments involving the abuse of power can occur—and both help to produce masochism. The first of these is the so-called double-bind communication between parent and child. In this situation the child, because she is the less powerful, the weaker of the two, feels obligated to listen to and understand the message being given by the parent. The parent, however (usually without realizing it), is giving out a message that is impossible to understand clearly because it contains two contradictory parts: its overt content and its latent, or covert, content. The child knows that if she makes any attempt to question the message, she can get in trouble.

"Come here, dear," a mother says to her child with an edge of hostility in her voice. The appellation "dear" indicates that this is a loving mother who might wish to do something for her child. That is the overt content of the message. The latent content, however, is conveyed by tone of voice— and perhaps even clenched teeth—which suggest that the mother is not loving at the moment; she is angry. If the child does not come immediately but asks, "Why are you angry, Mommy?" the damage may be compounded by a reply like: "You're imagining things. I'm not angry. You know how much I love you." Confusion, hurt, and self-doubt are generated in the child by this sort of exchange. The erosion of a child's ability to trust her own perceptions is one more factor that leads directly to masochism.

The second of the damaging mechanisms that occurs as a child learns to understand language is hypnotic suggestion, a parent's repeated designation of the child as bad or wrong: "You are bad." "You are naughty." "You are stupid." "Why are you such a pest?" "Why can't you be a good girl?" These assertions, heard often enough, become part of the child's image of herself as surely as if they had been hypnotically implanted. This is a child who will grow up with a belief in her own badness, her own wrongness, always feeling guilty about something despite the absence of a realistic reason for guilt.

In addition to establishing specific pieces of the child's self-image, this hypnotic process also intensifies the child's pattern of submission to someone else's will. Just as a wolf attempts to escape death by baring its throat to a conqueror, the masochist offers a gesture of subservience by attempting to anticipate what an authority figure wants and rushing to comply. But this is not effective in the adult human world because the masochist is attempting to second-guess what authority figures will do on the basis of her childhood learning. What was appropriate as a child's response is inappropriate to an adult out in the world.

Another psychological factor important to the development of masochism is an unresolved symbiotic attachment to the mother. It is necessary for a kind of symbiosis to exist between mother and child at the beginning of a child's life. They are not completely separate emotionally, and this furthers attention to the child. But if this attachment continues too long it fosters extreme dependency in the child. An overprotective mother binds her child to her by refusing to allow the child to move away from her. Unable to recognize the separateness of her daughter, unable to acknowledge the boundaries between them, such a mother refuses to let the child develop her own thoughts and perceptions. This symbiotic relationship breeds passivity and a sense of inadequacy in the child, two prime requisites for the development of masochism.

As the child becomes more competent with language, the parents begin to mediate cultural attitudes; they introduce the child to gender roles and gender-role stereotypes. Gender roles, of course, encompass the customary functions each sex is expected to perform, and gender-role stereotypes consist of the narrowest, most rigid interpretations of those roles, of what is "fitting" behavior for a man or a woman. Stereotypes play a large part in making women feel inferior, helpless, and guilty.

A mother may encourage a boy to go out and play while she keeps a girl at home close to her side. She may give her son a toy that involves the use of a hammer and pegs, her daughter a doll. But why shouldn't a girl have fun hammering? Why shouldn't a boy fantasize being a father with a doll? A mother may emphasize how her little girl *looks*, what her little boy *accomplishes*. Fathers do this even more frequently. And so gender lines begin to be drawn. As the child grows and moves into the culture on her own, she will, of course, encounter more and more insistence on gender differences. But her first acquaintance with them comes through her mother and her mother's own feelings about herself as a woman.

There are subtle psychological differences between men and women, and it would be foolish to insist otherwise. Women possess a quality I would call receptivity, which should not be confused with passivity. Passivity implies inaction caused by a feeling of helplessness. Receptivity signals action. It relates to reproduction, and in strictly biological terms it is reflected in a woman's being receptive to a man and in taking in the penis during sexual intercourse. It is also expressed by the uterus taking in the fertilized egg, by the womb surrounding the fetus, and by the provision of support and nurture for the infant. Metaphorically, women's receptivity is represented by a kind of openness in intellectual and work endeavors. Men, on the other hand, possess a penetrating quality. This is, in obvious fashion, reflected in sexual intercourse but also perhaps in such undertakings as the exploration of the world and outer space. But these differences cover only one facet of personality and do not exclude men from being receptive and women from being penetrating. That acknowledgment is a far cry from the rigid notions of sex-appropriate behavior that are perpetuated through gender-role stereotyping.

One last factor must be emphasized when one is considering the early roots of masochism: the favoritism toward boys that still exists in families. This bias immediately puts girls on notice that they are second-class, that they are not worth quite as much as their brothers. I saw a marked expression of this some years ago when I was house-hunting and looked through the home of a couple about to have a child. The mother-to-be was ready to leave for the hospital, her suitcase packed and near the front door. The father-to-be had made his preparations also: On a bench in the entryway lay a tiny baseball glove, a small bat, and a tiny football. The equipment this man had gathered said only one thing: It *had* to be a boy!

Dr. Shirley Press, a pediatrician connected with the University of Miami School of Medicine, reported in an article in the *Journal of the American Medical Association* that she noticed disappointment in the faces of fathers, and even mothers, when they learned their child was a girl. And once she encountered a patient who said that she and her husband wanted a boy, and she did not feel that she could love a girl. When Dr. Press said that if they felt that way, *she* would adopt and love the baby, the patient subsided, probably out of a sense of shame rather than any change in point of view. People often profess that all they want is a healthy baby, but Dr. Press has found that what they really hope for is a healthy *boy*.

There is a story about Freud himself that illustrates the preferential treatment he received as a boy. Freud's sister loved music and began to play the piano, studying and practicing diligently. Unfortunately for her, little Sigi wasn't a music lover and didn't like hearing his sister play. One day his sister arrived home to find that the piano had been removed in her absence. Mrs. Freud, deferring to her son's wishes, had had it taken away.

My treatment of the historical context of masochism must necessarily be rather simplified. But the first point to be made should be that masochism in women has its historical roots in two biological facts: Women bear children and are physically weaker than men. As a result, women have been vulnerable and men have been dominant. The reproductive function dictated from the outset of civilization that women would be tied to the home, that men would serve as the providers. And until very recently, when women gained control of their reproductive function, this was a great handicap for women, keeping them in a position of dependence that fed their powerlessness. This must have been as true for a female member of a nomadic tribe, whose mate foraged and hunted for food, as it is for a contemporary woman with no independent income, whose husband keeps her on an allowance.

Throughout much of history, women have lived as a devalued subgroup. One of the forces that has institutionalized this devaluation, sadly enough, is religion. I have no desire to attack any faith or to advocate that anyone relinquish it. Religion can serve as a great comfort, and if it helps anyone to travel more satisfactorily through this difficult life, I think that is fine. However, it is necessary to recognize that religion has been male-dominated and has promulgated views of women as decidedly inferior to men. The Bible itself, whether one regards it as the law of God or as an important collection of myths about humankind, was written essentially by men and reflects a skewed view of women. In the Bible, women appear in only three roles: as the wifely need-satisfier for a man, as the sufferer, or as the prostitute. That is a fairly narrow range of options. The Scriptures define God as "He," and that single pronoun perpetually reinforces the notion of male dominance. The appellation God the Father makes the male position of father important, while the female role of mother has no deistic significance. One could ask why God is seen as having any sexual attribute at all since He is One, above all living things.

Chapter 3 of the First Epistle of Peter outlines the respective duties of husbands and wives and accurately capsulizes the absolutely discriminating view of the sexes that holds sway throughout the Bible: "Likewise ye wives, *be* in subjection to your own husbands; . . . Likewise, ye husbands, dwell with *them* according to knowledge, giving honor unto the wife, as unto a weaker vessel." "Knowledge," as used here, has a sexual meaning. So wives are commanded to submit to their husbands, while husbands are directed to use their wives sexually at their pleasure and, at the same time, to honor them for their submission and weakness. What a crumb thrown to a trapped bird!

Then there is the covert content of many of the Bible's stories, content often at odds with the tale as stated. The story of Adam and Eve is a perfect example of this. We all know how it goes: Eve seduces Adam by causing him to eat of the fruit of the Tree of Knowledge and, as a result, they are banished forever from Eden, the paradise of innocence. But looking beneath the surface of this tale—just as one would look to decipher the latent meaning of a dream, it is interesting to note that coiled in the Tree of Knowledge, which stands for scxual knowledge, is the serpent who first tempts Eve with the apple before she succumbs and tempts Adam. Could there be a more perfect phallic symbol than the snake? Sexual excitement in the male cannot be concealed, and an erect phallus is a powerful sexual stimulus to the female. Is it possible, therefore, that the true story of the. Temptation is Adam's seduction of Eve, even though it is Eve who is punished forever for this alleged sin?

St. Thomas Aquinas fixed women firmly in their inferior position in his *Articles on the Production of Women*. A female, he stated, was a misbegotten male who must, by virtue of her sin, be under man's power. Subjugation was also dictated by the fact that reason predominates in men. Woman had been created only because man needed a sexual helper to carry out the task of generation. Man could perform other work efficiently on his own, Aquinas said. Then he pounds the last nail in woman's coffin by declaring that God's image exists in every man but in no woman, because woman was made in the image of man, not God.

In his book *Eve's New Rib* Robert Francoeur makes a wonderfully sly, satirical statement about the view of women that has grown out of Christian doctrine. The first human mother was Adam, he suggests because "From Adam's rib came the first baby and men kept her a social infant even when they left their father's house. . . . The child bride remained the emotional, half-human, imperfectly formed, miscarried male whose world would revolve around the men to whom she was meant to cater."

Christianity, of course, is not the only religion to give women exceedingly short shrift. Orthodox Judaism's morning prayer begins with a man giving thanks to God that he is not a woman. A *minyan*, ten male Jews, must be present for services to be conducted properly. Orthodox women are required to bathe in the *mikvah*, a special pool, to cleanse themselves after a menstrual period, before a marriage ceremony, and after bearing a child. Surely many Orthodox Jewish women experience this requirement as a humiliating punishment that makes clear their lack of worth—one that is hardly compensated for by the women's role of lighting candles for the Sabbath.

A patient of mine some years ago recounted the fight that erupted in her Orthodox Jewish family over whether or not she, who had her first menstrual period, should be allowed to go to the cemetery for the burial of her beloved grandfather. A menstruating woman was forbidden by Orthodox law to set foot on hallowed ground. She was finally allowed to go after her grandmother intervened and advocated bending the rules—she believed it would do no harm to the holy ground since there was no chance the blood would touch it.

The Muslim faith consigns women to an even lowlier place. Not only are they, as in Roman Catholicism and Orthodox Judaism, denied high religious office, but their legal and social rights are severely restricted. Their bodies must be covered by the all-encompassing *chador*, and a veil leaves only the eyes exposed. Thus men are shielded from their sexual attractions. A Muslim man can marry as many women as he wishes provided he can support them—and the degree of support is not spelled out. Further, he can divorce a wife simply by saying "I divorce you."

Nor did secular societies do much better by women. Roman law ordered women "to conform themselves entirely to the temper of their husbands, the husbands to rule their wives as necessary and inseparable possessions." To preserve their "property," Roman men were extended the right to beat their wives, to punish them for drinking and/or adultery. The insistence on premarital virginity in women—the only way to maintain certainty about paternity—was another way men sought to protect their property by insuring the pedigree of male children.

In ancient Greece, Sophocles asserted that "a woman's glory is in not departing from her woman's nature, which is to have no fame in the world of men whether for praise or blame." Socrates, at the same time, proposed that women be given equality in intellectual, political, and sexual activities. Is it surprising that

Sophocles lived to an old age, revered for his wisdom, while Socrates killed himself by drinking hemlock after being condemned to death as a corrupting influence?

Custom and code bolstered the tradition of female subjugation in succeeding centuries, too. French men were accustomed to beating their wives for contradicting them or for refusing reasonable commands. And it was men, I am certain, who decided what was reasonable and what was not. Laws governing the chastisement of wives and women began to be codified in the Middle Ages. As the English jurist Sir William Blackstone put it in the eighteenth century, looking back: "The husband also, by the old law might give his wife moderate correction. For as he is to answer for his misbehaviours, the law thought it reasonable to entrust him with this power of restraining her by domestic chastisement." Another Englishman, William Winter, eager that his countrymen be seen in the most favorable light, explained it this way: "It is not that the gentlemen of England are tyrannical and cruel in their treatment of women; but the predominance of John Bull in any question between him and Mrs. Bull is a cardinal doctrine of British law."

The whipping of female vagrants was permitted in England until 1791. Ducking stools, used to douse a "scolding woman" repeatedly in a pond or river, were in use as late as 1809. The brank—a particularly cruel sort of gagging device—was commonly used to punish "a certain sort of woman" during this same period. Not until the middle of the nineteenth century did the English, traditionally so noted for protecting animals against cruelty, begin a campaign against wife-beating. Until then it was an established principle of English common law that a man could beat his wife provided that the stick he used was no thicker than his thumb.

No one saw more clearly or wrote more cogently about the inequities in the treatment of women than the nineteenth-century philosopher John Stuart Mill. "At the present in the more improved countries," Mill pointed out in *On the Subjection of Women*, "the disabilities of women are the only case save one in which laws and institutions take persons at their birth and ordain that they shall never in all their lives be allowed to compete for certain things." This is considered part of the natural order of things, Mill wrote, because "the subjection of women to men being a universal custom, any departure from it quite naturally feels unnatural."

Mill's description of relations between the sexes reads like a blueprint for the development of masochism. "The position of looking up to another," he said, "is unpropitious to sincerity and openness with him. The fear of losing ground in his opinion or in his feeling is so strong that even in an upright character there is an unconscious tendency to show only the best side. How much more true then when one is not only under the authority of the other but has it inculcated on her as a duty to reckon everything else subordinate to his comfort and pleasure and to let him neither see nor feel anything coming from her except what is agreeable to him."

Addressing the question of marriage, Mill wrote that the husband was literally regarded as his wife's sovereign, while the wife was as much her husband's bondservant as a common slave. "She vows a lifelong obedience to him at the altar and is held to it all through her life by law. She can do no act whatever but by his permission." Then Mill noted that "a female slave has in Christian countries an admitted right and is considered under a moral obligation to refuse to her master the last familiarity. Not so the wife. However brutal a tyrant she may be chained to, though she may know that he hates her, though it may be his daily pleasure to torture her, and though she may feel it impossible not to loathe him, he can claim from her and enforce the lowest degradation of the human being, that of being made the instrument of an animal function contrary to her inclination. While she is held in this worst description of slavery as to her own person, what is her position in regard to the children in whom she and her master have a joint interest? They are by law his children. He alone has any legal right over them."

Acceptance of a heritage of brutality to women and wives has played a major formative part in shaping our modern societies. And women, traditionally, have responded to their subjection by accepting it and attempting to fit into the expected passive mold in order to avoid trouble. They have turned their anger inward and adopted a "suffering style"—the essence of masochism.

Originally handicapped by biology, women have been caught in a vicious historical circle that has been extremely difficult to break. In an industrialized world, skill, dexterity, and intelligence were the qualities needed for the production and distribution of goods. Women who shared those attributes equally with men were not given equal opportunities to gain economic or professional power, however, and their reproductive function was used as an excuse. To this day, we still hear women being judged unfit for certain jobs because of the supposed instability engendered by their menstrual cycle. When women did begin to gain a toehold in the professional world, the possibility of pregnancy was used to justify their low pay and to deny them promotions. It was not deemed necessary for women to be as well educated as men because they were considered unsuitable for the higher echelons of work endeavors. And so, because of their inferior education they were judged less qualified than men to hold certain positions. Thus the relentless circular diminution went on, keeping women unequal, keeping them dependent.

I recently came across a splendid example of how such erroneous conclusions have been drawn to women's detriment in Margaret Rossiter's book *Women Scientists in America: Struggles and Strategies Up to 1940*. Rossiter, writing about a book on men of science published in 1910 by James McKean Cattell, notes that Cattell was struck by the low performance of women in the sciences, giving the statistic that only 1.8 percent of scientists ranked in the top thousand were women. Rossiter says, however, that rather than concluding that something in the cultural environment favored the exclusion of women from scientific endeavor, Cattell suggested that women's poor showing indicated that they were genetically inferior. "There does not appear to be any social prejudice against women engaging in scientific work," Cattell wrote, "and it is difficult to avoid the conclusion that there is an innate sexual disqualification."

The greatest liberating force for women in our time has been the development of contraceptive means that free them from ex cessive and unwelcome childbearing. Today anatomy is *not* des- tiny. But attitudes that are centuries old don't just wither and die in a generation or two. History teaches that those who hold power do not surrender it without a struggle, and it seems unlikely that men will willingly relinquish or share the power they have enjoyed for so long. Women will have to wrest it from them, and women, unused to handling power, are fearful of doing that. In our present culture male dominance–female subordination is still maintained in a number of ways, and all of them contribute to masochism.

I noted earlier that gender constriction, which is what we might call the limitations that continue to be placed upon women and their capacity to exercise power, often begins in the home when the mother, and somewhat later the father, starts to trans- mit cultural attitudes and expectations to the children. This is the starting point of the gender stereotyping that will later be experi- enced more directly in the culture at large. The focus of a little girl's upbringing is still, more often than not, on being nice and being pretty rather than on being successful at accomplishing something, the focus for little boys. In this most competitive so- ciety, girls are still acculturated to be timid, docile, and self- effacing, attributes that are poor weapons in competition of any sort. Teachers still tell girls they can be nurses, not doctors. Boys are encouraged to go out and play; girls learn that it is dangerous for them to go very far afield. A girl may get less allowance than her brother, the implication being that it is more appropriate for him to handle larger sums of money, that his need for his own money is greater.

And girls have only to look around them—at television, the movies, very possibly at the relationship between their own parents—to see where the power lies in our society. It is evident that men are the important sex, the ones running things, whether it be the country, the broadcasting station, or the home. Of course there have been some changes in recent years, but still, when one observes a legislative body, a courtroom, a corporate board meeting, the floor of the stock exchange, one sees a sea of male faces. The gender stereotype that emerges from this sort of conditioning is this: A nice girl is one who does what her parents tell her, acquiesces to the needs and wishes of the males around her, and does not compete against men but tries to win them over.

Women who refuse to conform to this stereotype are subjected to certain, almost institutionalized, attacks. A woman who works hard at her career is labeled "aggressive." A man making a similar effort is complimented on his ambition. A woman who doesn't knuckle under to men is called a "ballbreaker" or a "castrating female." A man exhibiting the same behavior is described as admirably tough. A woman with exacting work standards is called a "bitch," while her male equivalent is praised for being meticulous.

When women, despite the odds against them and the resistance they meet every step of the way, do manage to succeed in a traditionally male-dominated area, the praise they receive will probably be couched in male terms. How often have we heard it said of a successful woman that she thinks like a man. I am reminded of the remark a friend of mine heard from an Israeli who was complimenting the Israeli prime minister at the time, Golda Meir. "She's all right," the man said. "She's got balls!" The implication is that only someone endowed with masculine characteristics could achieve such success.

Perhaps nothing does more to keep women in their traditional place, that second-class sphere of lower expectations and lower self-worth, than the image in advertising to which we are constantly exposed. Much has been written and said about this, particularly about those ads that show women as very marginal characters indeed, whose biggest challenge in life may be to get the ring off the collar, the hair out of the drain, or to turn up (in Maidenform bras and bikinis) where the men are. Medical journals, whose drug ads appeal mainly to male doctors and contain extremely distorted and misleading images of women, are culprits as well. But worst of all, I think, particularly in the wake of the women's movement and its struggle to free women of old notions of femininity, are the fashion ads that focus relentlessly on female sexuality.

Clothing has many functions, one of which is to convey impressiveness and power. When part of a person is revealed that would ordinarily be concealed by clothing, that person becomes less impressive. I was struck by this quite forcibly one night at the opera *Alceste* when I realized that the king, though magnificently garbed, suffered a slight loss of grandeur because he was bare-legged. Ads in which women are partly nude make women less impressive. It also seems to me that one is hard pressed these days to find a fashion ad in which a woman's legs are not spread. The message here is a masculine one, to be sure. Another damaging aspect of these ads is that they put women into competition with each other by focusing on sexual desirability as the primary characteristic that women project. This is made to seem women's stock in trade, with intelligence, ambition, talent, and competence nowhere in the picture. As long as the sexual self is stressed, it is difficult for the intellectual self to come forward and receive notice. Women's chances for success in business and the professions are severely undermined when they are assigned to sex-object status.

Then there is the sort of ad typified by the Saks Fifth Avenue fashion slogan: "We are all the things you are." The implication is that a woman is nothing but an assemblage of things, items from her wardrobe. And the further implication is that should she not have these things, she would be nothing.

An ad for the Lebenthal investment firm features Myrna Loy, looking as glamorous as ever, wrapped in a fur, saying: "I'm afraid I'm a novice at this. Please be patient with me." The sexual innuendo in these lines is unmistakable. Then she inquires: "May I ask a stupid question?" The notion this ad promotes is that it is all right for women to be inadequate, suffering, and stupid as long as they look nice.

Another cultural phenomenon that devalues women by making them sex objects is pornography. It is on the rise today, and it often takes an exceedingly violent turn. Women who are viewed as mechanistic entities whose primary purpose is to serve men sexually cannot be considered very worthwhile creatures. The tolerance exhibited today for pornographic films, publications, and bookstores underlines that sense of worthlessness.

The primary fact of female economic life—that women are paid less for what they do—produces a deadly feeling of inconsequence. The message cannot be clearer: You are not worth as much as a man.

Defeat of the Equal Rights Amendment was extremely damaging to the image of women in our society. A simple statement guaranteeing the opportunity to be equal, the amendment's defeat suggests that women are *not* equal and are not entitled to be treated equally. The defeat also suggests that women do not have what it takes to get this sort of law passed. They are neither skillful nor powerful enough. And one way that women's power is, in fact, abridged is by their fighting each other. Women have always been divided and conquered, and the ERA experience was a vivid illustration of that. Women who were afraid to risk losing what they had, women who were afraid to rock the boat, fought the amendment's passage. If women had stuck together and spoken with one voice, the ERA would never have been defeated. The fact is that the defeat harmed not only the image of its supporters but the image of those who worked against it as well.

Two less tangible influences that strike me as pushing our culture in a masochistic direction are the notion of "stonewalling," which Richard Nixon refined to an art in his last few years as president, and the emphasis on team-playing. One used to assume certain minimal standards of decency and conscience on the part of the public and of public officials. One expected appropriate behavior, and when that expectation was not met, one anticipated, and generally received, an acknowledgment of wrongdoing. Today, however, there seems to be a growing tendency to deny culpability—to stonewall. We have seen this repeatedly in scandals involving government officials: Faced with evidence of misconduct, impropriety, and even crime, the accused simply refuse to acknowledge that there is anything wrong with what they have done. I see this as well, and more and more frequently, in passing encounters I have with clerks in stores, for instance, or tellers in the bank. The motto today would seem to be "The customer is always wrong." The masochist, who always believes she is in the wrong anyway, has a harder time than ever in this sort of atmosphere.

People do not speak up today as much as they used to, and I fear that the time of the individual, the maverick, is rapidly disappearing. Today it seems almost dangerous not to be a member of one team or another. Deviation from a group brings on ostracism, which in turn promotes masochism. The masochist always fears speaking up, always tries to avoid offending the powers that be. In a society that stresses conformity, going along, and team-playing, the masochist will find it especially difficult to overcome her fear-ridden behavior.

Obviously, the roots of masochism are deeply planted. The last few decades have brought some changes and, unquestionably, women today feel freer to demand their rights. But even as laws, policies, and codes of behavior begin slowly to change through political action, masochism remains firmly, obstinately, entrenched. A woman who rushes eagerly to the barricades in the fight for women's rights may conduct herself in a self-destructive way when she confronts her landlord, her boss, her husband. As resistant as society is to change, it still yields more readily than does the individual personality. It is in their own psyches that women must struggle against their masochistic heritage. To do that it is vital that they understand the process of communication that lies at the heart of the problem; it is vital that they learn to recognize what I call the messages of masochism.

4

Sending Out
the Signals

"I'm probably way off base on this one."
"How stupid of me!"
"I don't mind if it's cold. I'll eat it anyway."
"I'm sorry. It must be my fault."
"I hope you won't be angry with me."
"I've just never been able to understand these things."
"It's nothing really. I was just lucky."
"Whatever you say."
"Just wait until your father comes home."

Masochistic communication has a distinctive style; its messages are the means by which the masochist exhibits and perpetuates her suffering. A masochist's aim is to appease or second-guess another person, someone she perceives as having power over her. Since the masochistic person perceives nearly everyone as more powerful than she, this strategy colors virtually all of her speech. The messages the masochist transmits, either through words or actions, are attempts to ward off the harm she fears and expects. Unfortunately, she is rarely a successful appeaser. In fact, her efforts to placate, to buy off, usually lead to further self-damage. Real communication between people involves give and take, a true exchange. The masochist, fearful as she is of the power of others, concentrates solely on keeping harm at bay. Her modus operandi is based on a system of anticipatory defense.

Masochistic communication is in many ways like a tennis match between an accomplished player and a duffer. The accomplished player serves, let's say, at high speed into the duffer's court. The duffer, unable to handle the powerful serve and afraid of it, may be hit by the ball, miss it altogether, or dink it into the net. Lost point! In the same way, the masochist, when a statement perceived as threatening comes at her, is paralyzed by terror, unable to position herself to reply properly. She may stand helplessly and just watch the ball (the statement) go by. She may allow it to plow right into her, causing a wound. Or she may make an ineffectual effort to return it that never clears the net. What she does not *dare* to do is to hit out strongly at the ball and return it forcefully to the server. She seems not to know how. The masochist is too fear-ridden for strategy of that sort. She always feels helpless and small; the server always looms large and powerful. When she muffs a shot, the best she can do is to murmur, "I'm sorry."

I will focus here primarily on verbal, rather than behavioral, messages of masochism since they are more easily conveyed. But, actions can impart messages just as definitively and forcefully as words do. Again, I emphasize that *all* masochistic messages, verbal or behavioral, are marked by an inability to express true feelings and by submission to another's power. And all of them are generated by the desire to appease. But beyond these general characteristics, there are some specific mechanisms one must examine to understand thoroughly the nature of masochistic messages.

The Use and Power of Apology

The masochist is an inveterate apologizer. "I'm sorry" is a phrase that comes to her lips all too readily, reflecting her low self-esteem and her sense that she is always in the wrong. She is the woman who, when someone bumps into her on the street, murmurs that *she* is sorry.

The apologetic message also demonstrates the masochist's more than ordinary belief in the power of apology. She uses it like a talisman that can turn away anticipated harm. If she says "I'm sorry" quickly enough, perhaps the damage and hurt she expects can be deflected. Most small children have a belief in the magic of words. After all, their initial experience of speech is that when a sound is uttered, all sorts of activity ensue. For the masochist, the phrase "I'm sorry" retains a kind of magical aura. More than likely as a child she was often found naughty, punished for her misdeeds, and made to apologize before being dismissed by her punishers. Saying "I'm sorry," or "I apologize," never helped her to understand why what she had done was wrong; it never helped her to learn anything. But it was the ritual expression that had the power to bring a painful episode to a close. She believes that "I'm sorry" is the statement that makes everything all right, in the same way that attending confession is supposed to wipe the slate clean. The phrase has great potency for the masochistic person, and she often utters it almost without thinking.

I was riding in the elevator with another woman and, having just picked up my mail, I was reading a postcard. It slipped out of my hand and I stooped to pick it up.

"I'm sorry," the woman said. "I should have gotten that for you."

"There was no reason for *you* to pick it up," I replied, "and besides, bending is good for me."

"I'm sorry," she repeated.

Her insistence on being wrong, her need to apologize was a defensive ritual: there was no realistic reason for her to attempt to placate me. She simply could not help doing it. And the result? I felt annoyed with her, a common reaction to this sort of self-abasement. People get tired of hearing the masochistic person's apologies; they weary of her rush to assume guilt and blame.

The husband of a patient of mine is extremely critical and demanding. One of the things he insists on is that his shirts be taken to the Chinese laundry every Monday. Usually his wife succeeds in meeting this demand; sometimes she does not. Her husband often asks her on Monday night whether she took the shirts to the laundry. If she has not, she immediately begins to apologize: "I'm sorry. I'll do it first thing tomorrow. But I'm really sorry that I didn't get to it today." She hopes her apology will appease her husband whom she knows will be angry. In fact, it makes him angrier and he becomes even more critical of her. What if, instead, she said to him: "Look, I run a big house and I have a lot to do and I'm not perfect, so the shirts don't always get to the laundry on Monday." Her husband might not be pleased, but this sort of statement would not provoke him to further invective the way her apologies do.

Accepting the Premise of the Other

The masochistic person, confronted with a powerful other, often experiences a state of what I call hypno-suggestibility. Related to hypnosis, but limited to the exchange at hand, hypno-suggestibility causes the masochist to accept whatever the other person says as correct just as surely as if she had been hypnotized into believing it. Totally paralyzed by the power and the idea of the other person, she loses any ability to think for herself and allows the other's viewpoint to be imposed on her immediately and totally. Having accepted the premise of the other, the masochist will then rationalize why it is so as a means of justifying her acceptance.

Hypno-suggestibility, as I noted in a previous chapter, begins in childhood vis-à-vis significant adults, and it is there that the masochist begins to accept the premise of the other as a defensive maneuver. Eric, for example, had a mother who frequently forced food down him. One item she always pushed was her chicken soup, which he abhorred because of the layer of fat that floated on top. "I'll eat the soup," he would say, "but can't you take the fat off?" "There's no fat on the soup," his mother would insist. "But," he would protest, "when the pot was in the refrigerator I saw the hard layer on top." "I took it off," his mother would answer even though Eric, looking into the pot, could see that the fat was now floating in liquid form on the top of the soup. Then she would force Eric to drink the soup. Eventually, he reported years later to me, he came to believe that, despite the evidence of his eyes, he must be wrong, that there was no fat on top of the soup. And he also believed that he must be very peculiar to believe that he saw fat when his mother didn't. Her constant, repetitive denials ultimately led him to doubt what he saw, to reject the proof he possessed. She implanted the hypno-suggestion that the fat did not exist and, as he yielded to her, he came to accept her premise.

A young woman who worked in an industrial firm ordered a twelve-dollar subscription to a trade magazine. When her boss got wind of this he was very annoyed. Despite the fact that the firm commonly made large outlays of money with little thought or scrutiny, the boss made a big fuss over the money spent on the magazine. Confronted by him, the young woman immediately accepted his assertion that ordering the subscription was wasteful. Panicky in the face of his annoyance, she apologized. Talking to me about it later, she said: "You know, this magazine is very useful. It's necessary to keep in touch with what's going on in the field. It's really not wasteful at all." When I observed that that would have been the perfect reply to her boss, she said she felt much too threatened by him to have thought of such a rejoinder; it only came out with me because she felt safe.

The masochistic person always feels in the wrong. When someone powerful comes along and says you *are* wrong and this is right, she has no capacity to fight that thesis. She succumbs instantly, as if she had been given a hypnotic command.

I ask patients of mine to keep a pad and pencil by their bedsides to write down dreams when they awaken and the dreams are still fresh. A male patient has been doing this for some time. One night when he got up and wrote down a dream, his wife said to him: "Listen, you're fifty-one years old. You shouldn't still be writing down your dreams." During his next session he reported this to me and revealed that he had accepted his wife's premise. "You asked me to write down my dreams," he said, "but my wife says I shouldn't have to. Why should I keep on doing this?"

There are many elements expressed in the wife's remark: her resentment that he still continues in treatment, her interference, her contempt for him. But the important thing here is that when this man's wife made an assertion, he immediately, unquestioningly, accepted it. Why did he not say to her: "Who the hell do you think you are to tell me what to do about this?" He did not say that because of fear, the same fear that caused him to accept his wife's premise with such alacrity.

Hypno-suggestibility is a striking element in man-womn relations. That should not be surprising in light of the cultural inequities that I outlined in the preceding chapter. And yet I am amazed at the degree to which women still continue to accept men's premises. Despite some social changes in man-woman relations, time has stood still for the masochistic woman, it seems. A friend of mine, a beautiful woman in her late forties whose body still looks almost the way it did twenty years ago, called me in a panic recently. "Natalie," she said, breathless with consternation, "I'm losing my figure. I'm going to start exercise and dance classes and go on a strict diet." Since I had seen her only a week before, and her figure had been as lovely as ever, I knew there was no basis in fact for her alarm. "Who said something to you?" I asked. She admitted that the man with whom she was involved had said something rather unpleasant about her figure—and she had taken it to heart with hypnotic effect.

Anna met Roger when he was in New York doing some buying for his firm in the Midwest. When his work was over and he was preparing to drive back home, he said to Anna, "Why don't you drive out with me and then fly back to New York? It'll be fun. We'll have a good time." Despite the fact that this meant giving up her own work at a time when she was quite busy, Anna accepted Roger's premise that this would be a great thing to do and, of course, she also counted on his implication that the trip would further their relationship with each other. She made the trip with him and they had an enjoyable time.

Over the next few months Roger called from time to time. Then Anna received a letter saying he was coming to New York to do some buying, he would be in town for two weeks, and he would like to stay with her. Thrilled, she took this as a sign that he was serious about their relationship. She made elaborate preparations for his arrival, getting her apartment in order, buying tickets to some Broadway shows, stocking her refrigerator with a lavish assortment of food. And when he arrived, she took considerable time off from work in order to drive him to some out-of-the-way places where he was doing his buying. When she did not drive him, she gave him her car to use and sometimes put gas in it for him. So solicitous was she that when Roger ran out of his favorite shaving lotion, she immediately noticed and replenished it, a gesture he acknowledged with pleasure but without thanks.

The night before Roger was to leave, Anna felt that his behavior was somewhat stiff, but she brushed aside her perception. The following morning, after some very satisfying sex, he told her that he would not be back in New York for quite a while. He had a vacation coming up soon and was planning to go rafting out west. When he was gone Anna found in her car a parking ticket he had received and never bothered to tell her about. Recounting this to me, Anna was plaintive about Roger's vacation plans. "He never even asked me to come with him," she said. And she was reluctant to write to him about the parking ticket because she did not want to seem petty.

The moment Anna accepted Roger's premise that it would be a fine idea for her to make the drive out to the Midwest with him, she sent him the message of absolute submission. Her unquestioning acceptance showed that she was willing to drop everything, that she did not consider her own affairs very important, that he was free to call the tune between them. And Roger obviously read that message clearly. When he returned to New York, he had no serious intentions about Anna; his raft vacation, probably with someone else, was already planned. But he did need a place to stay, a car to drive, meals, entertainment—and Anna furnished them all. Even as this gradually became evident to her, the thing she continued to worry about was whether she would appear petty to him if she asked him to pay for the parking ticket. At the outset of their relationship, Anna signaled Roger that she was vulnerable and submissive. Did signaling this serve her in any way? Did it cause him to treat her better, to respect her more? Quite the contrary. Anna's masochism alerted Roger to the fact that he need not regard her feelings at all. She did not, after all; why should he?

Avoidance of Questioning

Closely related to accepting another's premise is the masochist's fear of asking a question of the other person. Asking a question is the equivalent of returning the serve in a tennis game, putting the ball into the opponent's court, and forcing him to respond. Response, of course, is what the masochist fears. Hence, avoidance of the question. She also has no confidence in herself and her own views. Asking a question, returning a serve, feels dangerous and she avoids it.

I think of the junior executive I knew whose boss directed her to collaborate with a male colleague on a rather complicated project. After some deliberations, the male associate suggested they hire an outside firm to coordinate the operation. The woman felt she could have handled the matter herself, but her colleague persuaded her that to do so might be penny-wise and pound-foolish, so they engaged the outside firm.

When her employer learned of this he sent for this woman. "How could you spend all that extra money to hire another company?" he asked. "What do you think I pay you for?" The best she could do was to stammer that it was not her idea even though she had gone along with it. But this response did not appease her boss and his rebuke continued. The incident also jeopardized the woman's career.

How differently this encounter might have gone if she had been able, after her employer's initial accusation, to ask: "Why do you think this is a waste of money?" The question would have interrupted his attack on her and forced him to justify it. It would have, at the outset, erased the automatic assumption that she was at fault. And it would have allowed her then to focus on the real issue: why she and her colleague made the decision. Her avoidance of questioning her boss was an attempt to placate him, but it just encouraged further reproach and did nothing to support the notion that she had done what she considered best for the firm.

Equivocation

A masochist's uncertainty about herself and her opinion, her fear of taking responsibility for her own decisions, and her desperate desire to appease are on full display in a cartoon I saw some time ago. A woman sits in a restaurant, looking at the menu, and the caption reads: "Well, to be honest, maybe I'm way out of line on this one, but I'm pretty positive that I probably don't want the sole, I almost think." Of course this is caricature but, as with all good caricature, it is based on truth.

This kind of language is known in psychiatric parlance as tangential or circumstantial speech. In the former, the speaker constantly moves away from the center, away from the issue at hand; in the latter, she focuses on any circumstance that arises and talks about *it* rather than the primary issue. In either case, she is like a traveler who never reaches her destination. She starts down one avenue, then detours onto a side road, from there finds another path, and then another, each byway taking her farther and farther afield. These delaying tactics, she believes, buy her more time in which to attempt to second-guess the other person. They also keep her from being pinned down, from being stuck with any clear-cut position.

Repeating obsessively is another form of equivocation. Masochists find numerous ways of saying exactly the same thing, often prefacing each repetitive statement with a phrase like "I want to be sure you understand this," or "Let me just clarify what I mean," or "In other words, this is what I'm saying."

Language marked by ambiguity and lack of concision can only produce impatience. Will she ever get to the point? the listener wonders.

Polonius in *Hamlet* could well be called the Great Equivocator. When he is in the presence of royalty, his anxiety pushes him into tangential and circumstantial speech. He splits off first in this direction, then that, always avoiding any point that feels dangerous to him, ducking down any avenue that will keep him from having to make a direct, clear statement. Queen Gertrude, impatient with his indirection, chides him by saying,

"More matter, less art." Today she might simply say, "Get on with it," a phrase people often feel like directing at a masochist.

Circumstantial or tangential speech often has an underlying aim that goes deeper than concern with defensive maneuvering. This aim is to stave off abandonment. Masochistic people, by never getting to the point, hold on to their listeners and their listeners' attention. They don't recognize that the quality of the attention has been severely marred by the irritation and impatience the listener feels. They are simply interested in hanging on for dear life, and they try to do so by spinning out an endless stream of speech.

I'm reminded of a particular sort of stalling operation in an extremely masochistic patient of mine. She prefaced everything she was going to say with qualifying remarks that not only took up time but were also efforts to make me see her upcoming statements in a certain light. She never simply entered a session, sat down, and began to talk about what was on her mind. First she characterized what she was going to talk about. These are some of the phrases she used: "I have a lot to tell you today." "Today I'm going to deal with such-and-such." "I have something funny to tell you." "I have to say something very unpleasant." "I have something very complicated to discuss with you." "What I'm going to tell you about is a very difficult and terrible situation." "I'm going to change the subject now." These preliminary remarks allowed her to delay substantive discussion, and they reminded me of the remark of the mathematician/semanticist Alfred Korzybski: "The map is not the territory." This woman constantly handed me maps, delaying out of fear her entry into the territory.

Capitulation

The submission to authority that underlies all masochistic communication is perhaps most evident in the messages that turn on the mechanism of capitulation. Here the masochist exhibits her inability to hold her own, her tendency to collapse in the face of opposition, her failure to counterattack when such a maneuver is called for. The abandonment of autonomy is displayed with a painful clarity.

Evelyn had started her own business, which quickly became quite successful. In need of additional capital, she took in some partners, one of whom immediately began acting like her boss, questioning the hours she kept, referring to *his* business and *his* success. Part of his responsibility was to place an ad in which Evelyn had requested that she be mentioned as founder of the business. He had already "forgotten" once to include her name, so she raised the matter with him at a board meeting.

"Did you remember to put my name in the ad?" she asked.

"Oh, I forgot," he replied. "Remind me to call tomorrow morning at ten."

"I'm not sure I'll be able to call you then," Evelyn said.

"Well, I hope I'll remember," he said, adding, "Wait a minute. I think I did call . . . yes, I think I did."

"All right," she said, "case closed."

Evelyn's submission began when she accepted her partner's order that she be responsible for reminding him rather than pointing out that it was his obligation to remember. After all, she was not his secretary. By saying "I'm not sure I'll be able to," she revealed the degree to which she accepted his premise that it was her task. It deepened when she didn't question his obviously false last-minute recollection. And her final statement, "case closed," indicated total surrender. By saying that, she told him she would not cause trouble; she was a nice girl who just wanted to be liked; she would not fight. Appeasement—and where did it get Evelyn? Could she realistically have had any expectation that her partner would deal with her differently in the future? Of course not. She had just dug herself in deeper.

On her birthday, a patient of mine named Joyce was given a large camellia plant by her lover with whom she lived. The plant came from the florist shop of a friend of theirs. When, a day after she received it, the buds dropped off, Joyce picked up the heavy, rather unwieldy plant and returned it to the florist. "Keep it for a week," he said. "If it doesn't have some blooms by then, I'll give you something else in its place." So Joyce lugged the heavy pot home again.

A week later, when no blossoms had appeared, Joyce carried the large pot back to the florist again. He was not in the shop, but his assistant agreed to an exchange, and she picked a plant she liked and took it home. An hour later she received an angry phone call from the florist, who accused her of failing to water the camellia. He could tell this, he said, because the soil was dry. She had not watered it that day because she had not wanted to make it heavier than necessary for the trip to the shop, but she did not dare say so. The florist ordered her to return the new plant.

Joyce asked her lover if he would tote the new plant back and try to get a refund, but he refused. So once again she set out for the shop. When she arrived, the florist greeted her with annoyance and insisted that she take back her original camellia. Joyce acquiesced and hauled the moribund plant back to her apartment, where it failed to flourish and was eventually pronounced dead.

One last time, now carrying an obvious camellia corpse, Joyce returned to the shop and requested a refund. The florist refused, and Joyce left empty-handed.

Here and in the preceding example, there is evidence of submission to what can be called symbolic rape. Each of Joyce's heavily laden trips to the florist shop was a violation of her rights. And she submitted to these repeated violations without protest. Because she knew the florist socially, her fear was that it might be embarrassing to run into him if she was too demanding about an exchange or a refund. It never occurred to her that *he* should be embarrassed about giving her a flawed plant in the first place or by not telling her that camellias are temperamental. It never occurred to her that it might be more embarrassing to see him socially after she had let herself be exploited. And it never occurred to her that if she had been politely firm from the beginning, insisting that her unhealthy plant be replaced the day after she received it, the whole pathetic and outrageous incident could have been avoided. She felt she had no choice but to submit, to go along, to attempt to appease the florist by accommodation. And she ended up with nothing. Notice, also, that she capitulated to her boyfriend. After all, he bought the plant for her. Why was he unwilling to help return it? Why did she accept his refusal uncomplainingly?

Jennifer, a married woman with a five-year-old child, occasionally did some free-lance writing in a special field but she began to feel that she wanted to take on something more substantial. After mailing out resumes, she was offered an assignment that involved several months of work. She decided to take on the project and to work at home four days a week, a decision that curtailed the time she had to devote to her family. But she was delighted to be working and her husband seemed pleased also. When a bedroom lamp broke, she asked her husband if he would take it to the repair shop on a Saturday when he was free. He refused; he did not feel it was his job. She did not force the issue but took the lamp herself. In order to conserve time she began preparing simpler meals. Her husband complained. As a series of these clashes grew between them, Jennifer's anxiety mounted and she began to question whether she should continue with the work she was doing.

"Wasn't your husband pleased when you took on the job?" I asked.

"Oh, yes," she replied, "he's already decided how he'd like to spend the money."

Jennifer was capable of taking steps in her own behalf as long as she had her husband's approval. But the moment she encountered resistance from him, she capitulated. She suggested that he take a greater part in household tasks but when he refused she never asked again. When he complained about their less elaborate meals, she questioned whether she should be working rather than questioning his unwillingness to make an accommodation to their new circumstances. She tried to effect changes in the basic framework of their marriage that would make more room for her self-fulfillment but when he insisted that things remain the same she could not stand up to him. Her capitulation to his wishes was fear-driven: she was afraid to make waves, to rock the boat; her husband would be angry if she asserted herself; she must appease him or he would not think of her as a good girl, a nice wife. All of these are typical masochistic fears and, in this instance, they kept Jennifer from pointing out to her husband that if he wanted to share in the benefits of her work he should be prepared to share in the difficulties as well.

Spilling

This is manifested in the tendency to say too much, to overexplain, to be too self-revealing. Insecure about her own power, the masochist feels she has no right to keep her own counsel, no right to maintain a self-contained position. So she believes she can ward off harm by a stream of words, the way a fire hose directed at an attacking dog can keep him at bay.

A patient of mine afforded me a textbook illustration of this phenomenon when she told me of an exchange she had had with a man who was selling textiles to her company. She was the buyer for her firm and the seller quoted a price to her. "That's about what we can pay," she responded, "but I'd like you to do better." Already she had said too much. By indicating that her firm could pay this price, she handed him a solid reason to hold the line and not bargain with her. She then went ahead and gave him a lengthy explanation of why her firm could pay the price, a completely unnecessary contribution for her to make. She was not obligated to give him any explanation whatsoever.

At the outset of their encounter, she held the advantage: He wanted to sell to her. But she quickly squandered it by divulging things she should have kept to herself. Her tendency to spill cost her dearly. In the figurative sense, she gave away little pieces of herself by being unable to stand up to the seller and deal with him effectively. In the literal sense, the price was also high—$70,000 more than she needed to have paid, she told me.

Another patient was at an art gallery opening when an attractive man approached her and struck up a conversation. After they had talked for a time, he asked if he might see her the following Friday night. "Well," she answered him, "I'm going through a very difficult time in my life right now. I have a lot of things on my mind, a lot going on, and I'm in the midst of a divorce and that's hard. I don't know whether it would be a good idea for me to see you or not." And on and on. Why, I asked her when she reported the incident, could she not simply have said no thank you, if she did not wish to see this man again? She thought she might want to see him sometime in the future, she said. In that case, I pointed out, she could have said no to Friday night but asked him to call another time. Or she might have asked for his phone number and said she would call him when she had some free time.

She did none of those things, however, because she was afraid to say no, even to a man she barely knew. She was afraid to be definite, afraid to take the responsibility for making a choice. She did not owe him an explanation, but she gave one. She was not obligated to reveal anything about herself, but she chose to. Her litany of woes probably made the man sorry he had issued the invitation in the first place.

One of the functions of spilling is that the words that pour out of the masochist fill up pauses that feel threatening to her. She is fearful of silence because during such an interval an attack might come. She may associate silence with the times her mother picked on her during childhood. I think of a patient who recalled her mother's behavior when she would come upon her daughter sitting quietly and reading. "Why are you just sitting?" her mother would ask in an accusing manner. "Why aren't you doing something, like cleaning your room or putting away your laundry or straightening up the mess you made in the basement?" Eventually, quiet moments came to feel dangerous to this child; she learned that if she wanted to sit still and read she would have to leave the house and take her book elsewhere. This was her way of avoiding her mother's attacks. Masochistic spilling seeks that same end by filling every moment with words. If words take up all the space, the masochist believes, there will not be room for the attack she is always expecting. But in the course of spilling, she almost always lets the other person know something that does not serve her at all. The content of what she reveals may, in fact, precipitate a negative reaction, the very thing she was trying to avoid by her outpouring of words.

Acquiescence and Accommodation

Masochistic people are invariably compliant, willing to let other people call the tune, reluctant to put their own stamp on anything. They concentrate on not making waves, not rocking the boat. The messages they transmit that are marked by acquiescence and accommodation almost seem to be efforts to be invisible. Their own feelings play virtually no part in their exchanges with other people; they are utterly agreeable.

A woman began seeing a male gynecologist shortly after her marriage and from the time of her first appointment found his internal examinations rough and painful. Nevertheless, she continued under his care, and he delivered her three children. His hurtful, inconsiderate methods never varied over the years, and he was given as well to delivering condescending lectures on diet and nutrition though he was himself obese. When she told me of these experiences, I said it seemed that it might be time for a change of physicians. "How could I do that?" she answered me. "I'd be too embarrassed to tell him I was leaving him."

This woman submitted for years to a situation that caused her pain, acquiescing in the doctor's authority over her (appropriate if he had been considerate and capable), making endless allowances for him, none for herself. Once in the situation, she felt powerless to change it. To do so would have been to risk the doctor's disapproval, a risk she was unwilling to take.

Suzanne reported to me a phone call she had received from a young man who wanted to arrange a blind date. She said it had been a very long conversation, and it had interfered with some tasks she had intended to do and made her extremely uncomfortable as her need to go to the bathroom became increasingly urgent throughout the call. Despite this, she had been unable to cut it short, waiting instead for the young man to end it. That fact alone was a masochistic message.

One of his first comments to her was that she did not seem as aggressive as many women in her line of work. "I don't think of myself as aggressive," she answered him, "but I suppose I must be in order to survive." They talked further, and then he suggested that they go out. "I don't suppose there's anything much on the West Side where you live," he said. "Oh, there are places," she responded, "but I'd just as soon go elsewhere, if you like." "Do you like to get dressed up, or would you prefer to be more informal?" he asked. Although she had a new dress she was longing to wear, she said that informality would be fine. They decided to meet at eight o'clock at her apartment, but then, uncertain whether he would have enough time to go home from his office and change into jeans, he said he would call her just as he was leaving his apartment. At the end of the conversation he said, "Sorry to have kept you so long." "Oh, that's all right," she replied.

This entire conversation was a series of maneuvers in which the young man moved aggressively and Suzanne countered with a masochistic defense, acquiescing and accommodating, which is really no defense at all. Her responses constituted a reenactment of the way she had as a child responded to her tyrannical father.

Letting Others off the Hook

With this device, the masochistic person rushes to hand other people excuses, to justify their attacks on her, and to rationalize away her own feelings in deference to theirs. Returning to the analogy of the tennis game, it is as though she hits a good, firm shot, but when her opponent misses it, she says it was not really good, it must have taken a bad bounce, the sun must have been in his eyes, he must have been slowed up by a rough spot on the court, and so on. She will not just keep quiet, content with the knowledge that she has made an effective stroke. She fritters away her advantage, fearful of the response of this authority figure across the net from her.

A patient of mine who is beautiful, intelligent, and a success in her job had just begun a new relationship with a young man she liked very much. After they spent a lovely weekend together, he asked when they might see each other again. "How about Wednesday?" she replied but then added, "But maybe you won't enjoy it because it's so soon." She, too, was attempting to ward off disappointment by offering the young man an out. And the out she offered him was to suggest that she was not really enjoyable and that perhaps too much of her was not good. This blatant display of low self-esteem could have done little to enhance her in the young man's eyes. She handed him an excuse for not seeing her and did so in a manner that could very well make him think twice about continuing the relationship. A nonmasochistic woman would have said simply, "How about Wednesday?"

When another woman patient of mine was promoted, her employers offered her a car along with an increase in salary. She could pick any car she liked as long as it fell within a certain price range. She chose a sports car and, excited and proud, drove immediately to a neighboring state to show it to her mother. Her mother's response to her daughter's good news was: "Don't you think it's selfish of you to get a two-seater?"

My patient should have recognized this gratuitous insult as part of a lifelong pattern of exchange between the two of them. She always persisted in seeking her mother's endorsement, and when she received an attack instead, she justified the attack by responding defensively. A small car uses less gas, she now told her mother; it is also easier to park in the city, she pointed out. Inherent in her response was the tacit admission that her choice needed defending. This let the mother off the hook and shifted blame to the daughter. What a different tone the exchange would have had if she had been able to say: "The car suits me fine since I live alone in the city." That would have placed the ball firmly in her mother's court, where it belonged.

Avoidance/Evasion

In some human encounters, avoidance can be an effective, and healthy, device to employ. It can be good strategy. But the masochist, who evades out of fear rather than tactical maneuvering, uses avoidance in a neurotic way.

A woman attending a party was greeted by her host who said, "You have nice legs and you can afford to uncover them. This is the first time I've seen you in a dress rather than slacks." His remark was upsetting to her, revealing as it did the unflattering assumptions he had been making about her, divulging as well his presumption that he had the right to make such a comment to her. But fearful of offending, eager to appease, she said nothing to her host, and her lack of response constituted a masochistic message. There were any number of replies she might have made that would have prevented her upset over the encounter, but she did not dare to respond at all.

This same woman told me a story about her parents. Her father was a very demanding, authoritarian man, her mother the archetypal "good little housewife" who cleaned, cooked, sewed, and always agreed with her husband. During a recent visit, her mother had told her about a trip she and her husband had taken to Philadelphia, focusing on an unsatisfactory dinner they had had. As she and her mother talked, the woman discovered that this dinner had taken place in a "topless" restaurant her father had insisted on going to. When she asked her mother what her complaint was, the mother said, "The food was no good." Repeating this to me, my patient was able to see the blatant avoidance in her mother's remark. "Of course," she said, bursting out laughing, "my mother wouldn't dare say she hated being forced to go to a topless restaurant. She often evades when she doesn't like what my father does . . . and so do I."

Inability to Change Direction
of an Encounter

An obese woman ran into a friend she had not seen for some time. "Oh, dear," the friend said, "it looks to me as if you've put on some weight." This remark caused the woman to launch into a lengthy explanation of how difficult things had been for her lately, of how her troubles had caused her to overeat, and of how she had indeed put on weight. Undoubtedly, she believed that explaining away the weight was in her own best interests, that the explanation would lead her friend to be less critical and accusatory. In point of fact, she made matters worse by emphasizing the negatives about herself and left her friend with the image of someone who had no willpower, was preoccupied with her weight, and felt ugly and helpless. But what if she had been able instead to give her friend's remark a cursory reply and then move on to something else? The direction and nature of their encounter would have changed; the stigma of her weight problem would not have colored the entire meeting.

Masochistic people don't recognize that they need not be stuck with the topic raised by the other person. They don't dare to ignore it or give it brief lip service and then inject something new. Instead they focus on the topic like a fish drawn toward bait and then they hang on, hooked, unable to get free. Lawyers sometimes attempt to "change the venue" because they feel their clients will receive a fairer trial in another area. Masochistic people might receive a more favorable hearing if they were able to change the venue in a conversation.

Underscoring Mistakes

This characteristic is closely allied to spilling and to the use of apology. Fearful, guilty, certain that she will be caught out in her misdeeds, even if they are only imagined ones, the masochistic person rushes to point out her shortcomings. She hopes by doing this to disarm what she sees as her opposition. She will beat others to the punch, so to speak, underlining her errors before they can and, by doing so, deflect the negative judgments she anticipates. The woman in Salzburg who was "holding up the wall" certainly falls into this category.

At a dinner party I attended recently, the hostess sat with her guests and her quite critical husband in the living room for a while, and then got to her feet and said, "I'm terribly sorry but I have to go into the kitchen for a bit. I know I should have had everything absolutely ready so we wouldn't have any delays, but you do have drinks and hors d'oeuvres to tide you over, and I'll be as quick as I can getting dinner on the table."

What party does not require some last-minute attention? Our hostess could have excused herself simply and quietly. But she insisted on seeing her last-minute tasks as errors that could have been avoided; with apology and self-recrimination, she succeeded only in calling the attention of the guests to something we most likely would not have noticed at all.

I knew that this woman repeatedly acted out this same pattern with her husband. When she did something she construed as a mistake, she launched into profuse apologies that threw the spotlight onto her shortcomings. Many of the things she was at such defensive pains to point out might have passed unnoticed without her relentless underscoring—and the more she underlined her weaknesses to her husband, the more critical he became.

Rigidity of Language

The masochistic person is not free, to use again the tennis metaphor, to take a good swing at the ball and then wait to see what kind of a return she receives. Frozen in her defensive posture, she structures everything around that; her thought processes are carefully organized to effect defensive maneuvers. This necessarily produces a kind of rigidity of thought that is reflected in her language. She tends to see things in extremes and to express herself accordingly. Her speech is riddled with dualistic couplings like right and wrong, good and bad, weak and strong, and there is seldom much middle ground.

"Nothing I ever did was right—everything was bad or wrong. My outstanding work at school was ignored, except when I got less than a 95, and then I was punished. The punishment was so unyielding. I was confined to my room for a whole week for being a half hour late one afternoon when I was in high school. Now, when anything goes wrong, no matter how small, I blow it up out of proportion. I realize what I am doing, I know it's wrong, but I can't help it."

The language of this patient, a young woman who grew up in a harsh and punishing environment that left her always feeling "bad" and "wrong," was characterized by black and white extremes. Note the number of times she uses "right" and "wrong" in this one short speech.

The linguistic style of masochism often has an extreme tone

that comes from the liberal use of such words as "totally," "completely," "absolutely." While the masochistic persons uses these words freely, it is important to note that they generally go far beyond what the situation calls for.

Meta Messages

Words are not the only means by which human beings transmit messages. Often the tone or inflection of the voice, the body posture, or the gestures or actions accompanying the words say something as well. These communications, counterpoints to speech, are meta messages, and often they are even more important than the verbal message. Let me give a rather crude but clear illustration. A man says to a woman "I love you," but at the same time he kicks her. "I love you," the verbal message, conflicts with the kick, the meta message. In this instance, because the kick is more powerful, it is the true communication.

Meta messages can be conveyed by body language. Intimidated people, people with bad feelings about themselves, often fear looking another person in the eye. A direct look might be construed as a challenge or it might increase the possibility that one will be seen through. Masochistic people may reveal how they feel about themselves by their posture, which is often slouching, indicating their sense of servility and fear. They generally don't carry themselves with the air of erect self-assurance common to people who feel comfortable with themselves. Head-nodding is another bodily communication masochistic people frequently use. The moment someone else starts to speak they begin nodding affirmatively, eager to show just how agreeable they are.

Crying is another meta message the masochistic person transmits. Because masochists do not dare to be angry, they convert their anger into hurt. And when they are hurt, they frequently call upon tears as a way of getting themselves off the hook and warding off further harm. This is not a *conscious* choice, of course. Their crying is an unconscious mechanism that says: I'm pitiful, look at me cry, you must feel sorry for me, and if you feel sorry for me you won't hurt me anymore. The masochist's tears are no more effective a method of appeasement than any of the others I've mentioned. By evoking pity, the masochistic person seeks to evade harm. What her tears produce in reality are just more pain and suffering.

A physician told me of an experience of hers some years ago that illustrates the masochistic tendency to cry. She was an intern at the time and served as anesthesiologist, using the open-drop ether method, for another intern who was doing a tonsillectomy. During the operation he ran into some difficulty with bleeding, and the operation ended up taking longer than it should have. The next day the other intern approached her in the hall of the hospital and, in front of other people gathered there, said to her: "Goddammit, if you ever tell me what to do again during surgery, I'll get you." Stunned, she immediately began to cry. She tried to think back and remember if she had said anything to him during the operation and could not recall that she had. "I didn't say anything to you," she said, her assertion undercut by her continuing tears. "I was having enough trouble trying to keep the child anesthetized." "The hell you didn't," he said and stormed off.

The stand the young woman doctor took in this exchange— that she had said nothing—was rendered meaningless by the meta message of her tears. It signaled her weakness to him but did not deflect his attack. If she had delivered her challenge without crying, the outcome of the encounter might have been different. Also, she told me, she went over and over this incident, wondering what she had done wrong, accepting his premise that she had been at fault. Only years later did she realize that the attack on her had been a defensive projection on the other intern's part. He was embarrassed by the botched job he had done, and she had witnessed his inadequacy, which enraged him.

A patient reported to me that she had had a terrible week. She had slammed her hand in the apartment door, bruising it badly; she had burned her arm on the stove; and during a dinner party she had broken an old china dish she loved. Completing this recitation of damages incurred, she said, "I can't imagine why all this happened." "What are you angry about?" I asked her. She denied that she was angry, but as we talked further her denial began to diminish. She was in the process of getting a divorce, her husband had constantly delayed signing an agreement, and she had not pushed for a settlement even though she was desperately short of money in the meantime. This situation filled her with rage, but because she didn't dare to talk to her husband and urge him to move ahead on the agreement, she turned the rage on herself. The bruised hand, the burned arm, and the shattered dish were meta messages that said: "I'm angry at you, but I don't dare say so. I'm angry at you, but I'd rather damage myself than express it."

Misinterpretation of Visual Cues and Tone of Voice

Watching and listening for trouble, a masochistic person pays particular attention to the looks on other people's faces and their tones of voice. Unfortunately, many of these "signals" the masochist believes she is picking up exist only in her own fantasy. She may, for instance, look at someone who is expressionless and interpret the impassivity as anger. Or she may hear an inflection in someone's voice and read anger into it when, in fact, the person may have an abrupt style or a head cold or just have come from an unpleasant encounter with someone else.

This extreme attention to visual and vocal cues is rooted in the infancy of the masochistic person and based on what Harry Stack Sullivan called "forbidding gestures." These gestures, which include angry looks and angry tones of voice, come from a parent and indicate displeasure with the child. In order to appease and ward off harm from the parent, the child learns early on to try to interpet these gestures, and that predilection becomes imprinted on the child's psyche. These interpretations may have been correct in childhood and perhaps necessary adaptational solutions for the child trying to deal with an abusive and powerful parent. But carrying the mechanism into adulthood is extremely destructive. The masochistic person misinterprets a look or a sound, expresses that misinterpretation and, by so doing, creates trouble for herself.

Martin and Jack were brothers who ran a business together.

When Martin learned Jack was planning a trip to Massachusetts, he went into Jack's office, where Jack was studying some material spread out on his desk.

"What's the purpose of the trip to Massachusetts?" Martin asked.

Raising his head, staring at his brother, Jack said, "What?"

"Why are you looking at me like that?" Martin said.

Martin's response expressed his fear of some fantasied criticism by his brother. While he had asked a perfectly legitimate question, his fear made him feel he was somehow in the wrong and deserving of an attack. So he took his brother's "what?" coupled with his stare, as an accusation.

Jack's reaction to Martin's original question could have meant several things, and if Martin had not been masochistic he might have forced Jack to clarify it by saying, "What do you mean 'what?'" Or, "Didn't you hear me?" If he had hit the ball back into Jack's court, Jack would have had to explain himself. Perhaps he was reluctant to discuss the purpose of his trip. Perhaps he was bothered by being questioned. Or perhaps he was simply engrossed in his work and missed the sense of Martin's query. Martin never had the chance to find out, because he immediately focused on his own assumption that he was wrong to have asked Jack the queston, and that led him rather far afield from his original purpose. All he succeeded in doing was putting the spotlight on his own liabilities.

Rejection of Praise and Attention

Often when she is singled out for commendation, the masochistic person transmits a self-damaging message, snatching defeat from the jaws of victory, as it were. Unable to accept a compliment, she rushes to undercut it with a dismissive remark.

A thirteen-year-old girl was at a summer camp, and one weekend a dance was held with boys from a nearby camp. Slightly chubby and awkward and, like most adolescents, uncomfortable with herself, she sat with a group of other "wallflowers," watching the dancing and feeling wretched about the entire affair. Noticing one especially handsome boy, she thought how she would give anything to dance with him, and, to her astonishment, he approached and asked her to dance. As they moved out onto the floor, she said to him, "Are you a Boy Scout doing his good deed by dancing with me?" The boy gave her a searching look and soon excused himself. She never saw him again. One might dismiss this as just the behavior of a typical teenager who had not yet learned to deal with the opposite sex, but as the girl's later history confirmed, she had definite masochistic problems. And they were already showing themselves in an active fashion at the camp dance. Obviously she was not as homely or clumsy as she thought; the handsome boy did go out of his way to choose her. But because she felt she was worthless and unappealing, she was unable to believe that the boy's interest in her was genuine. Reacting defensively, she transmitted a message that drove him away, thus giving herself more ammunition to reinforce a distorted image of herself.

A common exchange one hears between women goes something like this: First Woman: "What a pretty dress." Second Woman: "Oh, I don't think I really like it. It's too frilly" (or tailored or drab or bright). The masochistic woman is unable to accept praise or attention; in fact, she seems to have an overriding need to push it aside. She is incapable of just thanking her friend for the compliment, whether she agrees with it or not, and then moving on to something else.

Unresolved Symbiosis and Poor Maintenance of Boundaries

As soon as Jane returned from her honeymoon, her mother began to nag her. "When are you going to write your thank-you notes?" she asked. "Don't you think it's about time you showed some gratitude for the nice gifts you received?" Exasperated, Jane snapped, "Are you going to keep annoying me?"

Because of their symbiotic relationship, the mother still regards Jane as a part of herself, as someone she can control. Even though Jane is now married, the mother's nagging is an assertion that her daughter has not achieved independence. She doesn't accept the fact that Jane is no longer part of her sphere of influence. Jane, because of her masochism, acquiesces in her mother's assertion of authority. Her response—"Are you going to keep annoying me?"—is an improvement over her past behavior, when she silently absorbed all her mother's reproaches. But it falls short of confronting the issue head on. It still includes a tacit acknowledgment of her mother's right to power over her. If Jane had been able to say something like, "Mother, you attend to your affairs, and I'll attend to mine," that would have been a direct, clear-cut statement of boundaries, putting the mother on notice that she was no longer the commanding authority in her daughter's life.

Symbiosis, especially in relation to a son, and usually an only son, has been called the "silver cord" syndrome, this standing for the umbilical cord that, symbolically, has never been severed. This is most common when the mother is widowed and wealthy and has the means to coerce her son into doing her bidding and dancing attendance on her. Clear boundaries have never developed between mother and son. But this cord attachment applies to daughters as well.

Occasional Negativism and Defiance

Masochistic messages exhibiting this characteristic are much less common than most of the preceding examples I have cited. However, they do occur. Continual self-abasement certainly breeds anger and resentment, and while the masochistic person guards vigilantly against any display of these feelings, occasionally they erupt. The docile, yielding accommodator can, every so often, lash out in a hostile fashion. At a glance, this may seem an improvement over her ordinarily immutable submissiveness. In fact, it is no improvement at all, for her anger is usually expressed inappropriately and ends up causing her just as much trouble as her subservience.

A physician had a difficult relationship with one of her male colleagues. She found his obsessive nature extremely irritating, and the two of them had had a number of unpleasant confrontations. One day, looking over a patient's chart, she saw his diagnosis and wrote next to it: "No. I do not agree with you." When the male doctor saw her statement he asked that she erase it. She refused, and the incident erupted into a heated argument. He was right in believing that her dissenting comment could support a malpractice suit if the patient or family were so inclined.

The female physician's remark was provocative, unnecessary, and inappropriate. When her primary concern should have been for the patient, she was focusing on her own need to pick a fight with her antagonist. Instead, she ought to have taken a positive approach to the medical problem by stating her impressions and substantiating the reasons for them. This would have allowed her to register her disagreement but in a constructive way. It could have been helpful to the patient, and it might not have triggered further difficulties for her.

The defensive communication style of masochism is a mosaic of all the different types of messages just described.

Often a single communication can contain several messages, and the characteristics I have delineated are present in masochistic speech all the time. They are like themes in a piece of music that recur over and over, sometimes stated plainly, sometimes phrased with elaboration, but always recognizable no matter how many instruments or notes have been added or taken away. The masochistic message, whatever its form, is always an expression of powerlessness and a plea for leniency. Unfortunately, the signal of weakness does not discourage injury. More often than not, it promotes it. The masochistic person, fearful though she is of the power of others, is truly her own worst enemy, the victim of a system of suffering that is self-fulfilling and self-propelled.

5

Active or Passive Voice

Chance plays a part in all human affairs. A hand of cards is dealt each of us in life; while we have no say in what those cards will be, the way in which we play the cards is very much within our control. And in life, as in a card game, there seem to be people who win consistently and people who lose with equal regularity. Masochists play the cards they have been dealt with a notable lack of skill, signaling their vulnerability at every turn, invariably saying or doing the self-damaging thing.

The messages a masochist transmits signal vulnerability at every turn. These messages are, of course, just the tip of the iceberg, that portion of the personality that is visible, the outward manifestations of the masochist's inner sense of fear and power-lessness. But it is important to recognize the messages if one is to explore and understand what lies beneath the surface. And equally important to understand is the difference between active and passive masochism, a somewhat artificial distinction, perhaps, but a crucial one nevertheless.

Active masochism exists when a person *initiates* something that is self-punitive; passive masochism exists when an outside event triggers a masochistic response. Hard though it may be to believe, if the masochistic person could just learn to keep her mouth shut, she would eliminate half her problems, the active half, the half she brings upon herself. But keeping still, refraining from using her anticipatory defense system, is one of the most difficult things for the masochist to do. Impaled upon the notion that things are made better by assuaging power, deferring to power, and apologizing to power, the masochistic person finds it almost impossible to believe that her best interests may be served by saying or doing nothing.

Genevieve was in the midst of a divorce and involved with a younger man in an enjoyable, though not serious, romance. He had made it clear he was not interested in a deep commitment for a number of reasons, but they did spend most weekends together. During one stay at his apartment, Genevieve saw tickets to the ballet on his phone table, but he did not mention them to her and she knew better than to press him. A few weeks later, however, he invited her to accompany him to the ballet. "Oh, I noticed those tickets," Genevieve said, "but you didn't ask me and I wondered if you were planning to take someone else."

This is active masochism. Genevieve could simply have said, "Thank you, I'd love to go." But her masochism pushed her to spill out self-revealing information that would do her no good whatsoever. She divulged to the young man that she was jealous, worried about her relationship with him, and desirous of greater commitment. By conveying to him her relief that the tickets were for her she, the powerless one in the relationship, put herself even further in his power. If she had been able to accept his invitation with thanks but without masochistic embroidery, she would have done herself a favor.

Some time later, when Genevieve had occasion to be in the man's office, she noticed that he still had on his desk a picture of his former girlfriend. She said nothing in the office, but when they came downstairs and got into his car, she could no longer contain herself. "I see you still have Elizabeth's picture on your desk," she said, a remark that enraged the man and constituted another example of active masochism. It may have been wise of her to note the picture for future reference, but it did her no good to spill it out to him.

Ralph and Sam are business partners who arranged with their burglar alarm company that Sam was to be called first if the alarm went off, since he lived twenty minutes closer to their business location. One night the company called Ralph to say the alarm had rung; he was annoyed they had not called Sam and told them to do so even though he was now awake and alerted to the situation. The next morning, Ralph asked Sam what had happened the night before. "How do you know about it?" Sam asked angrily. "They called me," said Ralph, "and I told them to call you." At this, Sam flew into a rage. Why would Ralph do such a thing, Sam asked, if he was already awake? Why would he be so inconsiderate? And, while Sam was at it, he might as well mention that Ralph had not been pulling his weight lately in a lot of ways. Sam claimed he was doing the lion's share of the work while Ralph just coasted along.

Again, this is active masochism. Ralph, who knew what his partner's personality was like and who also knew that it had been unreasonable of him to have Sam called, could easily have called the alarm company the next day to find out what had happened. But, instead, he volunteered information to his partner that was bound to boomerang and deal a blow to him. You will recognize both spilling and underscoring mistakes in the active masochistic message that Ralph transmitted. If he had just stayed quiet, there would have been no trouble with Sam. But he could not help saying more than was necessary.

When masochistic people feel defensive about something, which is most of the time, they invariably attempt to correct it, to fix it up. Just as invariably, that attempt makes things worse. They feed the flames rather than putting them out. Learning not to do that involves learning to say no to themselves: No, I will not rush to explain, to rectify, to mollify, to disarm . . . I will keep still. Few human beings find ambiguity comfortable, but for the masochistic person it is nearly unbearable. She would rather translate her inner discomfort into a sure loss than to remain in a limbo of uncertainty. She experiences a release upon ending the suspense. But what a high price she pays for temporary relief.

A patient of mine was invited to a party several weeks ahead of time. As the date approached, she called the friend who was giving the party and said, "I'm calling to ask if I should come to the party." "Well, of course," said her friend, "I'm expecting you." My patient's remark revealed unmistakably her sense that she did not belong, her belief that she did not deserve to be invited to the party, her pervasive self-doubt. If she had called to check on the day and time of the party, that would have been one thing. But to call and ask if she should come, when she had been invited and had accepted the invitation was another matter.

In this instance, her friend responded warmly, but that is not the customary response to masochistic behavior. In fact, people who are repeatedly on the receiving end of a masochist's messages come to expect certain behavior from her and may even treat her unfairly before she hands them the opening. In this way, over the long haul, masochistic messages encourage further aggression. Cumulatively, they create a climate where attack is more likely.

Susan has a friend who lives out of town, and each time the friend visits, the first thing she says to Susan is, "How *are* you?" The question, with its telling inflection, makes it obvious that the friend expects Susan to be perfectly awful. The friend's asking the question is an implicit put-down of Susan, something she has come to resent as she has grown healthier. In the past, the same question, asked in a conventional, polite way, was always the trigger for a recital of woes, and now, in a certain sense, the damage has been done. Even though Susan no longer jumps at any opening to catalogue her wounds, her friend continues to respond as though that were happening. She has been conditioned by her exposure to Susan's masochism to expect it, and her attack, subtle though it may be, occurs without Susan's doing anything. Now, of course, it is up to Susan to reverse the pattern, to change the direction of the encounters with her friend. The next few times her friend asks, "How *are* you?" Susan should say, "Things are great. What's going on with you?" or, "Just fine, thanks," and then move on to something else. Her friend will be puzzled because she has heard nothing but complaints for so long, but eventually she will catch on.

Active masochism also reveals itself in the masochistic person's propensity toward physical damage of the self or of possessions. Masochists do not dare to express their anger directly, but often that anger makes an appearance in the guise of destructive events that appear to happen by accident. Ludwig Eidelberg, a noted psychoanalyst, has observed that some masochistic people bring about their own discomfiture by a roundabout process in which they manipulate the reverses they suffer. It is a kind of self-mortification.

Karen had three very special Japanese cups and saucers that she treasured. A couple with whom she was somewhat friendly, even though she did not like them all that well, arrived from out of town and asked Karen to have dinner with them. She felt it would be incumbent upon her to take them to dinner, but since she couldn't really afford that, she invited them to come to her apartment for coffee and dessert, even though she preferred not seeing them at all. She had to rush that evening to get home in time to get things ready. As she was taking her irreplaceable cups from the closet, one fell to the floor and smashed, an expression, I think, of her annoyance at finding herself in an unwelcome position.

I will never forget the first sight I had of a patient who came to me very specifically seeking help for what she knew was her masochism. She was having a difficult time in her marriage, and the therapist she had seen previously had attempted to establish a sexual liaison with her. When I opened the door for her, I saw that she had an arm in a cast, a large purple bruise on her hand and her hair had obviously been singed by fire. She was a masochistic disaster area! We all know people who tend to be accident-prone; the blows that fall on them seem to be dealt by fate. But it is just as likely that their preoccupation with unexpressed anger causes them to be careless.

Very often, in the background of people who express their masochism in this fashion, there is an overprotective mother who constantly issued warnings: watch out, don't trip, don't fall, be careful, look out. Through repetition of these admonitions, the mother implants hypno-suggestions in the child. What she is really saying is that the child is clumsy, careless, worthless, and inept, and the child, out of defiant, masochistic rage, begins to act this out: All right, Mom, you expect me to break the plate? I'll show you. I'll break the plate. You think I'm going to fall? Okay, I'll fall. And so on. It is a kind of self-fulfilling prophecy and can be triggered by unconscious fear as well as by more overt defiance.

In passive masochism, the triggering event is unavoidable because it comes from outside. The masochistic person is not responsible for initiating the interchange. She is, however, responsible for her reaction. Apologizing when someone bumps into you is a perfect example of passive masochism. You may recall the young woman in the last chapter whose boss took her to task for ordering a twelve-dollar magazine subscription. The attack on her came from the outside, something she could not control, but she responded masochistically by becoming panicky and apologizing. That is passive masochism.

Passive masochism often consists of silent submission to a difficult or painful situation, an unwillingness to speak up, to make one's wishes or feelings known. A young woman was studying for her exams in her New York apartment when her upstairs neighbor began to play his stereo loudly. The noise interfered with the student's ability to concentrate, as did her anger, which grew as the noise continued. But she made no effort to change the situation; she just accepted it. Her fear of confronting the neighbor prevented her from acting in her own best interests.

Marcia went to the bank during her lunch hour to take care of a matter that needed the attention of a bank officer. Soon after she sat down, the woman officer took a phone call that was obviously personal and went on talking while Marcia waited in silence. There were other officers available to whom she could have taken her business, but Marcia stayed where she was, awaiting the end of the seemingly endless phone call. When the officer finally hung·up, Marcia did venture timidly that she didn't have much time and hoped they could take care of the business as quickly as possible. The officer, obviously annoyed, said, "My mother is sick in the hospital," a statement that caused Marcia to abandon even her paltry effort at assertion and lapse into an orgy of apology. "Oh, I'm so sorry," she said. "I feel just terrible. I didn't mean to be impatient. I didn't realize you were talking about your mother. I hope she'll be all right."

The provocation of this instance came from outside of Marcia in the form of the phone call. She made a half-hearted effort to protest the treatment she was given, but the moment the officer presented her with what appeared to be an excuse, Marcia capitulated and began to backpedal furiously to let the woman off the hook. In fact, the excuse was no excuse at all. Marcia could have replied, "I'm sorry that your mother's ill, but that doesn't mean you needed to stay on the phone for fifteen minutes. You could have said what was necessary and ended the call, or you could have called back after we'd finished our business." Instead, *she* ended up apologizing and feeling in the wrong.

Almost anyone is fair game for unprovoked abuse or rudeness, particularly in today's climate of ever-diminishing civility. However, the masochistic person reacts to these slings and arrows in a particular way. She absorbs the punishment, rather than deflecting it. Because of her fear, her feelings of guilt, and her persistent sense of being in the wrong, she doesn't put up effective resistance to the assaults she encounters. The neurotic defensive responses of passive masochism are in large measure due to the masochistic person's lack of a sense of her own limits and boundaries, the legacy of her still unresolved symbiotic attachment to her mother. She has great difficulty perceiving when she has been infringed upon. So meager is her sense of herself as a separate, autonomous person that she often does not even realize that an offense against her has been committed.

It is, of course, self-defeating to respond heatedly and pointedly every time someone shoves ahead of you in a line or keeps you waiting for an appointment or jostles you on the street. It is especially true that people who live in large cities could use up all their energy simply reacting to incidents of that sort. Obviously, one must bring a sense of proportion and judgment to exchanges with other people, a sense of what is appropriate and what is not. A minor brush with someone during the day may not rate much concern; its consequences may be insignificant. On the other hand, some slights or attacks absolutely merit a response; the failure to respond may, in fact, provoke further aggression. But making these kinds of distinctions is very hard for the masochist. Her perceptions are not grounded in present reality. She lives in a world peopled by the harsh phantoms of the significant adults of her childhood, and it is to these shadows that she is perpetually responding. Her anxiety-driven defensive behavior is a fantasy expression of something no longer real—not real, that is, until she recreates it over and over again by employing her system of anticipatory defense. In a situation that has the potential for passive masochism, it is necessary to determine whether true injury has been done, whether the failure to defend oneself may encourage further aggression, and whether one is in a position to defend oneself adequately. Masochistic people, bound to the past, indeed haunted by it, have not developed the autonomy that would allow them to ask these questions and then answer them objectively.

As I said at the outset of this chapter, the reason for making the distinction between active and passive masochism is that someone attempting to overcome her masochism must understand as precisely as possible the part she plays in the masochistic process: When is she the initiator, when the respondent? Both active and passive masochism exist in the same person, side by side, and both are equally destructive. But active masochism is perhaps more easily conquered. Here the masochistic person has her fate in her own hands. It is up to her whether or not she will hand someone the rope with which to hang her. If she can learn to keep quiet, to be self-contained, to refrain from volunteering information that will be damaging, she will have taken a major step toward eliminating her own suffering.

6

Masochism and the Maiden

I peeked in to say goodnight
And then I heard my child in pray'r,
"And for me some scarlet ribbons,
Scarlet ribbons for my hair."

All the stores were closed and shuttered,
All the streets were dark and bare,
In our town no scarlet ribbons,
Not one ribbon for her hair.

Through the night my heart was aching,
Just before the dawn was breaking,
I peeked in and on her bed
In gay profusion lying there,
Lovely ribbons, scarlet ribbons,
Scarlet ribbons for her hair.

If I live to be a hundred,
I will never know from where,
Came those lovely scarlet ribbons,
Scarlet ribbons for her hair.

The first time I heard "Scarlet Ribbons," which sounded like a folk song, was in the early 1960s as my daughter was playing the guitar and singing. I had just begun to do research on the menarche, the onset of menstruation, and the song struck me as a powerful metaphoric expression of that most significant event.

It had a dreamlike quality, moving fluidly between the symbolic and literal levels, and I felt almost as though it had been written for me.

The mother-daughter relationship reflected in the song is a positive one. The mother is loving and caring; she hears her daughter's prayer and yearns to be able to answer it. Metaphorically, I thought, what the daughter prays for are the scarlet ribbons of menstruation, the flow of blood that will signal her physical maturity. It is a request the mother would do anything she could to grant, but it is beyond her power to do so. Then, the ribbons do appear ("I will never know from where"), and the mother is delighted that her daughter's longing has been fulfilled. The song captures the anxiety and eagerness a young girl may feel awaiting her passage past this milestone, the mother's empathetic heartache as she feels her child's yearning, and the beauty and sense of reassurance of menstruation when it does arrive.

The girl in the song was fortunate to have a mother who really loved her and wanted to see her wishes fulfilled. At this crucial time in the girl's life, her mother wanted to give maturity to her, to support her development, rather than deprive her or hold her back. And it is likely that such a girl would not grow up masochistic, even though cultural forces could evoke masochistic tendencies. Certainly the mother's caring attitude would mitigate against the negative effects of the cultural input. Quite the opposite is true when a mother is uncaring and unloving; her insensitive, indifferent, or even hostile behavior will only serve to reinforce the cultural and social inclination toward masochism.

Adolescence, which generally begins with the menarche, is the last period of intensive interaction between mother and daughter, the time when a girl either receives an assist from her mother that enhances her chance of becoming an emotionally healthy young woman or suffers at her mother's hands the kind of ego damage that makes a healthy womanhood unlikely. The menarche itself, that first nodal point in the reproductive process that ends with menopause, serves as a focus for all the attitudes of mother and daughter relating to feminine sexuality and also con-

tains a summation of all the feminine feelings and attitudes that
have been established up to that point.

Contrary to much psychoanalytic thought, the menarche is
not a time of *capitulation* to femininity, a time when girls are
forced to give up their inherent desire to be boys and to succumb
to their incipient womanhood. It is a positive first step on the path
toward womanhood and reproduction and ought as such to be
viewed as an auspicious and joyous occasion. Mothers who behave destructively at this time give their daughters a substantial
push toward masochism.

Consider the damaging treatment afforded a patient of mine
on the occasion of her first menstrual period. She was eleven
years old and had been given no preparation whatsoever. One
morning she awoke early, feeling wet. Throwing off the bed-
clothes, she saw that she was covered with blood and ran in panic
to her mother's room. Her mother greeted her with a show of
irritation and slapped her face. She then told her daughter that
the flow of blood was a natural occurrence but added that it really
should not have appeared for another year or two. This left the
girl feeling that something was wrong with her. The mother instructed her daughter how to care for herself hygienically, advised
her to take to her bed for the day but gave her no other information. This was not an isolated experience, of course, although it
was a most significant one. The context of the mother-daughter
relationship was a series of experiences that resulted in the daughter's feeling devalued as a woman, viewing her menstruation as
something undesirable and carrying into adulthood a masochistic
heritage that was extremely difficult to overcome.

The slap on the cheek, by the way, is apparently a legacy of
the Jewish-Russian culture. It is said that the slap brings a blush
to the cheek, thus guaranteeing good color as an adult. Psycho-
analytically, one is hard pressed not to consider the slap a castrating gesture, suggestive of the mother's anger at her daughter's
newfound maturity and the potential threat it may indirectly pose
to the mother.

As a mother watches her daughter approach puberty, all the
anxieties and fears she felt at that time in her own life are fre-

quently evoked. The mother may also find her daughter's emerging sexuality threatening. She, after all, is heading toward menopause, the end of one part of her life as woman, while her daughter is poised at the very beginning of her sexual life. The sense of threat and the recapitulated fears and anxieties may cause great difficulty between mother and daughter, and often they struggle fiercely at this time.

A parable by the Lebanese writer Kahlil Gibran called "The Sleep Walkers" catches the ebb and flow of the currents and undercurrents that can exist between a mother and daughter at this time of life. It involves a mother and daughter who walked in their sleep. One night they meet in a mist-veiled garden. The mother speaks first, calling her daughter "my enemy," declaring that the girl has "built [her] life upon the ruins of mine." The daughter in turn calls the older woman selfish and accuses her of hatefulness in standing "between my freer self and me," and wanting "my life an echo of your own faded life!" When both women awake they revert to their polite and loving daytime selves.

Gibran's mother and daughter reveal their true feelings about each other when they appear in the mist-veiled garden. This is similar to a dream in which, under the conditions of sleep, the truth comes out. Each sees the other as her enemy, the mother resenting her daughter because she has sapped her youth and fed off her life in an almost parasitic way, the daughter bitter about her mother's desire to prevent her from becoming an independent sexual being. They wish each other dead. Yet when they awaken they slip automatically into a stereotyped sort of behavior, their deepest feelings obscured by a routine and superficial affability.

The emotions that are articulated in the garden, however, frequently come into play between mother and daughter at the time of the menarche. The fairy tale of Snow White and Rose Red, in which the old woman asks the mirror who is fairest of them all, also speaks of the sense of competition that can exist between an older and younger woman, between mother and daughter.

A masochistic patient who did not have many dates as a young

woman recalled how she felt when a date *did* come to pick her up
and her mother engaged him in conversation, going on and on,
not letting go until it was too late to go anywhere. The young
woman stood by helplessly, unable to intervene. Part of the
mother's success at this was due to the fact that she was an attractive and charming woman. She had never taken second place
herself and perhaps did not realize what she was doing to her
daughter. But the daughter did and felt murderous rage.

The fact is that a mother may find it difficult to witness her
daughter being launched sexually while she feels her own sexual
powers waning. This is especially true when the mother's life has
not been a particularly satisfactory or fulfilling one. The mother
wants to continue being declared the fairest of them all, but it is
usually evident that the daughter has, in fact, become the fairest.
The mother feels usurped. Very often at this time the mother is
also compulsively reenacting with her daughter the pubescent experience she had with her own mother.

Feeling threatened, beset by old fears, the mother may perceive her daughter as being out of control and make a last-ditch
effort to assert her dominance over her child. Her attempts to
rein in her daughter may be cruel and unduly suppressive. When
this occurs, the daughter generally responds by becoming more
defiant. Mother and daughter are then locked in a battle marked
by escalating cruelty on the mother's part, deepening defiance on
the daughter's. The other response an anxious mother may evidence is avoidance of the problem altogether, refusing to discuss
menstruation with her daughter, denying that it is happening.
Either response is clearly harmful to the girl's sense of her self-
worth.

The father may also play a part in this preadolescent drama.
To protect himself against any incestuous desires he may have for
his daughter, a father may accuse her of being seductive, of being
promiscuous. The daughter's behavior may be completely innocent, but the father projects his own fears onto her and then
makes accusations against her that are deeply hurtful. The father
of a patient of mine, as the girl approached adolescence, required
her to come directly home after school every day. He knew

exactly how long it should take her to make the trip, and if she was even slightly late, he would march her to the basement and beat her with his belt. Occasionally varying the punishment and making it even more cruel, he would require her to wait in the basement while he ate his dinner, and then he would come down and beat her afterwards.

It has become increasingly clear recently (Freud's interpretations of such reports as fantasy to the contrary) that sexual molestation and sometimes rape by a father or stepfather are far from rare. Sexual child abuse is often an ongoing phenomenon that occurs over a period of years. This does *not* make a young girl feel desirable. She recognizes the exploitative and damaging nature of such behavior even though she may be given rewards for enduring it. And the net effect of such exploitation is to make her feel contaminated and debased. Often such girls turn in desperation to their mothers to report what has happened, and often they are met by anger and denial on the mother's part, especially if the mother is totally dependent on the father who is being accused.

When a patient of mine reported sexual abuse to her mother, the mother's reaction was to begin accusing the girl of being a tramp if she put on lipstick or asked for high-heeled shoes, hardly suspect behavior in an adolescent girl eager to grow up. The mother was attempting to support her denial of the father's behavior by projecting blame onto her daughter for anything connected with sexual interest or sexual maturity.

A young woman who arrives at this time in her life having already developed masochistic tendencies will probably view the onset of menstruation with fear, the same way she views nearly everything. If, on top of this, her parents treat her cruelly or make accusations that further diminish her self-esteem, she will commence her life as a mature female with additional burdens of fear and a greatly increased inclination toward masochism.

The menarchal research I mentioned earlier was a study of premenstrual tension and the mother-daughter relationship. It is generally acknowledged that a large number of women suffer premenstrual tension, some estimating the proportion at 70 percent, my own study indicating it to be as high as 85 percent. By premenstrual tension I mean that wide variety of symptoms that includes feelings of tension, irritability, and quarrelsomeness; swelling of body parts (this is physiological, not psychological); headache (which may be either physiological or psychological), nausea, and vomiting; depression; hunger; desire for sweets; extreme lassitude; a tendency to cry easily; and a wish to call mother.

Because I found there was a virtual absence of any of these symptoms the first time the women in my study menstruated, I inferred that the behavior of significant persons, especially the mother, must account for the symptoms. Today the psychological connotations of PMS are being denied, and it is being ascribed almost exclusively to physiological causes. Contrary to this, I found that the mother's role in the daughter's menarchal experience was the crucial determining factor in whether or not she developed premenstrual symptoms. The following were the important elements: how the mother prepared her daughter for menstruation, her emotional and behavioral response to its occurrence in the daughter, and her other more subtly expressed attitudes toward womanhood that came to the fore at this key point in her daughter's life. A woman's menstrual periods throughout her life seem to represent a constantly recurring recapitulation of the circumstances of the first menstruation, a kind of hypnotic recreation reflecting a compulsive obedience to the demands and expectations, conscious or unconscious, of the mother. As the bodily climate is reproduced each month, so are the emotions.

Only 15 percent of the more than 100 mothers in my study reacted with joy to this sign of maturation in their daughters. An additional 25 percent responded in a generally positive, helpful way. The remainder, 60 percent, exhibited responses that were negative and damaging, and ten mothers had responses I would classify as extremely destructive. They failed to give any explanation of the meaning of menstruation, and/or they exhibited signs of annoyance, and/or they implied the girl was now in some sexual danger, and/or they failed to give help with the hygienic aspects of menstruation.

In those instances where the mothers responded joyfully to news of their daughters' first menstruation, and had adequately prepared their daughters for its onset, thirteen out of fifteen were free of any symptoms of premenstrual tension. In all those instances where women suffered seriously disturbing signs of premenstrual distress, there was either no preparation by the mother for the onset of menstruation or harmful action by the mother on being informed of it. Women in the former group made these remarks: "My mother was thrilled at having a grown daughter. She had prepared me with the necessary equipment and now showed me how to use it." "Mother said joyfully I had become a woman. She brought me flowers." Women in the latter group volunteered the following: "I had great difficulty telling my mother—I left the house to feel comfortable." "My mother told me if a man came near me I could get pregnant. I felt enormous fear." "My mother slapped me and called it the curse. I got no help from her. Somehow I adjusted." It is easy to see that the women in these two groups might grow up to be very different kinds of people, the former assured and unafraid, the latter fearful and vulnerable.

Women whose mothers responded negatively described their reactions to menstruation with the following words: fear, panic, embarrassment, bewilderment, resentment, alarm, terror. These reactions were occasioned not by the appearance of the blood itself but by the mother's response to its appearance. Negative terms, such as "the curse," reflect how damaging such negative responses can be.

Psychiatric News reported in its June 1983 issue that Dr. Uriel Halbreich of the Albert Einstein College of Medicine compared some forms of premenstrual problems to mild depressive disorders, especially the dysphoric changes, such as anxiety, the tendency to overeat, and so on. I believe this confirms my research findings because at the heart of depressive problems is object loss, the loss of the love of a significant person, leaving a feeling of bereavement that is characteristic of many premenstrual responses.

The symptoms of premenstrual tension have specific meanings that can be divided into two main categories. The first includes symptoms like hunger, need for love, craving for sweets, wish to call mother, depression, and weepiness. These suggest feelings of helplessness and vulnerability, emotional hunger, and a yearning for love. The second category, including such symptoms as irritability, tension, headache, anger, quarrelsomeness, nausea, and vomiting, suggests the need to defend against anticipated attack. Nausea and vomiting are also sometimes expressions of anger that say symbolically "I cannot contain it." Both categories suggest the cornerstones of the masochistic personality: helplessness, vulnerability, defensiveness, hidden rage, passivity.

It is natural for a certain amount of anxiety to accompany the menarche. It is a first experience of something unknown. It heralds the possibility of motherhood and, like all creative experiences, is linked with a kind of vulnerability. But the degree of anxiety, the extent of its perpetuation, and the sense of self with which a young woman emerges from this period depend to a great extent on the nature of the mother-daughter relationship. The onset of menstruation is a time at which there is great potential for enhancement or impairment of a girl's ego, especially in relation to her femininity, her approaching womanhood. A mother like the one in "Scarlet Ribbons," who is loving, accepting, reassuring, will surely give her daughter the gift of enhancement.

7

Sexual Masochism

The term *sexual masochism* conjures up for many people visions of whips and chains, bondage and flagellation, de Sade and Krafft-Ebing. They think of cruelty connected with sexual activity, the need to have pain inflicted by a sexual partner. And this form of extreme sexual masochism exists, of course. But it is a small part of the picture. Of greater interest to me, and far more prevalent—if less spectacular—is the everyday variety of sexual masochism, the reflection in the sexual sphere of the passive, power-fearing, suffering personality.

Sexual expression and experience are a distillate of the total person. A woman's essence is articulated in the sexual aspect of her life, just as it is in her family life, her working life, and her social relationships. In the sexual area, it may even express itself in its purest form because the intimacy of the sexual connection tends to highlight behavior and make it particularly intense. A woman who in general behaves masochistically and who operates from the defensive stance of the masochistic communication style will surely suffer from masochism in her sexual life. It is part and parcel of the same damaging conduct that pervades every other area of her life.

When considering this subject, I always think of the song by Carly Simon called "I Haven't Got Time for the Pain." The song reveals a lifetime of suffering and pain and a desire to overcome it through a relationship with a new sexual partner. In the lyrics, the line, "*Suffering* was the only thing that made me feel alive" is a clear statement of someone beset by masochistic tendencies. And, "That's just how much it cost to survive in this world" implies recognition of the high price that masochism exacts. The singer, declaring that she hasn't got time or room or need for the pain, wishes to leave her masochism behind. The only catch in this song, the only fallacy, is that she thinks this transformation will occur through a liaison with another man. To be literal about the song lyrics, that's highly unlikely. What is more probable is that her destructive patterns will come into play in the new relationship and, sooner or later, she will find herself crying herself to sleep over *him*.

Theoretically, when a man and woman meet they are equal. But if one of them is masochistic, as they begin to express their personalities, as they begin to interact with one another, the power situation quickly becomes loaded in favor of the non-masochist. One person (and, as we have seen, this is nearly always the woman) begins to surrender power, the other to acquire it. As the relationship progresses, this disparity becomes more and more extreme; the equation between the two becomes like a scale that is imbalanced: heavily weighted with power on one side, light with weakness and fear of power on the other. In other words, the relationship does not alter the basic personality patterns of the participants; it reflects, and sometimes accentuates, those patterns.

The slide into inequality can be set in motion the moment a man and woman first come into contact with each other. A beautiful, capable young woman who ran her own business received a phone call from a man she'd met on vacation months earlier and liked very much. When he suggested they get together, she immediately invited him to come to dinner although she was exhausted from a long day's work. Already she was responding masochistically and beginning to tip the power scales in his favor. Why didn't she wait to see what he had in mind? Why did she immediately volunteer to make a special effort? Since she was tired, it might have been nicer for them to go out. When he asked her at the end of the evening if he might spend the night, she said, "Well, I've been waiting since July for you to kiss me," a piece of information she might better have kept to herself. The sex that occurred that night was not particularly satisfying to her.

Fearful that she might not hear from him (worrying perhaps that since she had not enjoyed the sex, neither had he), she called the next weekend to say that she was having some friends over and asked if he would join them for dinner. He did and again he spent the night. The next day he suggested that when they went the following weekend to their summer places, which were near each other, they might go riding, a thought that delighted her. But a few days later he called to say he had studying and other things to do and would not be able to make it. She volunteered to come to his place instead so he would not have to interrupt his studying—yet another offer to put herself out. He agreed and said that if she would shop for dinner, he would reimburse her and cook dinner. Instead of graciously accepting his offer to share in the work, she said she had some leftovers and she would bring them along so that he would not have to cook. The next morning he told her that he did not want to get seriously involved with her. She was devastated.

Even in today's relatively free atmosphere, this woman was *too* eager, *too* willing, *too* compliant, *too* giving, and all of this *too* soon. Her eagerness to subordinate herself signaled how little self-worth she had. She went out of her way to let this man know that she considered herself a leftover, just like the food she provided. And I would imagine he found her behavior absolutely engulfing from the very beginning as she almost literally poured herself over him, revealing her lack of a sense of limits. Had this relationship continued, it is easy to see what the power alignment would have been.

In the following instance, the inequities in power were also established early on. At the end of their first date, which had been delightful, the young man escorted the young woman home in a taxi. As they rode along, he took her hand in his and held it on his lap. This was some years ago, before the "sexual revolution," and she was extremely uncomfortable when she recognized that she was touching an erect penis. But, despite her embarrassment, she did not dare to pull her hand away. "What if I'm wrong?" she thought. "What will he think of me?" This couple married quite quickly, and the marriage was a lengthy one marked by a decidedly sado-masochistic style and an eventual ending in wife-battering, marital rape, and, finally, none too soon for her sake, divorce. Looking back, it is clear to see that the power lines were drawn on that first date when she conveyed the message: I'll go along; I won't rock the boat; I'll do whatever you like; you're the one in charge here.

I have noted how women's history and acculturation have conditioned them for a masochistic role, and nowhere is this clearer than in the sexual area. Until quite recently, women were supposed to be virginal at the time of their marriage, and this lack of experience led them to suffer from sexual ignorance. They simply were not knowledgeable about sexual matters. This, in turn, caused them to feel that they had no rights in the sexual encounter. Both women and men operated on the assumption that it would be men who called all the sexual shots. Women felt it incumbent upon them to capitulate in this area, as in so many others; they were instructed to defer to their husbands.

Until the last several decades, marriages were often based on economic necessity, the desire to get ahead in the world rather than on any attraction that existed between two people; and women were often in the position of bartering themselves sexually for the sake of financial or social advantage. It was important for a woman to try to please or win over—certainly not to challenge—any man who seemed a good potential husband. This sort of pragmatic arrangement did nothing to allay their sexual fears. The severe inequities of power from which women suffered were made even worse in the sexual area by the addition of fear and ignorance.

These circumstances have affected female sexual responses in many ways, the most important among them being that they have deflected women's attention away from their own needs and feelings and directed it toward the pleasing of men. (This accounted for the large numbers of "frigid" women in the past, an unfair and entirely erroneous description that reflects the male viewpoint. More accurate terms might have been "impotent" or "unresponsive.") Women have obscured their own responses to such a degree that it is often difficult for them to determine what is an authentic sexual response and what is not. This uncertainty has not been helped by all the "experts" who have weighed in publicly and volubly with their notions of what women *should* want, prefer, and expect.

Pornography is a growing cultural force that continues to reinforce women's belief that the sexually masochistic role is rightly and properly theirs. Pornographic films and photographs generally show the woman serving the man, by definition a display of unequal power: The woman follows the man's dictates, does things that please him. Pornography also increasingly shows men hurting women in the course of sexual activity, tying them up, hitting them, attacking them in some violent way. And this is extremely destructive to women, lending support to the idea that they are inferior, that they have no right to say what they would like in a sexual relationship.

The extent to which women can be made to subscribe to such injurious views was evident in a recent "Letter to the Editor" column in *Ms.* magazine. Several letters responded to an earlier letter from a woman who said she enjoyed being spanked by her husband. More than one of the letters echoed this excerpt: "Unmarried, I have shared this desire [to be paddled] with only one boyfriend, and the results have been consistently terrific. When we tried role reversal of this particular activity, it turned neither of us on."

Sexual impotence in a woman is the ultimate expression of sexual masochism. When this condition exists, a woman has in effect castrated herself; she has rendered herself incapable of sexual response out of fear: a general all-pervasive fear of the other person, fear of his sexual desires, fear of asserting herself and refusing him what he wants, fear of asserting herself and requesting what would give her pleasure. These fears are a part of all expressions of sexual masochism in women, although they don't always lead to such a devastating result. Present in a less virulent form, these same fears make women feel that they must go along with whatever men want sexually, that they must put their own preferences aside. Whenever a woman does that, she is behaving masochistically. Sexual impotence may also reflect the fact that a woman has (for nonsexual reasons) chosen a man who does not appeal to her or who does not try to win her over in the sexual realm but is only concerned with himself.

Also at the extreme end of the continuum of sexually masochistic behavior was a patient of mine who was very hypnotizable and had gone to see a hypnotist for help with an obesity problem. She ended up working for him without salary and also became his compliant sexual partner. Therapy rescued her from this relationship, but she soon took up another man who had an especially disturbing sexual style: As orgasm was impending, he liked to put his hands around her throat and squeeze. Fortunately, in treatment with me, she was able to extricate herself from this relationship before anything seriously harmful occurred. But obviously the potential for violence was present throughout her association with this man, and she submitted to living with that threat.

Another patient of mine who exhibited very masochistic sexual behavior had actually been taught to be masochistic by the sadistic actions of her parents. They abused her mightily as a child and sometimes had kept her chained to her bed for as long as a week at a time. As an adolescent, she met men in the streets and went home with anyone who asked her. Sometimes she would have a brief sexual encounter with her pickup and leave. On a few occasions she was held prisoner for several days, being used and abused sexually before managing to escape. From none of these experiences did this young woman, who was a very isolated, alienated human being, derive any sexual pleasure. Her sexual involvements were a form of punishment, something her parents had taught her she deserved. The involvements obviously suggested that she felt herself to be utterly worthless, a piece of refuse. I think it is also possible, sad to say, that she gleaned some meager feelings of companionship from these encounters and that she paid for the momentary, fragmentary sense of relationship with sex. In any case, the punishment she absorbed was a high price indeed.

Masochistic women are wound-gatherers; they accumulate hurts, injuries, sorrow. In the sexual area, these are women who often manage to contract one venereal disease after another (a patient of mine once described herself as having "crotch rot"); they are women who need to have repeated abortions. They collect sexual wounds. The "crotch-rot" woman, by the way, was married to a very authoritarian man who constantly issued orders to her (which she willingly followed). When she left him she became involved with a succession of minor gangsters.

Caroline was a brilliant, attractive young lawyer who came to me in an extremely depressed state shortly after having an abortion. Her pregnancy had resulted from a sexual relationship with a married man who had been a law school classmate and had ended up in the same firm as she. This man had always been given to making sardonic and disparaging remarks at Caroline's expense, and she had felt he did not like her. Nevertheless, when they one day found themselves alone in a conference room, he locked the door and they had sex on the long table in the center of the room. Caroline did not experience any real pleasure from this, but the occurrence turned out to be the start of an ongoing arrangement. They never saw each other anywhere else; he still never had a kind word for her; they just met every so often in the conference room and had sex. Caroline submitted to this perfectly extraordinary behavior even though she found it humiliating. When she discovered she was pregnant, she did not tell him, for she knew he would either ridicule her and/or deny that the child was his.

Those people who need to have pain inflicted in order to participate sexually are seriously neurotic. My feeling is that they must have had a connection established during childhood between pain and erotic sensation. A woman reported, for example, that she liked to be shaken and slapped as a way of initiating sexual foreplay, which then soothed, comforted, and ultimately aroused her. When the rough handling was absent, she didn't enjoy the foreplay and became aroused very slowly. This is another example of how problems that occur in the sexual area are rarely purely sexual. This woman was reenacting, in transferential fashion, a prevailing condition of her early relationship with her mother whose style was to alternate punishment and beating with remorseful embracing and seductive forgiveness. I would also venture to say that women who exhibit this pattern, and it is not an uncommon one, seldom experience true sexual excitement. It is more likely that they make a trade-off: acceptance of pain in return for physical closeness and a semblance of attention that they might not receive any other way.

More minor expressions of sexual masochism occur when, for instance, a woman avoids initiating sex because she fears the man will think ill of her or, perhaps, ridicule her. To wait always for the man to initiate sex is self-punishing. If a woman feels she can never refuse sex, regardless of how she feels, this is self-punishing in a different way and constitutes another example of fear-ridden, masochistic behavior.

During sexual contact, if a woman would like to be kissed and held first but fears to request physical affection and foreplay, knowing that the man is eager to get directly to the sexual point, this is sexual masochism. If she prefers a particular position during sexual intercourse but does not dare ask for it, that is another manifestation of the same destructive syndrome. It is masochistic when a woman is afraid to discuss contraception with a man or to question someone she does not know well about venereal disease. In short, when a woman would like some change in the sexual encounter but does not dare request it, or when she would like some information but fears to demand it, then she is exhibiting sexually masochistic behavior. Clearly I do not mean that a woman should *always* have her way. But she is certainly entitled to it some of the time.

One would think that sexual masochism might be less prevalent in nonmarital relationships than it is within marriage, which carries with it certain obligations and demands, foremost among them the consent to a sexual relationship. Women engaging in sex outside of marriage should in a sense be freer, more able to exert their free will. Yet I have been interested and distressed to observe over and over again that once a sexual relationship is established, unmarried women adopt the most negative aspects of the behavior of married women: They become afraid to assert themselves sexually, they assign their own sexual interests a low priority, and they capitulate to the expectations of their male partner, even though they are under no obligation to do so. They are as quick to negate themselves sexually as are women bound by marriage.

Eileen came to New York to be near her lover, who was a medical student in the city. She, like so many of the young women I have described, was a bright, attractive person with a good job. When I first began seeing her, she was eager to hide the destructive nature of her relationship with the young man, and only gradually did its extreme inequity become clear. Because the boy was studying hard, it was understood that he would not come to Eileen's apartment to pick her up when they went out, nor would he call ahead and state a time when they might see each other. She was simply to be available, sexually and in every other way, whenever he was free. He would call, for example, half an hour before show time and say, "I want to see such-and-such a movie. Can you come?"

There was never any caring involved in their sexual contact. They had intercourse when they were together because that was when he had time. The sex was all right, she said, when I questioned her about it. I took this to mean that he probably did what he wanted to do sexually, and since it did not really offend or irritate her, and she got a little affection from it, she considered it "all right." She certainly did not experience much pleasure, however, and my guess would be that she was not orgastic, although she would never say so directly. Despite the paucity of regard, tenderness, or satisfying sex involved in this relationship, Eileen hung onto it tenaciously.

In an article called "Masochism in Love and Sex" in the *American Journal of Psychoanalysis*, Dominick A. Barbara questions why masochistic women let themselves be used sexually in relationships with men who treat them badly. His explanation, a correct one, I believe, emphasizes the masochistic longing for surrender and notes that in sex, of course, one merges with another person. The relationship between this yearning and the unresolved symbiosis to mother, or another significant adult, is obvious. The masochistic person seeks to return to the symbiotic state via sex, fantasizing that if she submerges herself in another, if she becomes part of him, she will feel safe and he will love her.

Something that I have long considered almost a diagnostic sign of masochism is the almost involuntary need to cry immediately after orgasm.

In an earlier chapter, I described crying as a masochistic message and mythology offers ample evidence that this has existed in women for a very long time. Niobe was a mother in Greek mythology who was punished for maternal pride—she declared her children to be like gods—by having her children slain. When this occurred she wept so copiously that her tears turned her to stone. She reminds us, of course, of Lot's wife, an obviously dependent, masochistic woman who was unfairly accused of looking back at Sodom and Gomorrah for salacious reasons. A poet I know has tried to set the record straight.

Women

Like Lot's wife
nameless
and forced
to leave her homeland
I know now
she looked back
having no way to look ahead.

Too long has the world
insisted
a willful curiosity
turned her head—
not even suspecting
unconquerable
ties to home.

But even this was
half truth:
the rest—that
no road opened.

She and I
sisters
could not move on
nor has history
recorded
it was torrents of tears
transformed us
to
pillars of salt.

Involuntary tearfulness speaks of a woman's lack of identity, her sense of worthlessness, her feeling that she is nameless, faceless, that she must follow her partner's dictates, accepting whatever he does or says. Her orgastic release leaves her feeling even more helpless and vulnerable than usual, and her tears are a plea that she not be attacked in her defenseless state and that he extend some sympathy and understanding to her at this moment when things between them ought to be tender.

Fantasy can play an important role in the sexual life of the masochistic woman. Coital fantasy, it should be noted, generally serves a diametrically opposed purpose in men and in women. Men usually employ fantasy in order to *engage* in sex despite problems; women use it to help themselves to *submit* to sex where it seems unavoidable. Harry Stack Sullivan used the term "long-circuiting" to describe the process of taking a complicated series of steps, like a lengthy detour, to achieve an end one is incapable of attaining directly and simply. And that describes very well the way many masochistic women use sexual fantasies. They need the assistance of an often elaborately constructed story to enable them either to tolerate something that is intolerable or to perform something that without the fantasy would be impossible. Such a story, encompassing many complicated steps toward a simple end, might be that the woman imagines herself a princess who has been brought into the grand hall of a majestic palace in order to be initiated into the rites of love. The initiation begins with many men in a variety of splendid costumes playing with the woman, teasing and exciting her, and ends with the men having intercourse with her.

The notion of being a passive, almost lifeless performer in the sexual act is at the heart of most masochistic sexual fantasies. Women fantasize themselves being bound or restrained in some way so that they have no ability to assert themselves sexually or to refuse the sexual involvement in the first place. Sometimes these fantasies extend to being raped or, in the most extreme cases, being raped and tortured. The latter, of course, indicates severe pathology. But the former, and more common, fantasy is simply another part of the masochistic stance I have been exploring. It grows out of that same sense of guilt and fear that the masochistic woman feels about virtually everything in her life. In this instance, she is guilty about her sexual desires and fearful of acknowledging them. After all, mother or father or both parents, those forbidding authority figures, would not approve. So the masochistic woman long-circuits that disapproval by concocting a fantasy that robs her of her own volition. When she is bound or restrained, when she is forced to submit to rape, there is no question of free will; she cannot be held responsible for her sexual involvement; she is, in effect, the man's victim—helpless, passive, compliant. In this way, via the extraordinary human capacity for rationalization, she can have her cake and eat it too.

The sexual fantasies of masochistic women sometimes become highly elaborated, reflecting the grandiose aspect of masochism that makes the masochistic person think all eyes are focused on her, that she is the center of the universe. They also frequently include the princess figure: The woman fantasizes herself a royal personage and thus special; she imagines that many people are serving her, that her clothing and her appearance are beautiful. If she feels extremely special, that balances the sense of defective ego and worthlessness from which she suffers. Rape occurs in many sexually masochistic fantasies not only because it allows the victim a completely passive role but also because it permits sex under violent, cruel, and painful circumstances. The masochistic person's need to receive punitive treatment expresses itself in this way during sexual relations. Not surprisingly, rape fantasies may frequently occur in women who have been the victims of sexually violent behavior within their own families. Their first sexual experiences were violent and abusive ones, and these elements are incorporated in their fantasies.

The sexual fantasies of masochistic women have another curious and, unfortunately, predictable element. They almost always focus on the woman imagining how she can make herself more desirable, more appealing, to the man. She turns herself into a princess; she glorifies her appearance. Virtually never does she envisage what she would find desirable in a male partner. In her fantasies she attempts to idealize herself, but she tends to include the man pretty much as he is. Of course there are exceptions, such as the woman who imagined herself a princess being sexually aroused by princes. But even in that instance the emphasis was on the woman's passive submission to the things that were being done to her. The princes were incidental, nothing very much more than the instruments of her initiation. This stress on being desirable so as to appeal to a man has interfered with women's true expression of their sexuality and taken the focus off what it is *they* find arousing, what it is *they* desire sexually. I am not denying that a woman must arouse desire in a man for true consummation of the sexual act. But the emphasis on physical appearance as an avenue to arousal has been exaggerated. Other factors are involved as well.

Most women in our culture probably suffer from some sort of sexual masochism because women generally have been led away from their own notions of authentic sexual response and had imposed on them, by the media as well as by professionals, a set of sexual standards to which they are told they should aspire. It is as though they have been handed sexual thermometers, told what temperature they should run, and instructed to check frequently to see how they are doing. Of course this is fallacious, and the result is to put more and more distance between women and their true sexual selves.

The only real indicator of authentic sexual expression is what is going on in the person, and being in touch with that requires introspection and self-awareness. It cannot be dictated from out-side. All living creatures are in a sense worlds unto themselves, containing within them knowledge of their behavioral and physio-logical functions and a sense of when these functions are operat-ing properly. If a dog breaks a leg, you don't have to tell it not to walk; it knows that it can't. It gets along fine without the benefit of expert opinion, operating instead from instinct that lets it know when something unhealthy has happened. Human beings have higher perceptive and cognitive levels, but they also contain within themselves the maximum amount of information about their own proper functioning. Women have been led to abandon this in the sexual area. They are singular beings trying to accom-modate themselves to general standards, with disastrous results.

In the past there was a greater belief in selectivity, a greater premium put on individual tastes. All women were not thought to find beefy, muscular men (the "hunks," as they are currently billed) attractive; all men were not expected to respond uniformly to a certain shape and size of breast (every woman did not have to be a "10" to be deemed worthy of attention). But gradually our own individual cues about what is sexually appealing are being eradicated. A woman used to know whether or not she wanted to kiss a particular man. Today, if he looks a certain way, if they are in a certain situation, she *presumes* that she wants to kiss him and she acts on that presumption.

This absence of sexual autonomy is reflected, for example, in a play like Neil Simon's *The Last of the Red-Hot Lovers*, in which an attractive woman involves herself in a sexual escapade with a dull, uninviting fish store owner who perpetually smells of fish and is married besides. I see it reflected also in what used to be called the May/December romance but might now more aptly be called the *April*/December syndrome because older men are get-ting involved with ever-younger women. Of course there is a trade-off involved in such a liaison, and the woman gets some-thing from it as well as the man. However, I believe it is masochistic on the woman's part, because a sexual relationship with such age disparity goes against natural human inclinations.

Adam and Eve were roughly the same age, whatever it was. And until quite recently relationships with a large age gap were exceptional.

The belief that it is all right not to have sex with a man if you don't feel like it has been chipped away at. The dilution of this belief and of individual cues certainly prepares the ground for sowing the seeds of sexual masochism. Women increasingly, I think, are doing things sexually that they do not want to do, submitting themselves to the power of their sexual partner, or partners, and their sexual autonomy is the casualty. They hew to external guidelines, ignoring their own feelings, moving further and further away from them until these authentic indicators vanish altogether. Holding out for what one wants, feeling powerful enough to be assertive about what one wants, constitutes true autonomy. But there is precious little of this being practiced by women today.

The great orgasm debate of a few years ago certainly highlighted the conflict between individual cues and "expert" opinion and illustrated as well the idea of the sexual thermometer, that gauge women were told they should regularly and rigorously consult. (Few people realize that Masters of Masters and Johnson, the "gods" of the sexual response arena, began his work studying the masturbatory habits of prostitutes. Perhaps this showed something about sexual physiology, but it had little to do with intercourse in which involvement with another person and feelings and responses to him are present.) Women's sexual responses were being debated, and out of the argument came more of those general standards: Women *should* feel this, they *should not* feel that, if they felt this it was real, if they felt that it was false, and so on. I could not help thinking as the discussion raged how unnecessary it would all be if women had not suffered such estrangement from their own feelings. For a woman who experiences authentic orgastic response needs no outside reassurance that what she felt was real or superior or legitimate. She knows what is genuine and what is not. But when a woman deserts this knowledge of herself, when she abandons her own preferences in favor of those espoused by a book on sexual techniques or a film or an "expert," when she relinquishes her sexual autonomy, in other words, then she is behaving in a sexually masochistic fashion.

8

Sado-Masochistic
Partnership

On a recent warm day, as I walked in a New York City park, I watched some people playing tennis, and I was reminded of the tennis analogy I had used to describe certain masochistic communications. One of the mixed-doubles players was a man who was built like a tank. Extremely compact, with virtually no protrusions destroying the solid line of his body (his nose did not even seem to break the plane of his face), he looked as though he could resist any assault upon him. His form was quite poor: He played aggressively, pushing the ball over the net with a vicious, slashing motion, rather than swinging easily and stroking it. But there was obviously something in his behavior that rattled the other players, even though they were superior, and he repeatedly came out on top. Somewhat later in a singles match with a man who was also a better player, his aggressive tactics became even more pronounced. He charged each ball as if hitting it were a matter of life and death, pounding it into the corners of the court, making no pretense whatever at playing a friendly game that might be made enjoyable by volleying a bit. And gradually the other, better player became demoralized and began to lose. This, I thought, is exactly what happens between a masochistic person and a sadistic one, most especially in a marriage. The masochist may be better equipped in all sorts of ways, but as the sadist exercises his abusive skills, those advantages are nullified. The masochist, as she succumbs over and over again to the power of the other, becomes more and more inept and self-destructive.

Nowhere are the effects of the historical and cultural forces that predispose women toward masochism more keenly realized than in marriage. St. Paul's epistle to the Ephesians, echoing the passage I cited earlier from St. Peter, lays the groundwork for the inequities that often exist between husbands and wives. "Wives," Paul writes, "*submit* [italics added] yourselves unto your husbands, as unto the Lord." The submission Paul speaks of is primarily sexual, but lest there be any doubt that it also includes all other areas of marital life, he adds: "For the husband is the head of the wife, even as Christ is head of the church." "Head," in this context, has more than one symbolic meaning: The husband is the ruler of the wife, the one who possesses power over her; he is also the thinker, the one with brains enough for both of them. Although Paul softens his admonition somewhat by directing husbands to "love your wives, even as Christ also loved the church, and gave himself for it," he exhorts wives to *revere* their husbands in addition to loving them, another indication of the higher level on which the man is placed. I cannot help but feel that Paul gave a substantial push to the sado-masochistic marriage with the arrangement he outlined (and, of course, he had plenty of help from others). For bestowing the gift of power on one partner and withholding it from the other virtually guarantees that a great inequity will exist between them. The fact that husbands are often sadistic and wives masochistic stems from the unequal power balance in marriage. The sado-masochistic marriage is characterized by an ongoing battle between the two parties as they engage in a kind of primitive struggle for power.

I once overheard a group of single men talking about women and one of them said, "Women tend to gravitate toward men who treat them badly. I have a great deal of trouble understanding this." Probably he could not understand simply because he was a man. The early, heavy weight of acculturation toward submissiveness that women receive would be incomprehensible to him. But what may have eluded him as well was the notion of the repetition compulsion, that tendency to engage in relationships with people in the present who bear a psychic resemblance to significant and powerful figures of the past.

It is a common psychoanalytic mistake to believe that people marry someone reminiscent of the parent of the opposite sex. My view is that people generally marry a surrogate for the more powerful parent, the parent whose behavior has had the greatest impact on them. The sex of that parent is irrelevant. Masochists tend to marry surrogates for the more dangerous, hurtful parent. Meeting a man who evokes the repetition compulsion, the masochistic woman deludes herself into thinking he is strong. She knows herself to be weak, she admires strength, and she believes she has found it in him. What she sees as strength is most likely the same kind of coldness or cruelty that existed in her damaging parent.

A patient gave the following description of how she perceived her husband when she first met him. "He was quite noncommunicative, but I thought that indicated he was self-contained, self-sufficient. I admired this. I thought it meant he was strong." In fact, her husband turned out to be an extremely brutal man who was incapable of true, intimate interaction. And in many ways he resembled the patient's mother—who had held her daughter captive for years.

Psychoanalyst Reuben Fine said that a sado-masochistic marriage does not begin as a love affair, but as a *hate* affair. It generally is of long duration, often lasting a lifetime, and becomes the center of the psychic lives of both partners, with each seeing the other as the enemy. Fine noted that both people involved in a hate affair are extremely dependent. Neither has resolved the symbiotic attachment to mother; neither has firm boundaries. They become part of each other, clinging to the attachment, unable to give it up despite its destructiveness. This suggests that what they fear most is not being attached to another person. Men may function well sexually in such a relationship because the sexual activity is allied to rape in its hostility. A man in a hate affair may have the fantasy of destroying the woman, and that fantasy will give him potency, Fine said. One woman cited had the fantasy of the man's penis breaking off inside her. Obviously her goal was destruction of the man. Interestingly, the superegos of both partners involved in such a relationship are similar. They have harsh, punitive consciences and tend to project all blame for wrongdoing onto the other person. The relationship involved in sado-masochistic marriage is that of slave-master, Fine observed, the master being the sadist who possesses the power, the slave being the masochist who is subservient to that power and victimized by it.

This, of course, relates directly to early experience and, again, conjures up the repetition compulsion. The parent is always the powerful figure, the source of supply of all things; the child possesses little on its own and is dependent upon the parent's desire and ability to give. In a sense, this earliest relationship in life is a form of the master-slave relationship. If love is present, the power between parent and child gradually evens out, and the master-slave framework disappears. If it is not, the child suffers from the parent's coercion and may become either submissive and passive, or assaultive and destructive. The sadistic husband in a sado-masochistic marriage attempts—through cruelty, blame-projecting onto the wife, humiliating her, inciting guilt in her and sometimes even through raping her—to gain the control he did not have as a child subject to powerful, abusive parents and to destroy those early, hurtful figures. The masochistic wife— through capitulation, submissiveness, and acceptance of the premises of the husband—attempts to appease, to placate, the stern authorities who governed her early life. Both are immature, anxiety-ridden people displaying transference reactions and irrational distortions, deeply dependent on each other as partners in what one therapist has called the "choreography of unconscious dissociated tendencies."

The absorbing, all-encompassing nature of the sado-masochistic connection was illustrated in Ingmar Bergman's film *Wild Strawberries*. A doctor picks up a couple as he is driving along a road. Once in the car, the couple ignores the fact that anyone else is present, continuing the horrendous argument they were in the midst of when the doctor stopped for them. All social amenities are displaced, all notions of proper social conduct obliterated by the couple's obsessive need to continue their struggle.

One thing that keeps the partners in a sado-masochistic marriage locked together is that each one's sense of self depends upon the responses of the other. The sadistic husband develops his self-esteem by denigrating, humiliating, and criticizing his wife. The masochistic wife gleans her meager self-worth from the occasional kind, or at least nonabusive, word from her husband. Masochistic women, it has been said, pay the price of suffering in a sado-masochistic relationship in order to receive what they believe is love. I would add that a woman who has been driven by the repetition compulsion to marry a sadistic person finds it very difficult to understand the ruling negativisms of her husband's behavior. She continues to labor under the delusion that the marriage began as a love affair, not a hate affair.

The sadistic partner in such a marriage is just as wretched as his wife, although that may not be evident, since he is the one who appears to be inflicting all the wounds. His victim, the masochistic wife, is sacrificed to his need to have a companion in misery. The sadist may also show little overt evidence of the guilty feelings so prominently displayed by the masochist. But he, too, suffers from a deep sense of guilt, although it is most often unconscious, and from a need for punishment.

The sado-masochistic marriage and its detrimental effects on both partners was eloquently depicted in Federico Fellini's film *La Strada*. As a daughter reaches puberty, her mother sells her to the strongman in a traveling circus, a man neither of them knows. This relationship automatically has a masochistic inception for the daughter because she enters it filled with feelings of abandonment. Her mother's action has told her in effect that she is unloved and that her mother is willing to exploit her in order to fight against her own crushing poverty. The girl, who plays the horn, is a sensitive, tender sort, and when she and the strongman first have sex together it awakens love in her and the expectation that they will establish a close, caring union. He does not share her feelings, however, and when she learns that he has had another woman, her hurt and despair are overwhelming. She then learns that he has killed a man, and she suffers terribly from this knowledge; she attempts once to escape but finally capitulates and rejoins him; she develops a hiccough, a psychosomatic expression of her inability to contain her distress completely; she grows sicker and sicker, and he becomes correspondingly taciturn and attempts to care for her; and finally he puts her out by the side of the road and leaves her behind. When he returns to this spot some time later and inquires about her, he is told that she has died. Hearing the news, he is obviously disturbed. Most perceptively, Fellini shows that the sadistic partner in a sado-masochistic marriage is just as pitiful as the masochist and, even though he is the one doing the punishing, he is being damaged, too. The relationship ultimately destroys both people.

As the power struggle continues between partners in such a marriage, they may at times seem to reverse roles, sadistic elements expressing themselves in the woman, masochistic elements in the man. A woman who has been repeatedly degraded by her husband may decide to fight back, and when she does her attack will be fueled by rage.

A patient of mine was a sensitive woman who was subjected by her husband to constant criticism. Every so often, her anger at this would reach a certain pitch and she would erupt. Once this occurred as they were getting into bed at night. He began his litany of criticism about how she ran the house, handled money, disciplined the children, and behaved sexually. Infuriated, my patient put her feet against her husband's body and gave a shove, pushing him onto the floor. This retaliation was mild, of course, compared with some we have read about in the newspapers: Wives no longer able to suppress their rage at being abused have turned on their husbands and killed them.

Behavior of this sort is what has led to the theory that each person has both sadistic and masochistic tendencies. But I do not subscribe to this. The masochistic wife's retaliation, or eruption of rage, is more likely due to the fact that even the worm turns when it has absorbed all it can tolerate. Then the anger is such that life is no longer meaningful and any risk is acceptable. Desperation is the name of the game, not sadism.

I came across a particularly blatant example of sado-masochistic interaction in a newspaper article recounting a divorce proceeding in which the wife maintained that the main problem in the marriage was her husband's "authoritarian dominance." To say the least, I thought as I read on. The husband, a physician, disciplined his wife with a demerit system, forty demerits, for example, each time she left the patio door open. For each demerit he required that his wife give him an hour's pay. To avoid demerits he also required that she cut her hair to his specifications, lose weight, lower the pitch of her voice, become a movie buff, and take dancing lessons. As if this was not enough, the wife, during the time her husband was in medical school, had to type his papers, clean the house and cook the meals, maintain the family cars, and work to support both of them. She and her parents, the wife said, had also contributed $32,800 toward her husband's medical school expenses.

This case not only illustrates the sado-masochistic marriage in full bloom but spotlights an unhappily typical attitude of the courts as well. In granting the divorce, the judge awarded the wife $24,600 and noted that this was a "very clear case of a woman putting a guy through medical school and wanting some good back from all those years." The judge never even addressed the obvious suffering this woman had endured, or the curious system of control her husband had employed. And the monetary award was $8,000 less than she and her family had spent and did not take into account in any way all the extra work this woman had done (in and out of the home) during the time her husband was in school. Judges are all too commonly unsympathetic and unfair toward women.

Witness the recent case in Colorado in which a judge sentenced a man to two years in jail for *killing* his wife, a case that caused an enormous outpouring of protest. The man maintained that his wife provoked him into killing her by leaving their home without any warning (we have reached a sorry state indeed if every woman attempting to get away from an abusive man is required to warn him of her intentions). Obviously, the defendant's reasoning fell on sympathetic ears, despite the prosecution's evidence that there had been a history of abuse in the marriage. The furor triggered by the two-year sentence (protesters included the governor of Colorado and his wife) eventually caused the judge to reconsider—and the sentence was changed to *four* years, still making the life of the dead woman rather cheap.

Judges have also been reluctant to validate the idea of marital rape, although it certainly exists. For some time, ironically, Israel was the only country whose courts had convicted a husband of rape. Recently, a marital rape conviction was handed down in a New York state court.

Relatively minor, but deeply wounding nevertheless, was the behavior of the husband who arrived at a party separately from his wife, went around the room greeting every woman with a kiss on the lips, but when he reached his wife he turned away and did not kiss her at all. This common tactic of a sadistic husband not only evoked jealousy in her, it publicly humiliated her in a sexual way, an especially vulnerable area. This same husband refused to stop when his wife had to go to the bathroom while they were driving. When they finally arrived home and she asked him please to open the door in hurry, he refused to put the key in the lock, instead hopping about from foot to foot and taunting her about her discomfort.

Another woman reported to me that her husband's way of tearing her down was never to compliment her, no matter what she did. This woman, who was "just a housewife," said, "I work so hard to please him. I keep the house nice and I try to have a good dinner ready for him when he comes home at night, and I take good care of the children, and I try to look attractive. After all, I get no other rewards. But he refuses to comment. He never says I look nice when we're going out. The most he might ever say is that it's not a bad dinner. That's the height of his praise."

Allied to this is the "silent treatment" that some sadistic husbands give their wives. In general, women tend to be loquacious; they are meant to be the entertainers and carry the burden of social involvement. Men, on the other hand, are often more taciturn, not as likely to feel obliged to speak, knowing they maintain more control when they keep their mouths shut. But the sadistic husband may punish his wife by refusing to speak at all, for hours, days, or even weeks. Some psychoanalysts maintain in regard to the parent-child relationship that indifference, not hatred, is the opposite of love. I think that applies here as well.

Silence is one of the most painful punishments the sadist can mete out. Hatred at least contains some emotion, some passion. Indifference, conveyed by the refusal to speak, the refusal of a husband even to acknowledge his wife, says: You do not matter, you are not really there, you do not exist.

That was communicated by the behavior of Sylvia's husband on their return flight from a European vacation. A film was being shown that she had seen several times and did not want to see again. An hour or so into the flight, the husband disappeared and was gone for two hours. When he returned he told her he had been watching a different film in another part of the plane. "Why did you just disappear?" she asked, quite upset. "Why didn't you come and get me and see if I was interested in watching it too?" He just shrugged and said he hadn't thought it was important.

With this as background, Sylvia then told me of her husband's shopping habit on Sunday nights when they returned from their weekend house in the country. He never asked her what she wanted from the store, and he never bought anything extra to stock the refrigerator after their being away. He only purchased those things he liked and wanted to eat on Sunday night, and the two of them had quite different tastes.

She also recalled the time her husband had plans to meet a friend for dinner and said she was welcome to come along. She pointed out that she would have to be a little late because of her work schedule but suggested that the others have a drink first and wait for her. When she arrived she found that they had not waited for her. They had, in fact, arranged to meet even earlier and were already through with their dinner.

Her husband, Sylvia said, displayed no real warmth toward her, even during sex. He didn't kiss her, there was no foreplay, and his only communication was to ask her afterwards if it had felt good, a query she felt was a demand for her to give a report on his performance, something she resented. When she told him this, he said that she took things too personally. I wish Sylvia had been able to reply that perhaps he took things too *impersonally* and perhaps their sexual life was not gratifying because it was devoid of feeling.

Sylvia's husband also displayed his indifference toward her by disappearing on weekends to play tennis for hours at a stretch, always without consulting her about their plans, often leaving her with a completely empty weekend. His behavior transmitted the message that Sylvia's existence did not matter to him. Any one of the incidents I've mentioned might seem minor standing alone, but when this sort of behavior is woven into the fabric of a marriage, it is undeniably sadistic.

Despite elaborate exhibitions of indifference, however, husbands in these partnerships do not generally want to see the marriage break up. And to this end they develop a kind of sixth sense that tells them just how far their masochistic wives can be pushed. When a sadistic man senses that his wife's tolerance for abuse has reached its limit, he will often pull back and sometimes even do something nice to disarm her and make her feel that perhaps her reactions were exaggerated, that he was not really as mean as she thinks. This is how, with her husband's collusion, the masochistic wife manages to keep fooling herself that she loves him. She mistakes dependence for love.

The issue of money is often the focus of sado-masochistic exchanges within a marriage. This was even more common no doubt when women worked less and a husband's cruelty took the form of squeezing his wife where money was concerned. I think of a patient whose husband was a doctor with a substantial income. The allowance he gave her for years and years was fifty dollars a week, even though during that period the cost of living escalated steeply. Out of that she was supposed to feed the family, buy clothes for herself and the children, pay any entertainment costs for the family, give the children their allowances, and so on. When she objected that she could no longer manage on that amount, he told her that she was not handling the money correctly. If she were, he said flatly, fifty dollars would still be sufficient to cover her expenses.

Another battleground for the sado-masochistic power struggle is the children. The woman whose husband gave her fifty dollars a week was frequently humiliated in front of her children by her husband's countermanding her instructions to them. This conveyed the message to the children that their mother's ideas were insignificant and her discipline worthless. It bred disrespect in the children and made them potential adversaries as well—two more people who would regard her as ineffectual and helpless.

The practice of wife-swapping we heard so much about during the so-called sexual revolution is something that could only occur in a sado-masochistic marriage. The term alone makes it clear that it is something generated by the husband, something the wife would probably feel powerless to resist. When a husband insists that switching partners is acceptable and suggests it to his wife, she is faced with a choice that is really no choice at all: She can refuse and risk ending her marriage, or she can go along, knowing her husband will do it anyway, and at least she will not be left out. I believe men are aware of their wives' position when they make the suggestion. Another common occurrence when the swapping actually takes place is that the husband questions the wife afterward, simultaneously robbing her of any privacy and claiming her back, while withholding from her any information about his own experience.

I mentioned earlier the projective blaming of the mate that occurs in sado-masochistic marriages, most especially by the sadistic partner. This can cover an extremely broad spectrum of offenses, the husband holding his wife responsible for everything from his performance at work to the cut he incurred shaving in the morning. The masochistic wife, no matter how hard she works to avoid giving offense, is fighting a losing battle—for her husband's complaints frequently have little basis in reality.

A woman invited her family to Thanksgiving dinner. When the time came for the meal, she set on the table a beautifully prepared turkey on a large platter. As her husband began to carve, a piece of turkey slipped onto the table. Then he unwittingly tipped the platter slightly, so that some juice spilled from it. The moment he made these mistakes, he began loudly blaming his wife for not having used a big enough platter. His harangue ruined the dinner. He attempted, of course, to hide his own inadequacy by accusing his wife of incompetence—and perhaps he took special pleasure in doing this in front of her family.

The sadistic husband may also use physical assault and rape in his ongoing offensive against his wife. When he attacks his wife physically, however, the assault is likely to be different from that of the run-of-the-mill wife-batterer. These latter men tend to be either passive-aggressive males, who feel helpless and vulnerable themselves and react with rage and anger in interactions with their mates, or obsessive-compulsives, who explode and attack when their defenses are threatened; or men, usually paranoid, who live with congealed rage and will assault anyone close to them.

Usually, a trivial event triggers the batterer, and his actions are never warranted by the triggering occurrence. For instance, his wife's breaking a yolk while cooking his breakfast eggs, or the first piece of birthday cake's being offered to a guest instead of him may send him into a battering fury. Wives have reported that wearing a ponytail or saying they did not like the pattern of the wallpaper resulted in beatings. Or the wife herself may not do anything, as in a case I know of in which a man beat his wife because his driver's license had been suspended. These triggering actions are simply pegs on which to hang the hat of rage.

The sadistic husband, on the other hand, uses a beating as just one of many weapons he wields against his wife in his campaign to destroy her. His attacks are not heated but calculated. On the surface, while administering this punishment, he will seem neither irrational nor out of control and unbalanced. His manner is more likely to be marked by icy calm. Any resort to brute force, of course, signals that the husband's resources are taxed to the limit. It also indicates that he is insistent on employing power as a means of resolving differences: His wife *must* defer—he *must not* compromise.

Certain special problems, most especially addictions, also add to the probability of a husband's becoming assaultive. If the husband is alcoholic, for example, he is particularly dangerous, because rage is a component of his personality and, while he may drink to anesthetize the rage, the effect is to increase it, making assault more likely. The narcotics addict, on the other hand, is not likely to be a threat when he is high, but when he begins to withdraw and needs a fix, he is given to explosive rages and can become very dangerous.

Marital rape, which exists whenever a wife is coerced into having sexual relations against her wishes, can also be an element in the sado-masochistic power struggle. In some marriages it may constitute the basic sexual style and occur quite frequently; in others it may happen rarely and perhaps serve as an indication of a severe crisis in the relationship. In a marriage illustrative of the former condition, the husband was crude, impulse-driven, and cruel, the wife sensitive and friendly. She chose a man who was a replica of the father who had belittled and ridiculed her; he behaved like his domineering, threatening, aggressive mother. His sexual behavior was always sadistic, forcing relations without his wife's consent. He had long ago identified with the aggressor and now behaved as one himself. Another patient whose marriage has been decidedly sado-masochistic but free of assault and rape found that those elements entered in as the deterioration escalated. She and her husband were at a party and when he did not introduce her to some people he knew and she asked why not, he got angry and walked away from her. At home later that evening, he beat her up for the first time in their lengthy marriage. The next day she went to a lawyer. He said she still seemed to love her husband and suggested that perhaps she was not really ready to leave him. She returned home although she was extremely fearful. But when, a few months later, her husband raped her, she visited the lawyer again and ended the marriage.

This same woman, looking back on her marriage, expressed puzzlement that the sexual area had not been troubled by difficulties until the end. "The sex was pretty good," she said, "and that's hard to understand in light of the problems between us." What she did not realize, until she uncovered it in treatment, was that it was the potency of rape, not a positive, loving orientation based on mutuality, that fueled her husband's sexual performance throughout the marriage. She began to recall that her husband had refused to kiss her during lovemaking; she remembered that there was virtually no foreplay. She also told me of his habit of issuing commands at the beginning of the day. "I expect sex tonight," he would say to her as he was leaving for work. This unromantic, uninviting approach to sex also reflected his hostility to her, as did his habitual comment after they had had intercourse. "That was a good one, wasn't it?" he would say, referring to his prowess rather than to anything mutually gratifying that had happened between them. Even if the sex had been satisfying for her, this was his way of obliterating any pleasure she might have felt. That he was also frequently involved with other women was something she managed to deny to herself until she left him.

Sometimes the sadistic husband may literally become murderous. One thinks of Claus von Bülow, sentenced to twenty years in prison for the attempted murder of his wealthy wife, appealing his conviction but still living free in society. A patient of mine, whose husband did not precisely fit the profile of the murderous exploiter but who was a bona fide sadist nevertheless, recounted to me how her husband took out double indemnity insurance on her life before they were to take a trip to Europe. On two separate occasions he attempted to maneuver her close to the edge of a cliff so that he could push her over. Once her own instincts saved her; the second time the fortuitous arrival of other tourists caused him to back off.

As I have said, the repetition compulsion is the basis for these marriages. But how do they evolve into such extreme situations? What is the process that takes place? Even when a woman makes a poor choice and picks a sadistic man, things can't be all that bad, all that unequal, at the outset. How do they get that way? When I say that the masochistic wife bears a major share of the responsibility for the negative direction the marriage takes, I want to be clear that I am not *blaming* her. I am simply attempting to describe what occurs in a sado-masochistic partnership. Because the wife is fearful of standing up to her husband, fearful of asserting herself and making her own wishes, needs, and opinions clear, she adopts a submissive stance, capitulating to her husband at every turn. As she succumbs and exhibits her fear and uncertainty, the husband's sadistic tendencies rise increasingly to the fore. The more he witnesses her fear, the more he pressures her with his cruelty. She, in response, exhibits greater and greater weakness. He, in turn, steps up his brutality. She has demonstrated to him that she will not take a stand and stick to it, that her protests, should they arise, will be hollow, that she will always, ultimately, give up and give in. Faced with such a willing and pliant victim, he cannot resist attack. And one must remember that such a woman, especially if she has children, may have no place to go if she decides to leave her sadistic husband. Until very recently, there has been little help and support from society for women in this position.

Let me cite what may seem like a minor example of the submissive, acquiescent behavior that can become so destructive when established as a pattern in a marriage. This comes from a story by Mary Kay Blakeley in the *New York Times.* Shortly after marrying, she was out shopping with her husband and saw a pint of ice cream she wanted to buy. It was a special flavor she liked and more expensive than many other brands. Her husband objected. There was no way, he said, that he would pay $1.95 for a pint of ice cream just because the box said "hand packed by Agnes." They did not get the ice cream that day and Ms. Blakeley recognized that this had something to do with the marriage vows she had taken, although she did not recall saying at the time of her marriage "I defer all ice cream judgments to you." She recognized, happily for her, that capitulating on the ice cream decision would also mean forfeiting her opinions in the areas of vacuuming, children, entertainment, sex, and so on. Ultimately, she got herself the ice cream, later recognizing that moment as the beginning of the end of her marriage. "We did not fully understand," she writes of women of her generation, "how much a husband's sense of *entitlement* and a wife's sense of *duty* reflected their decisions."

The struggle over a $1.95 pint of ice cream may seem trivial, but it is not. A woman's acquiescence on such a matter is symptomatic of much more than whether or not there will be butter pecan in the family freezer that night. Giving in on the ice cream would indicate that she has already made a crucial choice in terms of the equity of power in the marriage. It would mean that she accepted her husband's premise without questioning it, capitulating to him, letting him off the hook without objection or discussion. She would have abandoned her own rights, set aside her own desires in deference to his. By her total surrender she would have played a key part in her own victimization. Could she not say to him that she loved the ice cream, so why not indulge her now and then as she would him? After all, $1.95 was involved, not a million.

A woman need not always have her own way, of course, but the point here is to recognize when she has succumbed because she didn't dare defy her husband or assert herself. Once the balance of power begins to swing toward her husband (and it is through the accumulation of just such "trivial" incidents that this takes place) the masochistic woman becomes less and less able to stand up for her own views, the inequity between husband and wife grows progressively greater, and the marriage moves increasingly in a sado-masochistic direction.

9

Long-Suffering Wife and Mother

"Sorrow-Acre," a poignant and moving story by Isak Dinesen, describes the return to his ancestral home of Adam Rosenkrantz. Since the death of his father, the home has been owned by Adam's uncle. When Adam meets his uncle, he reports that someone has set fire to his barn, and it is believed that Goshe, a widow's son, is guilty, although he swears his innocence. Goshe is locked up. His mother, Anne-Marie, comes to the lord of the manor, Adam's uncle, to plead for her son's release. In a voice cracked from days of weeping, she maintains Goshe's innocence and begs the lord to save him. Staring out at his wheat field, the lord replies that if between sunrise and sunset she can mow the entire field, her son will go free. Anne-Marie kisses his hand in gratitude. But Adam is appalled when his uncle tells him that mowing the field is a three-day job.

The next day, as Anne-Marie begins her work in the rising heat of the day, Adam asks his uncle if he believes Anne-Marie can fulfill her bargain. She might, the uncle says, because her work is extraordinary, and he orders the bailiff to bring Goshe to the fields to see his mother struggling for his sake. As Anne-Marie advances through the fields hunched over, stumbling, hair plastered against her head with sweat, moving like a tired swimmer, people stand by watching. At one point when a young boy tries to help her, the lord calls out for him to desist. Adam finally can stand it no longer and pleads with his uncle not to force her to continue. "Do you not see she is dying?" Adam asks. He has given his word, the uncle replies. It is obvious that she is prepared to die for her son, Adam points out; is that not enough? If he were to nullify the terms now, the uncle says, Anne-Marie might feel he was making light of her feat. Adam, although he tells his uncle he can no longer sleep under his roof, is swept by a series of realizations: that his uncle has had much suffering in his own life and even watched his own son die; that all living creatures suffer; that his uncle is old and dreads death; and that to die for the one you love is an idea too sweet for words.

As sunset approaches, the old lord dresses in his brocaded court suit and goes to the fields. Anne-Marie completes her mowing, and when she sees there is nothing left, she seems confused and drops to her knees; her son drops to the ground beside her. Then the lord steps forward. "Your son is free," he declares. "You have done a good day's work, which will long be remembered." When it is obvious that Anne-Marie cannot hear him, the lord tells her sobbing son to relay the message. Collecting himself, Goshe repeats the lord's words. His mother raises her eyes to him, reaches out to touch his cheek, then slumps against his shoulder and dies. Some time later, the lord raises on the spot a stone to Anne-Marie's memory, and the peasants ever after call the field Sorrow-Acre.

This Dinesen story reflects a concept of mother love that held sway in an earlier day. At its core was the dictate that a mother would make any sacrifice for her child. And in life, as in the story, it used to be assumed that the love between mother and child was reciprocal, that the child understood and appreciated the mother's sacrifice, that the child loved the mother for her generous gift of herself.

How radically times have changed! Now it seems that perhaps there is some reason to question whether or not love begets love between mother and child, to question whether or not children generally appreciate the sacrifices made for them, even when they are freely given. Perhaps the loaded question is: How often is maternal self-sacrifice really only masochistic martyrdom, destructive to the mother and destructive to the child as well?

The poem that follows was written by a patient of mine, a

bright but quite disturbed young woman whose mother had refused to let the symbiotic tie dissolve and allow her daughter to
grow up and become an independent person. It conveys, however
amateurishly, the punishing consequences to the child of a
mother's masochism.

> She stuffed her ears with cotton
> and violently shook her head—
> the masochistic mother with
> the blue eyes said:
>
> "I don't believe you love me
> and I'm better off dead."
>
> "Mother I love you,
> you're not better dead—
> how must I convince you?"
> I sincerely said.
>
> WELL (she said)
>
> "You must do everything I say,
> for mother's always right—
> just to tell me that you love me
> is not very bright.
>
> "You must come to me with problems,
> you must come for advice,
> and if you really love me
> you will also come at night."
>
> "I love you, mother—
> that's all I have to say,
> but I've a mind of my own—
> don't turn me away."
>
> She turned to the door,
> and dropped on the floor—
> and the masochistic mother
> with the blue eyes said:
>
> "I don't believe you love me,
> and I'm better off dead."

The mother in the poem uses her own negative feelings about
herself to incite guilt in her child, an extremely damaging course

to pursue and one that will more than likely cause the child herself to be masochistic.

Many masochistic mothers either imply the following or state it directly to a child: If you don't do what I ask, it will kill me. Coercing behavior in this way makes the child, who can take such a statement literally, feel responsible for hurting the parent and, as a consequence, guilty. Constant repetition of this sort of threat makes guilt all-pervasive.

The masochistic wife and mother often experiences a sense of conflict between her need to appease her husband and her obligation to her children. Whom should she strive to please? If she does not maintain control over the children and meet her sadistic husband's disciplinary standards, she risks angering him. If she hews to his standards, it may be at the expense of the children. Often her efforts to be good to her children cause her husband to become envious and angry. Infantile himself, he feels in competition with his children rather than fatherly toward them. He resents the attention she pays to them and attacks both them *and* her. Conflicted and fearful, a mother may simply abandon her authority and resort to an old dodge vis-à-vis her children: "Wait until your father comes home," she says, rather than disciplining them herself. This is a disastrous step: She yields still more of her dwindling reserves of power to her husband, loses important ground with her children, and digs herself even deeper into her masochism.

Even today, women's dependence on men increases their vulnerability. As homemakers, they are largely cut off from social contact and, in the absence of other resources, they may focus an unhealthy attention on their children, endowing them with inappropriate power. Imagine what it is like—I'm sure some of you readers know—to live in fear of your children because you cannot discipline them and in fear of your husband because he will find fault with everything you have done in the course of the day, especially in relation to the children. The more he criticizes you in front of the children, the less will they respect you and follow your orders, no matter how much you have done for them. It is truly a no-win situation. And very often, of course, the sadistic husband will play the children off against their mother, countermanding her directives, ridiculing her in front of them, doing whatever he can to erode their respect for her. As the children fall into line behind him and disregard her orders, the husband sees even more shortcomings to chastise her for.

Sociologist Judith Wallerstein, in her study of divorce, verifies that children often feel greater respect for their father and notes that this imbalance can become even more pronounced when a family splits up. Children often fantasize about and idealize the absent parent, who is usually the father, and resent the caretaker parent, more frequently the mother. Even when she has abdicated her authority before the divorce, afterward she is a single parent and must serve as disciplinarian. She may find, as she attempts to take on this role, that her children simply will not respond to her as an authority figure.

A woman with two adolescent sons was having great difficulty with her husband who was extremely critical of her. Her response to his assaults was to apologize constantly, thus inviting him to believe even more deeply that she was always wrong about everything. When it was discovered that their younger son was ill with leukemia, and advanced treatment was unavailable in the town where they lived, she arranged for a housekeeper to look after her son and her husband and traveled with her sick son to a distant medical center where chemotherapy and radiation therapy took about three months. This experience turned out to be a kind of Sorrow-Acre for her. She went through it alone, living in uprooted fashion in a hotel room, trying to keep up her son's spirits and hold herself together psychologically. Her husband called occasionally to see how their son was progressing and to complain about how things were running at home, and he visited her and their son a few times, generally seeming annoyed by everything he encountered, including the fact that she wasn't very interested in sex (he chose this period, she later learned, to become involved with another woman). During this extremely difficult time, his criticism of his wife increased, and when he was not criticizing her, he gave her the "silent treatment." She ended the marriage soon afterward, a positive step for her and one that is extremely difficult for the masochistic wife and mother to take.

A woman who was referred to me by a neurologist for a consultation was married and the mother of three daughters. She was suffering from the following symptoms: migraine headaches of increasing severity, dizziness, blackouts, blurred vision, difficulty hearing on occasion, buzzing in her ears, occasional difficulty seeing food on her plate, loss of taste sensations, weak feelings in her thighs and arms, and, on one occasion, an inability to raise herself out of a chair. The neurologist wanted to know whether I thought she was suffering from multiple sclerosis or whether her symptoms were psychological in origin. Laboratory tests had been inconclusive in regard to any neurological or brain damage.

Although uneducated, she was a bright woman who had married young (her husband was only the second man she ever dated) and immediately been subjected to explosive expressions of anger from her husband when she was reluctant to submit to his sometimes bizarre sexual behavior. He began to criticize her constantly, accusing her of being incompetent, although she worked as a bookkeeper and cared for their home and three children. He especially delighted in putting her down in front of the children, undermining her disciplinary efforts.

What were her parents like? I inquired. As a small child she had been scared to death of her father, she said. Most of the time he was punishingly silent, but he also beat her occasionally. Her mother was a timid, submissive woman. Her own marriage, it was clear, mirrored her parents'. How was she feeling right now? I asked at one point. "I've been away from the noxious source of my difficulties for the last few weeks, so I'm feeling better," she replied. This was a direct, and surprisingly incisive, acknowledgment that her problem lay in her relationship with her husband, not in any physical illness. She had chosen, however, to retreat into sickness rather than to consider leaving her husband, a common masochistic solution to a difficult problem.

This woman's experience was characteristic of the masochistic wife/mother in many ways. Her marriage represented a shift from one dependency to another, the transference of the symbiotic tie from one person to another. She never had the opportunity to develop social interpersonal ties that might have served to strengthen her enough to leave her husband or to acquire the skills she would have needed to survive on her own. Because of her tenuous sense of her own boundaries, she did not feel herself to be a separate, independent person. In addition, she suffered extensive feelings of guilt that caused her to doubt herself even further and underscored her hesitation to consider divorce: What about the children? Would she not be hurting them? How could she deprive them of their father? The consideration of whether or not he was a good father played no part in her thinking. Nor did the idea that the children might possibly be better off in a more peaceful home. She clung to her marriage, turning her anger in upon herself instead of expressing it outwardly, making herself sick and thus providing yet another rationalization for staying put: Now I'm sick . . . I can't possibly leave under these circumstances. Her masochistic anxieties and fear of the unknown outweighed the familiar misery of her current situation.

I am happy to report that this woman, however, as she began to receive support from treatment and from her own mother, who had grown more independent since the death of her husband, was able to begin confronting her situation in realistic terms. Her recognition of her husband as a damaging, "noxious" influence was not just a fleeting insight that occurred in a conversation with me. She no longer needed to deny this at such a high price to herself. And I think it is likely that she will eventually dare to leave her husband and attempt to build a new life for herself.

A seeming contrast to the brutality this woman experienced occurred in the marriage of another patient of mine. But the results were equally destructive. She had hypertension, a mild cardiac problem, and was somewhat obese. Despite these problems, she was far from being an invalid. Her husband, however, had a great need to promote her dependence on him, and he constantly stressed that she was sick and helpless; he cast himself in the role of benevolent caretaker. In social situations, he discussed her illnesses so that whenever she ran into people they always inquired, "How *are* you, Georgia?" When they traveled, he insisted that she ride in a wheelchair to the airport gate although she had no difficulty walking. "I wonder what's wrong with that poor woman?" she recalls hearing people say. He issued daily reminders to the children not to upset their mother. The result was that the children turned to him for everything, and their mother became virtually invisible to them.

Finally, feeling quite desperate, she came to me for help. In treatment, she grew increasingly strong, began to assert herself and to challenge him, and the children once again became aware of her as a mothering figure. She did not consider divorce, as she was getting on in years and could not contemplate spending the rest of her life alone. But because she was able to recognize that her husband was not always right and to hold her ground without feeling threatened, their relationship underwent substantial changes. His earlier treatment of her, which had the veneer of loving care, was an expression of hostility and anger just as surely as are physical abuse and the silent treatment. It damaged and undermined her just as effectively as if he had beaten her regularly. And the end was the same; only the means differed. He had been killing her with kindness.

"To Room Nineteen" is a Doris Lessing story that speaks to the subject of the masochistic wife/mother in an especially affecting way. It tells of two bright, handsome, successful young people who fall in love, marry, and seem to have everything. Whatever they do is right and appropriate and graceful, and for a time their life together is charmed. When the young woman becomes pregnant, she quits her job, as seems fitting, and they have the first of four delightful children. They live in a beautiful home. They have a housekeeper to make life easier still. Then, in the midst of all this perfection, the husband confesses that he has had a sexual involvement with another woman, a one-time thing, not an ongoing arrangement. The wife says nothing—what is there to say after the fact?—and life goes on as it was. But beneath the unruffled facade of their existence, the wife thinks about this constantly. How could he experience with someone else the pleasure he has shared with her whom he loves? There is nothing she can do, she knows. She has no other resources. All the joy has gone out of life for her, and she feels a kind of deadness in her heart.

At one point the wife announces that she must have a room in the house where no one will bother her. It will bring her some kind of peace, she thinks, if she has a place of her own. Once she has the room, however, she finds it is not satisfying because now she is aware that the children can get along without her and that the housekeeper does not really need her to help run the house. She feels superfluous. Rather than adding to her life, the room seems to have diminished it further. She decides she needs to get a room outside of the house.

She has very little money, and the room she settles on is in a small hotel. The hotelkeeper is suspicious, believing she probably wants the room to bring men to, but she gives it to her grudgingly, and the wife sits for a day looking out the window at the Thames. When the hotelkeeper will not give her the room again, she tells her husband that she needs to have enough money to take a hotel room once a week. He gives her the money, and she asks him if he suspects that she is meeting a man. It is just as well you told me, the husband replies, because I have become involved with another woman.

The wife goes to a poor neighborhood, where she finds a room in a dingy hotel with a manager who keeps intrusively offering her things for the room when all she wants is to be left alone to sit quietly within the four walls. After a day of this, she returns home and feels even more acutely how unnecessary she is. No one has missed her. One day she goes to her hotel room and sits for a number of hours. Then she gets up and pushes a rug under the door, puts money in the gas meter and turns it on, and lies on the bed and waits to die.

This story focuses on a phenomenon I have encountered often in my practice but one that is never really addressed by psychiatry and psychoanalysis. This woman, like so many others, has had certain expectations imposed on her by her sociocultural surroundings. Society has, in effect, promised her that certain things will come to pass if she is a good, loyal, caring wife and mother. If she cares for her husband, depends on him, lets him call the shots, nurtures him and their children, and maintains a nice home, she will be rewarded with certain satisfactions. The corollary, of course, is that she must sacrifice her own needs and desires along the way. But the woman keeps her part of the bargain and gives in to the masochistic tendencies that are a part of it. When she is betrayed in this bargain, the results are catastrophic. Life never again has the same meaning for her. When the means of betrayal is infidelity on the husband's part, as is so often the case (male infidelity being socially acceptable, after all), it literally kills something in the woman, something that can never be restored. Because she makes her trade-off for this man, his faithlessness is especially devastating.

The masochistic wife/mother is in a situation where she may have *several* people aligned against her. No matter how good and caring a mother she is, she loses status by her husband's constantly criticizing her in front of the children. The powerlessness she feels becomes an increasing, and debilitating, reality. Like it or not, power is what children learn to respect, and someone who is without it sinks very rapidly in their estimation. Deprived of respect and caring from either husband or children, the masochistic wife/mother suffers from feelings of isolation and abandonment that make her existence sometimes seem unbearable. She is often unable to contend with this and begins to withdraw more and more in a variety of ways. Depression is one form of withdrawal. Suicide, as in the Lessing story, is another.

10

Vulnerability
to Violence

In our increasingly violent society, violent crimes against women are on the rise. Certainly there is greater recognition of their incidence. Awareness of rape, wife-battering, and marital rape has increased sharply in the last few decades. And at long last, professionals are studying and attempting to understand these disturbing crimes. But there is great disagreement among those conducting the studies as to what factors produce such violence, disagreement about the personality traits and situational elements vis-à-vis the victimizer and the victim as well. Some victimologists have concluded that victims *do* contribute to their own victimization in some ways; others maintain that victim-blaming is a cruel and unwarranted stance that ignores the random nature of most personal crime.

I would certainly agree that victim-blaming is neither helpful to the victim nor productive of understanding. *She asked for it. It was her fault.* These are common responses to violent crime against women that are almost always inaccurate as well as being investigatory dead-ends. However, I do believe that the victims of violent crime may sometimes play a part either in triggering or exacerbating those crimes. That this is especially true of masochistic women there can be no doubt.

Let me stress that to say a victim has in some way contributed to her own victimization is not to say that she is to blame for it, that she is responsible for it, or that she in any way desired such an assault or deserves it. The lack of compassion for the victim that exists in our society today dismays and saddens me. Bizarre though it is, people seem more inclined to rally around and identify with the victimizer than with the person who has suffered an attack. Eager to distance themselves from the victim position, influenced unconsciously, I suspect, by the pervasive taste for violence that infects our national life, people all too often direct their interest and even sympathy to the perpetrator of a violent crime rather than to the victim. I want to make it clear that when I examine those ways in which a victim may contribute to her own victimization, I am not judging her to be blameworthy. I am, rather, suggesting that she may not have taken all the preventive steps available to her.

All violent crime constitutes a drama of power and danger that is played out between the victim and the victimizer. All violent crime turns on the issues of fear and control, these underlying the more easily discernible issue of gain, be it for money or sex. The raison d'être of the victimizer is to seek power and control, those elements of which he was deprived in his early life when he was himself a victim. In the moment of committing a violent crime, he possesses both. The victim of a violent crime, on the other hand, is riddled with fear and overwhelmed by a sense of powerlessness and lack of control.

The latter description fits the masochistic person in general, not just at the moment of crisis. This very fact puts the masochist at greater risk when it comes to violent crime. Because of her tendency to provoke self-destructive events and to submit abjectly to a perceived powerful other, she is in greater danger than, say, a woman who is comfortable exercising her own autonomy and unafraid to assert herself. That is why this issue, sensitive though it is, bears thinking about. How can someone with masochistic tendencies keep her masochism from igniting a potentially dangerous situation?

Psychologist Lenore Walker and others have recently disputed that female masochism plays any role in the violence that erupts in wife-battering. They have, in fact, thrown out the term "masochism" altogether—feeling it too readily recalls Freud's notion that women seek suffering instinctually and enjoy it—and have replaced it with the concept of "learned helplessness." I, too, disagree with the idea that masochists derive satisfaction from their suffering. And, of course, I subscribe to the idea that women's sense of powerlessness is culturally and developmentally— not biologically—determined, an idea implicit in the phrase "learned helplessness." However, it is not a phrase or a concept I find particularly useful. Its essence is a kind of amorphous and overwhelming sense of impotence. It seems almost to imply that there is very little women can do to combat this deficiency that has been imposed on them by conditioning.

On the other hand, my concept of masochism and the communication style that reflects it allows one to focus on specific aspects of behavior that may be harmful and to learn to do something about them. Masochistic women *do* do things that make them more vulnerable than they need to be. They *do* send out messages signaling inadequacy, helplessness, and fear, which in a dangerous situation may make them more powerless than they need be. No one does women a favor by denying this. The term "masochism" has been in use for so long, both generally and professionally, that I think it is useless to try to eliminate it. It is better to reinterpret it, to use it appropriately.

Of course chance plays a large role in violent crime. There are times, no matter what precautions one has taken, when there is no way to escape a dangerous confrontation. We must recognize that there are situations in which there is absolutely nothing a woman can do to help herself: The cards are totally stacked against her. If I make suggestions of how a woman might best handle herself in dangerous situations, I am not implying that those suggestions will necessarily make the difference between life and death. But I *am* talking about raising the odds in her favor. As I said earlier, there are people who consistently win at cards because of the skill with which they play. By the same token, there may be times when, facing potential danger, a woman can override her masochistic tendencies, play her cards right, and make a difference in the situation that does result in saving her life.

Listening to the news one evening, I heard Alexander D.

Lehrer, prosecutor of Monmouth County, New Jersey, offer what I consider a gem of advice. "Conduct your life with care," he said, "and you won't be a victim." That may seem simplistic at first, but it actually says a great deal.

Treating herself and her life with care is one of the most difficult things for a masochistic person to do. Preoccupied with her own narrow field of vision, suffering from the perpetual anxiety that keeps her thinking confused, she is ill-equipped to respond properly to the world around her, prone to overlook real danger signs in favor of perceived threats that are based on her projections from childhood. So busy is she warding off these phantom dangers that she often fails to see or respond to real peril. She tends to be care-less in the way she conducts her life.

For example, a woman is standing alone in a loft building waiting for an elevator. A man arrives and stands waiting with her. Although something about him makes her uneasy and she is nervous about the prospect of boarding the elevator with him, she stays because she is concerned that if she walks away he will be offended and will assume she is thinking unpleasant things about him. This woman is not taking care with her own life. In fact, she puts an absolute stranger's opinion of her ahead of her own safety. She risks endangering herself just so that a man she doesn't know and will never see again will think she is a "nice person." This is the masochistic victim psychology in a nutshell.

Or, to give another example, a woman is walking alone on a deserted street at night and a man approaches her, asking for directions or a match or a quarter toward subway fare. She feels uncomfortable but stops to assist him anyway. Otherwise, she reasons, he will think she is unkind, ungenerous. This woman, too, is setting herself up to be victimized.

It is distressing that we live in a world where it is necessary to be so wary of our fellow creatures. I dislike advocating that people not help one another and, of course, where it is responsible—and safe—to do so I think we should offer assistance freely. I dislike promoting what appears to be selfishness. But I am not talking about selfishness; I am talking about self-preservation—and self-preservation is not something that comes naturally to the masochist. It is, in fact, at the bottom of her list of priorities, far below concern with another's opinion of her (another who is automatically powerful in her eyes) and acceptance of his premise (that he needs a match or dime or whatever).

Psychologist J. Selkin, who conducted a study of rape resisters, reported that the first act of resistance is a refusal to stop and talk to a strange man, a refusal to agree to help or to be helped by him. He also noted that those women who resisted were far more flexible than those who did not. Flexibility accompanies an autonomous personality, whereas rigidity—narrow options, the inability to think for herself or to trust her own perceptions, compulsive defensive reactions to any threatening situation— prevents the masochist from being careful with her own life. She gets herself into trouble by not daring to seem unkind or disagreeable, by being unable to assert herself, and by being unwilling to use her own premises as the basis for the encounter, rather than the premises of her victimizer.

Laura was a patient whom I invited to hear a lecture I was giving on a subject of particular interest to her. She sat next to a pleasant-looking, attractively dressed man who told her, at the conclusion of my talk, that he had been a student of mine some years earlier and that I had also invited him to attend the lecture. She had no way of verifying this but accepted it as true. It was a cold winter night and quite late when the lecture ended.

"Let me give you a ride home," the man said to Laura. "We'll stop and get a cup of coffee on the way."

"It's late but I do need to get right home," she said hesitantly. "I can easily get a cab."

"No, no," he insisted, "I'll drop you off. Besides, it's very cold and we can stop for coffee or a drink."

At this point, his insistence was showing, and a cup of coffee had begun to metamorphose into a drink. Laura could have given him a definitive no and headed for the cab. But she did not. Fearful of offending him, she continued to equivocate and finally let herself be persuaded to get into his car.

Once in the car, she continued to protest that she didn't want to stop, but her protests, like her initial demurral, were weak and ineffective.

"It really is late," she said. "I really ought to get home."

"Oh, come on," he said, "let's just have a quick drink and then I'll take you right home."

Each time he insisted, she yielded.

Once in the restaurant, he ordered a drink and she had a cup of coffee. As he drank, he talked and talked, and she grew increasingly concerned about the time.

"Look," she said finally, "I appreciate your bringing me this far, and it will be easy for me to get a cab from here. So why don't you stay and finish your drink and I'll just go on home?"

He wouldn't hear of it, he said. He had offered to take her home and he would. He finished his drink and they got back in the car. By this time Laura was quite aware that she was involved in a situation in which her voice carried no weight whatsoever, and she found her companion's persistence alarming.

As they approached her building he said, "I'll walk you to the door to make sure you're safe."

"That's not necessary," she replied pointedly. "There's an elevator man in the building and I'll be fine."

She put her hand on the door handle and when the car pulled up to the curb in front of her building, she said, "Thank you very much, I have to go," as she pushed open the door and ran inside.

As it turned out, I did know the man with whom Laura had this encounter, and I doubt that he would have harmed her. But certainly his insistence had ominous undercurrents in it and suggested his intention of a sexual encounter. Perhaps one has to say that there is always a potential for danger when someone is so tenacious. There can be no doubt, however, that Laura's behavior was masochistic.

First of all, she accepted the premise that he knew me, though she had only his word for this. He was a complete stranger to whom she owed nothing, but she was concerned that he think well of her, so she let him accompany her. There were so many points during the enounter when she could have extricated herself, but she capitulated to his wishes rather than defend her own. Her responses, until the final one, were always dilatory, never definitive. It took her a long time to register how completely he was disregarding her wishes. If the man had been truly dangerous, Laura could have been in deep trouble.

R. J. Gelles in *The Violent Home* gives a detailed accounting of factors that conspire to create violence within the family. First among these is the *offender's identity*, characterized by a vulnerable self-concept and low self-esteem. The *family of orientation* and *socialization* (including violence to which the offender has been exposed, violent role models, and self-devaluating experiences) are among the factors that shape the *offender's identity*; I will deal with these in some detail in my chapter on the victimizer. Gelles also enumerates other violence-producing factors such as *family structure, social isolation, structural stresses* (unemployment, financial problems, health problems) and *situational factors* (such as gambling, drinking, and so on). But there is one crucial factor he omits from his construct: the *victim's* personality and identity. This can play a part in evoking violent responses, in society at large as well as within the family.

The masochistic person cannot read power relationships accurately. She sees virtually everyone as more powerful than she, and she is automatically fearful of them. Any potential victim, facing a dangerous situation, is likely to be overcome by fear and a sense of powerlessness. But how much worse is such a confrontation for the masochistic person, whose daily life is pervaded by those feelings. To make the best of a bad situation, it is necessary to exert autonomy, to be self-assertive. This is extremely difficult for the masochist. But it is *not* impossible; the masochistic person can learn to be more powerful in a potentially dangerous situation.

I have already mentioned taking care ("prevention is ninetenths the cure") as one inportant part of lessening one's vulnerability to violence. Do *not* put yourself on a dark street alone at night. Do *not* stop to answer the requests of strange men. Do *not* get onto an elevator alone with a man who makes you feel uneasy. Do *not* place yourself in positions of potential jeopardy.

If a volcano began to spill lava and you were in its path, you would move swiftly to get out of the way. If you find yourself actually confronting a potential assailant, run if you can. If screaming for attention will help, scream. Don't consider what the other person will think of your behavior. Don't wonder if you might be making a mistake about his intentions. If you are, so what? It truly is better to be safe than sorry. If there is any chance of escape, take advantage of it quickly and resolutely. Vacillation will keep you frozen in place as well as advertise that you are an easy mark. Decisive action will make you a less appealing target. Just as a thief might be discouraged from breaking and entering if he saw that the only means of entrance was the noisy smashing of windows, so an assailant might be less likely to tangle with someone who does not readily submit.

Let me make a point here about something that is never mentioned in discussions of this subject. Fear and excitement often affect's one's bodily functions, causing some people to feel like urinating; others feel the urge of a bowel movement. We are socially conditioned to think that to lose control in an inappropriate setting is among the worst things that could possibly happen to us. But it is well to remember that it is not worse than being killed. So if you are in a dangerous situation, don't let your concern with propriety get in the way of your thinking clearly. Don't be distracted. Simply let go if you must. Leave your brain free to address the exigencies of the crisis confronting you rather than take up precious thinking time with worry about your body's needs.

If escape is impossible and you are truly embroiled in a violent encounter, you still need not accept the idea that all is lost. In fact, if you do accept that, chances are all *will* be lost. You still have an opportunity to raise the odds in your favor. Maybe you will only increase your chances from one in a hundred to ten in a hundred, but that margin could make a difference. It may buy you an extra few moments of time during which, for instance, someone might appear to assist you. It may deflect your assailant temporarily and offer you a new possibility of escape. Of course, much of your behavior in such a confrontation will be determined by whether or not your assailant is armed and by what you construe his motives to be. If someone is holding a gun to your head, your method of resistance will be different from what it would be if he were unarmed. If it is clear that he wants only your money and intends no physical harm, your behavior will be governed by those circumstances. Flexibility and a belief in your own perceptions will serve you well.

The question of physical self-defense arises here. My own view is that women are not well served by studying karate or other self-defense methods and, in fact, may even be saddling themselves with dangerous illusions by doing so. Mastering these tactics in class is a far cry from being able to employ them effectively in a moment of attack. In a class, a student is performing a known ritual. In a moment of violent confrontation, everything is unknown. The victim is taken by surprise. She has no way of knowing what effect such a situation will have on her. Studies have shown, in fact, that people trained in self-defense skills (both men and women) have sometimes had these skills desert them in a moment of crisis. The belief that you are equipped to defend yourself physically may lead you to stand and fight, with disastrous results. It may prevent you from seizing an opportunity to escape.

If you cannot escape from your victimizer, how can you raise the odds in your favor? First, try to keep from transmitting any of the masochistic messages outlined in Chapter 4. These will be just as provocative to your attacker as they are to your boss, your lover, or your husband. If you signal that you are vulnerable and fearful, your fear will in fact excite fear and anxiety in your attacker and perhaps make him even more violent.

But remember never to threaten a potentially dangerous person. Never indicate that you don't believe in his capacity for violence. Appeal to his power but never question it. Enhance his ego, don't try to diminish it. The victimizer is full of hate and rage that mask an underlying sense of utter worthlessness. Anything you do that strikes that chord of worthlessness brings you closer to a death sentence. Anything you do to inflate his self-image gives you a better chance of escaping alive. When you challenge or degrade the victimizer, he is likely to feel even more threatened. Your challenge is equivalent to an accusation that he is not potent enough to carry out his threat. Questioning his power undermines still further whatever pitifully fragile sense of self-esteem he already has, and that is what makes questioning it so dangerous. Now he *must* prove his potency by fully unleashing his rage. let me repeat: I am not saying that if you do this or that you will get off the hook entirely. I am simply talking about increasing your chances, buying time.

A few years ago there was a homicide in New York City that seemed a particularly brutal, senseless, wasteful crime. A gifted and attractive young violinist with an orchestra playing in Manhattan was sexually assaulted and murdered by a stagehand in the Metropolitan Opera House. It is sad beyond expression to think of such a life being eradicated in this way, and in my speculation about what may have happened between this victim and her murderer, I'm not implying that she was in any way to blame for what befell her. Fate dealt this young woman a truly horrible blow. Once engaged with her assailant, perhaps nothing could have interrupted his brutal crime. I use this case simply as a framework to illustrate those elements that are present in violent confrontations, to show the common responses that occur in such situations, and to suggest alternatives responses that *might* be lifesaving. Let me stress that the following account is purely speculative.

During the intermission of that evening's performance, the young woman found herself standing at an elevator with the stagehand in the labyrinthine backstage area of the Metropolitan. It seemed legitimate for him to be there, and when the elevator came they got on together. By definition, given the act he committed, this young man was disturbed, alienated, and very dangerous. Also, it was reported that he had been drinking heavily that night. None of this may have been apparent to the young woman. My hunch is that once they were on the elevator, he made an obscene remark to her and she responded as many women would have, with outrage. Whatever her words, the tone would probably carry an assumption of superiority. And that note may have been what triggered the consequences. Why? Because this was a vicious young man whose self-esteem was abysmally low and whose fear of women was great; a scornful response only pushed him further in the direction of fear and rage. It emphasized the disparity between him and the young woman. "I'm a lady, you're a brute" was probably the essence of her remark. Registering that, he responded out of the great accumulation of disturbance within him and struck her.

Is there anything that young woman might have done to alter the outcome of this confrontation? Perhaps not. Perhaps the odds against her were insurmountable. But let me speculate about responses that *might* have prevented this situation from deteriorating into a vicious murder. He makes an obscene remark. She, instead of deflating his already frail ego, says something that will support it. "You're such a nice-looking young man," she might have said, "I can't believe you meant to say that. Perhaps it was a mistake. Or maybe I didn't even hear it right." If there was anything she could have said to make him feel better, rather than worse, about himself *maybe* she could have bought those few seconds in which luck or new opportunity could come into play. Perhaps she could have pushed the elevator button on the next floor and then gotten out and run. Perhaps the elevator would have come to a stop and opened of its own accord. With any gain of time, there is the possibility that something or someone might intervene.

Another tack might have been to change the premise of the encounter and move it into more neutral territory. "I wonder," she might have said, "since you work here, do you like music?" She might have gone on to ask what kind of music he liked or if he played an instrument. This would have enhanced rather than diminished his ego. She would have moved the two of them onto an equal footing, placing him on a par with herself. She also would have changed the venue from the inflammatory province of sexual interaction to the relatively bland terrain of musical taste. By doing so, she might have gained time for possible intervention, time in which fate might have offered her a way out.

Perhaps even if he had made a physical pass at her, rather than just uttered an obscene remark, she might have been able to delay and deflect him for a precious few extra seconds. "Oh, please don't," she might have said, thus making a direct appeal to his power. She admits her own helplessness and speaks to whatever is benign in him, asking that he be merciful to her. Ordinarily, of course, one would not want to exhibit abject helplessness. But what you might do trapped in an elevator with an assailant is very different from what you would do confronting an attacker in the street where you might be able to get away.

I realize that these possibilities of escape are extremely flimsy. I also realize that none of the responses I have suggested would be easy to effect. They call for keeping a cool head, refusing to panic, exercising a flexibility that allows one to put aside conditioned reflexes, and responding autonomously and assertively to the situation. That is a tall order when one unexpectedly finds oneself in a dangerous situation, particularly so for the masochistic person. But just because these are long shots does not mean they are not worth thinking about. At least they offer a chance of raising the odds in your favor, whereas contempt or hauteur, I am convinced, remove absolutely any possibility of escape.

Let me recount a series of incidents in the life of a patient of mine whom I'll call Estelle. Each of these contained the potential for her to become a victim of violence, but she emerged from each safely, due in large part to her own behavior. The first incident occurred when she was twelve and walking home from school with a friend. They had decided to take a shortcut through a somewhat empty, rundown neighborhood, certainly an unwise choice. When they were about halfway home, Estelle became aware of a group of a dozen or so boys massed on the stoop of a building ahead of them. She could see that they were leering, and she approached them with an ominous feeling. Surely the best thing would have been for Estelle and her friend to have turned and run back in the direction of the school, but they did not and quite suddenly the boys surrounded them, shouting obscenities, grabbing at their breasts and genitals. Estelle's friend somehow managed to escape, but she herself was still surrounded. Feeling a surge of adrenaline from her rage at being assaulted, she shouted "Get away," swinging her heavy school bag around her in a circle, scattering her tormentors enough to allow her to run off toward a busy thoroughfare.

Estelle made one mistake in taking a shortcut and another in not turning back the moment she saw the boys. But once she was in a dangerous situation, she played her cards right. She did not consider, when surrounded, that all was lost. She did not yield to her attackers. Nor did she provoke them further by talking back or taunting them in any way. She said two brief, decisive words ("get away"), took a definitive action (swinging her bag), and made her escape. All her actions were assertive.

Some years later, when Estelle was in her early twenties, she again had occasion to pass through a rather rough area of New York City, and it seemed that the earlier incident was about to repeat itself. Looking ahead, she saw a tunnel that served as a subway underpass and, in the block before it, a building stoop with a group of leering boys sitting on it. The sight, kindling memories of the earlier episode, terrified her. Her first thought was to turn and run; but she knew that if they chased her she couldn't run fast enough to elude them. So she went ahead and, as she approached the stoop, one boy separated himself from the group and came toward her. "She's my girlfriend and you're not going to hurt her," he told his cronies. Then he held out his hand to Estelle. In a split second she assessed her options: ignoring his offer and running forward, rebuffing him verbally, accepting him as an escort through this dangerous territory. She decided to gamble on trusting the young man. She took his hand and he led her away from the other boys and through the tunnel. Safely on the other side, she thanked him. "You're a nice lady," he said to her.

Once again, Estelle did not vacillate but took decisive action. She said nothing nasty, nothing provocative, to her would-be attackers. And she trusted her own perceptions: She sensed something decent in the young man's offer of assistance and chose to gamble that it was genuine.

The third incident occurred when Estelle was on an outing with her two young children, one of them still in a stroller. They were in a park near home, picking blueberries. The bushes were heavy with fruit, and Estelle and the children eagerly moved along, filling their baskets with berries. Absorbed in the task, Estelle didn't realize that they were no longer on a path and had moved deep into an area of thick shrubbery. Suddenly, just ahead of them, a man darted out of the bramble, uttering obscenities. Estelle turned and said quietly and firmly, "Children, come." With them in tow, she moved swiftly away from the man—and fortunately, he did not follow.

The last incident occurred years later when Estelle attended a meeting in the Columbia University area of New York. Heading home afterwards she boarded the wrong subway and ended up in a completely unfamiliar neighborhood, one that appeared quite rough. It was late afternoon, and the few people on the nearly deserted streets were, as Estelle described them to me, "the most horrendous characters" she had ever seen. She was concerned and frightened. Looking around, she saw a bus stop with a police car parked at it and she went over to the police. She told them she was lost and asked if they could possibly escort her to safer, more familiar territory. No, she should take the bus, they told her; they could not leave their post. Immediately thereafter, however, they drove off, and Estelle was left standing at a deserted bus stop. After a few moments she looked up to see a fierce-looking man with a decidedly menacing air coming out of a building and heading straight for her. She knew she could not outrun him. All she saw to do was to move farther into the street where she would be more visible; perhaps a car or bus would come along. She did that, hanging on tightly to her purse and briefcase. Suddenly, just before reaching her, the man veered away, turned sharply back in the direction from which he had come and reentered the building. Looking around for an explanation of this seemingly miraculous reversal, to her surprise Estelle saw, standing on an opposite corner, the largest policeman she had ever seen, easily six feet six, sturdily built, complete with luxuriant handlebar mustache. It seemed he had appeared out of nowhere—or perhaps from Gilbert and Sullivan's *Yeoman of the Guard*. He watched over her silently until the bus came a few minutes later.

One could say that Estelle was blessed with extraordinary good luck in each of these instances, that fate was on her side. And indeed fate, luck, chance—whatever one chooses to call it— probably did play a part in these events. But I think it is also important to note the part that Estelle's behavior played. Although she was afraid in each of these dangerous situations, she didn't panic. She stayed cool, thought clearly, examined her choices rapidly and took definitive action. Hesitation could have been deadly in any of these instances, but Estelle didn't temporize. She decided quickly what was the safest thing for her to do in an unsafe situation, and then she acted decisively. She didn't send out any masochistic signals that might have served to invite further attack. Quite the opposite. Her autonomous behavior acted as a deterrent. This was particularly interesting because Estelle *was* a masochistic woman and was not always capable of bringing this autonomy to bear in other areas of her life. But she had the rare quality of being good in emergencies. They caused her to tap into assertive reserves ordinarily she did not have access to.

It is important to recognize that there *is* a connection between masochism and victimhood, even though every victim of violence is certainly not masochistic. Denying that connection is a disservice to women, eager though some of them are to sweep it aside as part of the patriarchal baggage that must be shed if women are to claim, and fully exercise, their independence. An example of this was the remark a woman made to me after recounting how she had been harassed by a man at the beach. She had gone alone to one of the many beaches surrounding New York City and found it deserted. Because it was empty, she decided to take off her shirt and bra and lie topless on the sand. Soon a man appeared and struck up a conversation with her. Even though she made it clear she wished to be left alone, he refused to leave. Then he began making suggestive remarks to her. While she did finally manage to get her clothes on and get away without being harmed, she found the incident upsetting and frightening. "But I'm not going to start thinking I had any responsibility for this," she said to me, "because that will just lead into 'she asked for it,' and we've all had enough of that."

This woman believed it was constructive and self-protective to deny that she played any part in the incident. She believed that her denial represented a sloughing off of old, negative conditioning. In fact, her denial just reinforced her ignorance about her own behavior, and that ignorance most likely doomed her to repeat her behavior. How much better it might have been to recognize that it was careless in the first place to put herself in the position of being a woman alone on a completely empty beach. Certainly, the situation—lying on the sand topless, without her shirt at the ready, oblivious to a stranger approaching—comprised a masochistic act, one that left her completely vulnerable. Recognizing one's own masochism and becoming willing to examine it is not the same as saying "she asked for it."

The she-asked-for-it syndrome is delineated with great clarity in "The Murderer and His Victim," an article by David Abrahamsen, a brilliant forensic psychiatrist with whom I differ strongly on this point, although often agreeing with him on other matters. He cites the case of a woman who went to bars to pick up men and who eventually found her own Mr. Goodbar and was murdered. Abrahamsen says that neurosis impelled this woman to frequent bars, that she wanted to be killed, and was searching for a means to that end. In other words, he says that "she asked for it." On the contrary, I believe that this woman placed herself in the position she did in an effort to live, although the effort was a somewhat pathetic and misguided one. She was an older woman, suffering from loneliness, from the dearth of possibilities that exist for older women to meet men, and from the lack of interest that men today have in older women. She was rather desperate, as many victims are, and her desperation drove her to take risks and put herself in potentially dangerous situations. But none of this came from a desire to die. I would say that her behavior was generated by a desire to live.

The she-asked-for-it syndrome blames the victim. My notion that women may contribute to their own victimization by feeling powerless and conveying a message of vulnerability does not. Self-blame just adds to the accumulated suffering that is caused by the masochistic system of self-punishment and does no good whatsoever. Examining one's own actions, however, attempting to see where anxiety, helplessness, and carelessness may have led one into trouble, is worthwhile for the simple reason that it may help prevent it from happening again.

Dr. F. Pepitone Rockwell of the University of California Davis Medical School asked convicted rapists how they selected their victims, and he contrasted these characteristics with the characteristics of women whom the rapists were not successful in assaulting. The data he compiled are valuable aids in counseling women how to be less vulnerable to rape or any violent crime.

The rapists chose victims who seemed innocent or uncertain. They avoided women they described as "rude," an appellation I would interpret to mean definite or resolute. The rape victims were likely to be polite, friendly, and obliging, the nonvictims suspicious. Women who avoided rape thought of resistance methods and recalled advice about rape prevention when confronted with an attacker; actual rape victims focused on survival and death. They were so rattled by anxiety and confusion that they were unable to think of anything but whether or not they would be killed. Women who avoided rape used more verbal and physical resistance at the onset of the attack than did actual rape victims.

It is important for women to believe that they can resist violent attack. It is important for them to counter the socialization that causes them to behave politely and submissively, i.e., masochistically. Confronted by an attacker, they must believe they are automatically helpless and have no choice but to give in. It is this attitude that leaves women feeling depressed in the aftermath of a rape. They translate their failure to defend themselves into a belief that they must have done something to invite the attack in the first place.

In *The Assertive Woman*, S. Phelps and N. A. Austin, writing about battered wives, observe that these women are not the domineering shrews that male psychiatrists, unfortunately, have long portrayed them to be. According to those who operate shelters for battered women, they are generally inhibited, passive, and helpless. "In anxiety-arousing situations, they are unable to act," Phelps and Austin report. "They are at a loss to come up with an effective response—in fact, any response at all." Debra Dalton and James Kantner support this in their article "Aggression in Battered and Non-Battered Women as Reflected in the Hand Test." Non-battered women, they note, show a higher activity score, while battered women show a lessened capacity to manipulate their environment constructively and a more passive, yet hostile, dependence and helplessness. This, of course, is a description of the masochistic woman. She exhibits these characteristics in all her life situations, including potentially dangerous ones, and these masochistic qualities increase her vulnerability to violence.

What tendencies do you possess that get you into trouble and might make you more vulnerable than someone else in a dangerous confrontation? Might your masochism get in the way and make things even worse than they are? How can you prepare yourself to deal more adequately with a situation that possesses the potential for physical harm? How can you learn to raise the odds in your favor?

The responses I have suggested are not guaranteed to get one off the hook. Being able to respond effectively may not make the difference between life and death. But it will raise your chances of escape as opposed to lowering them. Anything that can do that is worth studying, and thinking about and trying. Being willing to do that can be the beginning of learning to conduct your life with care.

11

The Victimizer

Victimizers come in many different shapes and sizes. Some are easily recognizable, others much less conspicuous. They exist at all levels of society. The degree to which they injure their victims varies widely. And, of course, every instance of victimization is shaped not just by the victimizer but by his victim as well. The personalities and characters of both people color and govern any interchange. There are, however, three broad categories into which most victimizers fall.

The first type is certainly the most innocuous, and the injuries he inflicts are of a nonviolent, almost prosaic nature. He is the person who perpetrates the garden-variety slights the masochist encounters in the course of the day. He may be someone who has no relationship at all with his victim, someone who encounters her in a transient exchange: the clerk who ignores her in the store, the bank teller who treats her with contempt, the insurance company representative who patronizes her. Or he may be someone who maintains ongoing contact with the victim, her gynecologist, for example, or her accountant or perhaps a casual acquaintance. When any of these people are abrupt, impatient, intolerant, they are inflicting a small injury upon the victim. This category includes those everyday instances where the masochistic person, feeling powerless, places herself in the power of the other person who then attacks her in some way. Many of these victimizers, I should add, may be perfectly decent people. But when the masochist extends her jugular to them, so to speak, they can't resist slashing at it because she has been so gallingly submissive.

The second type of victimizer is someone who has an established relationship with the victim, a relationship that could be called sado-masochistic. The masochistic person, as I have indicated, often forms an alliance with someone who has sadistic tendencies. He tends to be cruel, to sense that he has power over his partner, and to be decidedly egocentric, his needs taking precedence over anyone else's. His victim is useful to him, usually providing him with an operating household, perhaps extra income, and a sexual outlet. She thinks that he loves her, but, in fact, he is just exploiting her. The paradoxical nature of his tie to her is that he wants both to possess her and to eliminate her. At the heart of sadism is devotion to the complete defeat of the other person. In pursuit of that end, the sadistic person can become increasingly brutal. Many acts of suicide, in fact, are due to this progressive cruelty, although psychiatry generally tends to blame the suicide. In my years in practice I have seen things that lead me to think it is often the victimizer who drives the masochistic person to suicide by his continuing cruel destructiveness.

I have already discussed these first two types of victimizers at some length in preceding chapters. The third category is the one we read about in the headlines of our newspapers all too frequently, the one to which television news broadcasts devote an inordinate amount of time. He is the killer, the rapist, the man who commits both those atrocities, the mass murderer, the terrorist, the man who holds innocent people hostage in pursuit of his own pathological goals. These victimizers suffer from a grandiosity that is not so prevalent in the other two categories, a grandiosity built upon ever increasing isolation from society and other people. These victimizers are vicious; their rage increases as their isolation deepens. Whereas anxiety makes one feel helpless and vulnerable, rage imbues one with a sense of power and invincibility. These victimizers come to feel above it all, larger than life. They don't believe they are subject to the same laws, the same forces that govern ordinary people. Without any ballast of connective social ties to hold them down, they exist in a stratosphere created by their own madness. Many of these victimizers are sociopaths or psychopaths, men without conscience who feel no remorse or shame for their acts. Generally held social beliefs and values are absent in them. They live at odds with society, not as part of it. Like sharks, they navigate the societal waters searching for fodder to satisfy their needs, utterly unconcerned with how they get it. These are the victimizers I will focus on now.

Psychological traits are learned at mother's and father's knee. Children are formed by the treatment they receive from their parents or other caretakers, by the examples set for them, by the values they see espoused. And inevitably, I would say, those people who are given to violent behavior surely suffered from violence themselves early in their lives. The victimizer has himself been in the victim position; that more than anything is responsible for the genesis of the rage he takes out on others when he is grown.

The stereotyped image of the cruel child is the little boy methodically pulling the wings off a fly. Occasionally, this is rationalized away as the first signs of scientific curiosity, a young mind exploring the outside world. I would wager that budding inquisitiveness never takes that form. The little boy who pulls the wings from a fly is a child who has himself been abused. He knows that what he is doing is painful and destructive to the fly. He knows because he has been on the receiving end of such harsh treatment. His cruelty to the fly says one thing loud and clear: I am doing to the fly what has been done to me—I want to have power over someone or something, too.

A patient once wrote me a letter of apology that included a very explicit expression of this element of the victimizer's personality. "I have been an abusive person," the letter said, "compulsively abusive to people I care about and to people who care for me or begin to like me or want to help, doing what has been done to me by others, as if my hurts give me the right, as if the hurt would be less if I hurt others. . . . When I look at the messy state I got myself into, as I do now, I ask how much of this struggle is because I have not forgiven the hurts caused me."

Psychologist Stanley Rosenman, discussing anti-Semitism, points to crucial elements of the victimizer psychology. Individuals, like nations, help build self-esteem and insure the ego's coherence by participating, either directly or vicariously, in the decimation of others, Rosenman says. The violent victimizer regains a lost sense of omnipotence by his violent behavior. Frequently dependent and ineffectual, the victimizer helps to conquer his fear of debility or death by killing his victim. When he kills or rapes, he is the godlike creator. By destroying, usually symbolically, the powerful person whom he blames for his weakness, he hopes once again to regain control of his own destiny.

The victimizer and the masochist both grow up in great fear, as both are the victims of abuse during childhood. But in the victimizer, who has generally suffered more flagrant abuse and abuse that is more often physical than verbal, rage at the mistreatment takes over and supplants the fear. The masochist, on the other hand, remains mired in the fear. But these two types, who often come together in a terrible conflagration, share a common wellspring in childhood.

The ill-treatment a victimizer receives from his caretakers may be physical or psychological, intentional or not. Unintentional psychological harm may be done to a child by a mother, for example, who is trapped in a role she never wanted and angry because of it. Her anger, unfortunately, will be turned on her child. A reluctant mother inevitably damages her child no matter how hard she tries to be caring (a powerful argument for abortion, I believe).

Basically, there are three fundamental stances or attitudes toward motherhood that recur continually throughout a child's development. They are based on the reproductive experience itself, the motivation for the pregnancy, and, finally, the basic acceptance or rejection of the child. Two of these stances can be very damaging to the child. Two of them could produce a potential victimizer.

The first stance involves denial: You have not really been born, you are still a part of me and cannot grow without my constant care. M. J. Zemlick and Robert I. Watson conducted a study that demonstrated a relationship between maternal rejection and the development of overprotective behavior as a defense serving to deny the mother's true feelings about her child. The mother, seeing the child as part of herself, demands that he grow and develop as she wishes. To this exploitative end, she uses a variety of manipulative, coercive, and seductive techniques that can be extremely damaging to the child.

David Levy, writing about the development of the criminal, addresses the question of maternal overprotectiveness. When this is combined with an absentee or cruel father, Levy found, it is a factor in creating a criminal personality. This mothering stance produces a vulnerability to seduction, as well as a rage at it, and it also fosters the charm-boy aspect that so many victimizers seem to possess. They learn early how to get around their mothers, how to charm them to achieve their own ends. They practice this charm on their mothers even as they are filled with hatred of them for their tenacious, clinging, or seductive behavior.

The second maternal stance can be expressed like this: You have been born, but I cannot abide it. Here there is less denial and more overt rage on the mother's part. She participates as little as possible in taking care of her child, exhibiting inattention, distraction, isolation, and a variety of other distance-creating techniques. In extreme instances, this woman may become an attacking mother and treat her child with cruelty and murderous rage. The potential for damage to the child is obvious here as well.

The third, and ideal, stance says to the child: I will help you grow up in the way that is best for you. This generally produces a psychologically and emotionally healthy child.

When a child receives ill treatment, he comes to believe that his parents do not love him. That translates into his believing that he is not lovable. Since he is not lovable, he must be worthless and bad. Otherwise, he would not be abused. To compensate for feelings of worthlessness, he begins to formulate a sense of his own power in a negative, dangerous way and to develop the grandiosity I mentioned earlier. "I'm better than all the rest of you," this young man begins to think. "I'm stronger, more important, more potent." This grandiosity, present in almost all violent victimizers, is most easily detected perhaps in the presidential assassin: "If I kill the president, I'm more important than he is."

The rage that grows in a child who is seriously ill-treated leads him to see first his abusers, then all other people, as the enemy. And he is never concerned with what the enemy feels. He is concerned only with himself, his own needs, his desire to avoid being hurt, to avoid being a victim himself. The enemy has hurt him; therefore it doesn't matter what he does to retaliate. He sets himself up against society, and as his isolation and antagonism grow, he fails to see the part he himself plays in this process. Now he is the victimizer, preying upon other people as he was once preyed upon. In a perversion of the golden rule, he is now the dispenser of violence, doing unto others what was done unto him.

Unquestionably, the victimizer suffers grave wounds in his early life. But I want to repeat that that does not seem to me sufficient reason to extend sympathy to him. It is tragic that his has been a blighted life. But more tragic is the harm he inflicts on innocent lives. His victims are the truly deserving recipients of our compassion.

All violent victimizers are filled with hate and rage. In rapists, the hatred is for women; the rage is with mother. Rapists are not oversexed demons. They are men in whom impotence is common in ordinary sexual situations and in whom there is a strong link between sex and violence, sex and force. Their only sexual satisfaction may come in relation to violence. It has been said recently that rape is not a sexual act but an act of aggression. It would be more accurate to say that rape is a sexual act in which the violent degradation of the other person is the primary goal.

Freud provided the first important insight into this. In a paper titled "A Child Is Being Beaten," he noted that some patients connected feelings of pleasure with expressed fantasies of being beaten and that these feelings excited considerable shame and guilt. He also observed that being beaten on the bare behind was a common element in these fantasies and that sometimes the fantasies reflected genuine childhood experience. Inevitably, a spanking on the bare bottom carries with it penile stimulation, especially if the child is either across the knee or lying down on something. These fantasies illustrate the link between pain and erotic stimulation. It is not a very big leap from this to see how hatred and sexual stimulation come together. Violence and cruelty in childhood can impart a legacy of resentment and hate and erotic arousal linked with pain. The rapist in effect says: I was the beaten, powerless, sexually stimulated child; now I am the powerful, sexual, punitive parent.

This kind of turnaround is evident in the styles of many criminals. The form their violence takes is not arbitrary. They enact upon their victims what they feel has been done to them. Strangling is a quite common example of this. Men who strangle their victims most likely had mothers who were extremely controlling and who tried to shove things (food, concepts, points of view) down their throats. This made them feel they were choking to death. These men grew up with tremendous rage against women, and they carry out on their victims the feeling they had of being strangled by their mothers.

I mentioned that the victimizer often develops considerable charm. This results from his looking for a way to get by, looking for a mode of behavior that will allow him to deflect the harshness he expects and to disguise his true feelings of hate. He may stumble upon this quite by accident, usually in relation to his mother, when one day something he does gains him approval rather than punishment. He notes what seems to be winning behavior; he sees that it gets him what he wants. And he begins to develop his charm the way someone else would set out to learn how to use a new set of tools. He knows it is a skill that will stand him in good stead.

Charm is something the victimizer studies and learns, though not necessarily consciously, to carry him over the hurdles he faces; it is something that allows him to "pass." This charm, though highly developed, is only skin deep, of course. Someone with a discerning eye, someone autonomous, might be able to see through the superficial charm and note those signs of underlying hate and rage that are bound at some point to show through the victimizer's efforts to hide them. The masochistic person is less likely to penetrate the disguise, more likely to be taken in by the charm, leaving her more vulnerable to victimization. Chaplin's film *Monsieur Verdoux* provided an excellent portrait of the victimizer as charmer. Verdoux is a man who utterly captivates and wins over older women before he strangles them.

There are three other types of victimizer who also belong in the third category: the voyeur, the exhibitionist, and the obscene phone caller. These men are allied with the rapist in that their hostile feelings find sexual expression. They possess the same psychic ingredients as the rapist, but the ingredients take a different form in them. The voyeur hates women, as does the rapist; he can't experience genuine sexual involvement but must keep his distance. The exhibitionist certainly suffers from the same kind of rage toward women and he has the same desire to humiliate them as the rapist does. The obscene phone caller stays more remote from his victim but his act is nevertheless an attack, a form of symbolic rape.

The professional view has been that these types are essentially harmless, that they would never commit actual sexual assault. But I am not so sure. I think it is entirely possible that any one of them might be capable of genuine rape; given the right circumstance, he could move easily from the symbolic to the actual realm of attack. In fact, I know of more than one instance in which rape eventuated from a background of exhibitionism.

The necrophiliac should also be mentioned here. In *The Anatomy of Human Destructiveness*, Erich Fromm makes the point that the necrophiliac is death-preoccupied, that his drive is to create death out of life. This comes through graphically in the French film *Le Bonheur*, which tells the story of a seamstress who is married to a sadistic charmer. One day while they are on a picnic, the husband, completely indifferent to his wife's feelings, goes off and seduces another woman. The wife drowns herself, and when the husband returns and sees her body, which has been pulled from the water, lying on the ground, he throws his own body across it and begins miming intercourse. Her death gives birth to potency in him. In death he can love her, in a sense, because now there is no person there to deal with, only a corpse.

I think it would be instructive at this point to take a detailed look at someone established as a violent victimizer. Surely there is no better example of the species than Ted Bundy, currently on death row in Florida State Prison for the murders of two women and suspected of having killed perhaps dozens more. It was Bundy who, in 1978, entered the Chi Omega sorority house at Florida State University in Tallahassee and, in a matter of just minutes, killed two women with the club he was carrying and battered two others into unconsciousness. One of the dead women suffered such a powerful blow to her forehead that her brain was exposed. The other was sodomized with a can of hair spray, and one of her nipples nearly torn off by a bite, and had another deep wound in her buttock, where she had also been bitten. Directly after leaving the scene of this slaughter, Bundy attacked another sleeping coed in a nearby apartment; she survived only because the thumping noise of Bundy's club as he dealt blows to his victim awakened her neighbors, and he was frightened away. When he was arrested a month later, he was also indicted for the kidnapping and murder of a twelve-year-old girl six days before his arrest. He had begun killing several years earlier, when he was a law student. His young women victims numbered at least sixteen and came from four different states: Washington, Oregon, Utah, and Colorado.

After Bundy was convicted in Florida and revealed as the likely perpetrator of the baffling murder spree in the Pacific Northwest, a number of books and articles were written about him. The emphasis in all of them was how unlikely a candidate Ted Bundy was for a mass murderer, how in fact he was the antithesis of everything that role conjures up. Nothing about Bundy, apparently, appeared monstrous. He was handsome and well educated; people described him as intelligent, caring, and compassionate, the devoted son of an adoring mother, charismatic, politically adept and, some even said, a possible future governor of the state of Washington. He had even come close to being appointed director of Seattle's Crime Prevention Advisory Commission, a notion almost unbearable in its degree of irony. These accounts presented him as a terrific, talented, marvelously likable fellow whose life, inexplicably and horrendously, suddenly went bad. I submit that the picture can be neither so simple nor so rosy.

While I have no firsthand knowledge of Bundy, and the information I possess about his background is limited, what I do know tells me that the seeds of his psychopathy were sown early, as they always are. He is, first of all, often described as his mother's darling, and that in itself can be a dangerous position for a child. It usually indicates that the mother is getting vicarious satisfactions from an offspring that she ought to be getting from another adult, from a mate. In the case of Bundy's mother, no such figure existed. She and her out-of-wedlock child lived with her parents, his illegitimacy obscured by the fiction that Ted was the child of her parents, that he and his mother were brother and sister. One can imagine the conflicts, tensions, and anxieties that existed in that household. The parents must have resented and been deeply ashamed of their daughter, who had defied them and their religious code; the daughter must have resented their judgments and the child with whom she was saddled, denying these latter feelings by adopting a doting attitude toward her son.

Currents of hate, anger, guilt, and resentment must have continually washed over the adults and the child, and, presumably, they became unbearable because when Ted was four he and his mother moved to Tacoma, Washington, to live with other relatives. Even after they made this move, the fiction was maintained that Ted and his mother were siblings. Knowing no more than this, I can say that this is a child with an extremely disturbed family background. Add to it that when his mother finally married a man named Bundy, Ted took the man's name but refused any fathering from him; that Ted in elementary school was the butt of humiliating teasing from his classmates (teasing is very commonly directed at disturbed children); and that growing up he was never seen to date or to be involved with girls—and the picture changes considerably from the one of relentless normality that is usually presented.

That Bundy was charming I have no doubt. As I said, the development of charm is a commonplace among psychopathic people. It is their stock-in-trade, their means of passage, and as such it becomes a single, overdetermined trait that can be almost overwhelming. This accounts, I think, for the descriptions of

Bundy as charismatic, prepossessing, "Kennedyesque." But despite his considerable charm, there must have been signs of his underlying disturbance that would have been visible to the discerning eye. Unfortunately, none of his victims, nor any of the people who knew him in his "normal" life, had such a capacity, apparently.

Bundy has always maintained that he is innocent of any murders, those with which he has been charged, those he is suspected of committing. In the course of doing a book about him, with his supposed cooperation but frustrated by Bundy's constant refusal to address the issue of his guilt, journalists Stephen G. Michaud and Hugh Aynesworth devised a format they thought might appeal to Bundy's ego and penetrate his denial. As the suspect in these cases he had amassed a great deal of knowledge, they pointed out. He also had been a psychology student. And obviously he had a keen intelligence. Why, they suggested, didn't he *speculate* about the sort of person who would commit such crimes and about his motives for doing so? Bundy was willing, even eager. Psychiatrists who have listened to the tapes made by Michaud and Aynesworth say there is no doubt that Bundy is talking about himself.

Bundy describes the progressive growth within "the killer" of an "entity," a "distorted self," a "malignant being." And most interesting to me was the part that pornography played in this growth. Pornography, Bundy says, pushed him along the road of increasing violence. His thoughts about sex had begun to center on ideas of sexual violence. Pornography gave him permission to pursue these thoughts, to consider acting on them. Essentially violent toward women, pornography, which is tolerated by society and even by many professionals, set the societal seal of approval on Bundy's vicious tendencies. It lifted such limits as he possessed; it removed the restraints.

The late Alexander Bickel, who was professor of constitutional law at Yale University, was one of the few courageous voices in the legal profession willing to declare unreservedly that pornography is a menace. In his book *Morality of Consent*, he asserted that it is not always possible to carry out the intent of our laws, but he argued that nevertheless our laws represent a consensus of how we feel; they express society's general beliefs of what is right and what is wrong. Removing antipornography laws from the books, he said, was to declare that pornography is acceptable to us as a society.

In *Understanding Sexual Attacks* by Drs. West, Roy, and Nichol, the authors point out that group therapy among imprisoned rapists revealed how unhappy and conflict-driven rapists are. Their compulsive behavior is aggressive and violent in all its aspects; a preoccupation they all shared was with pornographic materials and fantasies. Of course, this preoccupation can be seen as a defensive response to their alienation and lack of relatedness. But it also sets off still further alienation through violence. Bundy certainly picked up in pornography the message that violence toward women is acceptable and, with that message, his sickness escalated.

Diana Scully and Joseph Marolla, professors at Virginia Commonwealth University, believe that rapists are in many ways no different from most men, that they are products of a culture that teaches that sexually aggressive behavior is all right and that rape is just the extreme example of that learned attitude. Not only do these men learn sexual violence from the culture, Scully and Marolla maintain, they also learn to master a vocabulary that can be used to explain violence against women in socially acceptable terms.

Bundy recounts how violence against women and sexual activity merged in "the killer's" mind, how he stalked his victims, and how he began to kill. He makes clear that the killer's exhilaration came from the capture and degradation of women. Describing one killing in some detail, he tells of how he picked up a young woman hitchhiker, invited her to come to a party at his place, flattered and entertained her on the drive there ("for the purpose of making the whole encounter seem legitimate and to keep her at her ease"), once there, giving her more alcohol on top of the drinks she had already had that evening, drinking a great deal himself, and eventually strangling her after having sex. What a perfect example this is of a woman's contributing to her own victimization. She put herself in a dangerous position by hitchhiking, particularly after she had had a few drinks. She agreed to accompany Bundy—an unknown person—to his house, accepting his premise that a party was in progress there. She failed to hear any discordant notes in his conversation in the car, although they were bound to be present. When they arrived at his house and she saw there was no party, she failed to leave immediately, if that was still possible. She continued to drink heavily. She submitted to "more or less voluntary" sex with him.

A second incident Bundy describes quite fully contains another cautionary message. Disturbed by the murders, suffering remorse in the aftermath of each, the killer decided on a compromise of sorts: He would rape his victim instead of murdering her, making sure there would be no possibility of detection so that he would not be forced into killing. To this end he set out one evening, cruising through the suburbs of the city in which he lived. Spotting a young woman walking alone on a dark street, he parked his car some distance behind her, made his approach brandishing a knife, and pushed her off the sidewalk into a wooded area. He told her to submit and do what he wanted. She began to argue with him, saying she did not believe he would do anything to her. He tried very hard to focus on his intention of not harming her; she continued arguing and began screaming as well. He began to panic, fearing someone would hear, and he put his hands around her throat and squeezed, "just to throttle her into unconsciousness so that she wouldn't scream anymore." Then he raped her, not realizing until afterward that she was dead. My hunch is that this was a real act of necrophilia, that Bundy knew she was dead and enjoyed it because she was dead and he had killed her.

When this young woman challenged Bundy by saying she did not believe he would hurt her, she signed her own death warrant. A rapist or murderer reassures himself about his own inadequacy through his violent act. Any challenge to his veracity is extremely dangerous, constituting as it does an accusation that he is not powerful enough to carry out what he has threatened. Accused of impotence, he is bound to prove that he means what he says, and the chances increase of his viciousness escalating. As I've said, when one is locked into an encounter with a violent assailant, it is important not to do anything that threatens his fragile self-esteem. One should concentrate instead on doing everything possible to bolster it. It is also well to remember, as Bundy indicates, that the victimizer is frightened, too, struggling to maintain a delicate balance between his fear of getting caught and his need to act out his savage compulsion.

Near the end of his "speculative" session with Michaud and Aynesworth, Bundy remarked on how vulnerable society is to the depredations of people like himself. "The really scary thing," he told them, "is that there are a lot of people who are not in prison, a *lot* of people who were far more successful than I." And therein lies the point of spending time thinking about a mass murderer like Bundy. These people exist. Their primary emotions are rage and hate, and their self-preoccupation is enormous. Other people serve only as fodder for their needs. Isolated, alienated, they are separate from other people but constantly studying them. And they become, in some ways, quite acute in their judgments of people. They develop a large fund of knowledge about their prey. Just as a fisherman learns about the movements of fish, the currents in which they swim, the times and seasons at which they run, the bait they rise to, so a victimizer learns where to find his victims, how to spot who is a likely prospect, who is not, and how to hook them. Bundy more than once used the ploy of putting his arm in a cast, traveling to a resort area, launching a small sailboat, and then requesting help of a young woman when the time came to take the boat out of the water and secure it atop his car. More than one responded to his plea, rode along with him to help unload it, and ended up a murder victim because of her willingness to assist the handsome stranger.

Recently at a legal conference, I heard a judge describe a particular victimizer's modus operandi. This mugger/rapist carefully chose a set of conditions that would be advantageous to him. He frequented suburban areas that had large supermarkets but also a fair number of apartment buildings, and he watched for a woman entering her building with packages in both arms. Going into the building after her, when the elevator came he would ask if he could press her floor. After doing that, he would press the floor below hers, making it seem he belonged in the building and also indicating to her that he would be getting off before her, just in case she had fears that needed to be allayed. Once the elevator closed, he would attack her and grab her bag. If he was not done with the robbery when the elevator door opened, he would put his foot in the door so that the elevator wouldn't operate. If he saw that there was no one around, he would rape her. Here the odds were entirely in favor of the victimizer. He has picked his own situation and environment. He knows he is operating from a position of strength because he has waited for someone who is alone, whose arms are full, and who will be inclined to be trustful because he has offered to help her. He knows, in other words, where the fish are running and the lure to which they will respond.

In this connection, I think of a patient of mine, a professional man who had the clean-cut good looks of a grown-up choirboy. His habit was to go to a singles bar and pick up a young woman, invite her to his apartment, have sex with her, and, as soon as it was over, kick her out of his bed and his house. "Get your clothes on and get the hell out of here fast or you'll regret it," he would say. As soon as she left, he would take a shower so that he could feel "clean" again. This man was potentially very dangerous, and the young women who accompanied him were taking a great risk, but he seemed to have no trouble finding willing partners. Women went home with him knowing nothing about him and without anyone else knowing where they were.

While superficially this man must have seemed like God's gift to women, I am certain he exhibited clues to his true nature during his approach to a prospective conquest. A self-contained woman would pick up on these clues, whereas his victims (and indeed he victimized women in his utterly selfish use of them), masochists all, I'm afraid, did not. His behavior was undoubtedly arrogant and grandiose, focusing exclusively on himself, showing little or no interest in the woman. He would have no natural curiosity about her because he would not really see her as a person in her own right. She would be simply the catch he was going to hook. And why should he bother feigning interest in her when it was not necessary? After all, he would know it was going to be just a one-night stand.

I am sure he also displayed a persistence in pursuit of his own ends that might have been a clue to someone perceptive. And no doubt he flattered the women profusely. The compliments he bestowed were, I feel sure, obvious attempts to get the woman to respond to him and had probably very little to do with her. But a person with masochistic tendencies would not understand or detect this; her focus would be on how nice it feels to be flattered. If she felt any disbelief, she would ignore it. Succumbing to flattery that has no depth is a masochistic trait.

The one thing a victimizer must have in order to commit an assault is opportunity. And he will seize it whenever and wherever it presents itself. He is always looking for a chance to strike. That is why the notions of self-protection and moving away from the masochistic tendencies that undermine it are so important. Any potential victim can play a definite part in her own destiny, denying the victimizer opportunity by her own prudent behavior.

12

Dream Worlds, Fantasy Lives

The daydreams, or fantasies, of masochistic people are fueled by a pervasive sense of ineffectuality; predictably, they exhibit a distinct split along gender lines, since boys and girls receive such different parental and cultural conditioning. The masochistic man who feels himself to be helpless and passive will tend to have fantasies of the Walter Mitty variety: He will imagine himself *transformed into another person*, someone of great appeal and accomplishment—a pilot, a politician, a mathematical genius, a movie star. He will tend to be like the Woody Allen character in *Play It Again, Sam* who has Humphrey Bogart alongside him at all times, coaching him in how to assume a tough-guy stance.

Masochistic women, on the other hand, daydream of overcoming their helplessness and passivity by meeting and attaching themselves to someone who possesses power. It is borrowed power they fantasize. They will *fall in love with* the pilot, the politician, the genius, the movie star. And they often arrange to establish this liaison with a minimum of initiative or forcefulness on their part: They will bump into someone electrifying on the street, and he will evince a sudden interest in them, and one thing will lead to another, and soon romance will blossom. A masochistic patient of mine would visualize herself walking down Fifth Avenue, being hit lightly by a car or twisting an ankle and falling. A gorgeous man would come along and either transport her to the hospital or, if she was not badly hurt, suggest they have a cup of coffee, and out of this a love affair begins.

This fantasy of rescue is very common. Chance and accident are prominently featured as the means by which the masochist overcomes her sense of inadequacy and incompetence. It is, of course, the Prince Charming or Cinderella story. The transformation that occurs for the masochistic woman is almost invariably through the agency of someone else. It is a sad commentary that even in their fantasies women do not often imagine themselves as powerful people; they imagine themselves *attached* to powerful people.

The same woman who fantasized the Fifth Avenue accident recalled to me a childhood daydream of hers that contained some of the same elements. She and her family lived in New York, and her mother forbade her to have a pet in their city apartment. When they went on vacations to a beautiful wooded area of New Jersey, the girl was particularly taken with the bushy-tailed squirrels, and she wished she could have one of them as a pet. She fantasized that a squirrel would go out on the limb of a tree, the limb would break, the squirrel would fall to the ground, hurting itself, and she would then nurse it back to health, care for it, and keep it as a pet. Her masochism is evident in the helplessness she felt in obtaining a pet in any way except through a disaster. Though the accident happens to the squirrel, not to her, the feeling behind the fantasy is the same.

Erich Fromm observed that the quality of daydreams, due to their being largely wish-fulfillment, is often slightly cheap. They seem rather simplistic and unelaborated, almost adolescent in their emphasis on easy gratification, revealing of the fact that the masochistic person is not quite grown-up.

Suicide is a frequent masochistic fantasy and one that also occurs fairly often in adolescents, another indicator of the common denominator of powerlessness in these two groups. The adolescent, while beginning to be free, is still dependent upon parents who may be mean or unkind or involved in an ongoing negative relationship with her. The masochist has been mired in a prolonged sense of dependence and tends to see nearly everyone as a stern authority figure who has the capacity to mistreat her. The purpose of the suicidal fantasy for both groups is to say to their adversaries: You will be sorry you treated me this way; when I am dead and gone you will regret that you treated me badly. The suicidal fantasy of the masochist is nearly always directed toward someone, and thus there is a coercive element in relation to the significant other person on whom the fantasy is focused.

Dreams express things in a much more complex way than do daydreams or fantasies. Many people view the world of dreams as a phantasmagoric one, filled with enigmatic images that share more of a kinship with the theater of the absurd than they do with the dreamer's daily life. Dream content seems arcane, fractured, and destined to stay clouded by mists of unintelligibility. We have all heard people say, "I had the craziest dream. There's no way any one could figure this out." Or, "You won't believe the dream I had last night! It made no sense at all." But despite the dreamer's assessment, you can rest assured that it *did* make sense, for the dream world is neither as cryptic nor as inaccessible as it appears to be. Montague Ullman, a psychoanalyst who has done a great deal of work on dreams, puts it this way: Dreaming is nothing more than thinking under the conditions of sleep.

Dreams may serve as a time for the mind to relieve and clear itself, offer a theater for the enactment of wish-fulfillment, or constitute an arena for working on the problems of our waking lives. But whatever their purpose, dreams are bound up with those things of the preceding day. However obscure they may seem at first glance, dreams are not arbitrary visitations from another realm. They come from us and belong to us. They are reports from the unconscious about what matters most to us.

"Why does the mind see more clearly in sleep than the imagination of the day?" Leonardo da Vinci asked, his question accurately reflecting the fundamental quality of the dream, that distillation of essence that occurs during sleep when all the day's distractions are set aside. Dream time is not interrupted by diversion of eye or ear. It is solitary, silent time in which the dreamer focuses intensely on the issues arising in the dreams.

The language of dreams is different from the language we use when awake. Dream statements are expressed in metaphoric or symbolic terms, a fact that accounts for their seemingly elusive nature. But one can come to understand dream language in the same way one masters any foreign tongue, by study and exposure. This was recognized in the Old Testament, in which Joseph was shown rising from captive to right-hand man to the pharaoh on the strength of his accurate interpretations of dreams and his predictions based on them. All dreams are predictive in the sense that they are expressions of the present illuminated by the past and pointing to the future.

Very often, dream language can be highly individualistic. I am sure, for instance, that if I were shown accounts of dreams from my patients, I would know which dreams belonged to which patient. Each dreamer has his or her own language or style. And it is important to note that to be understood a dream need not be examined in minute detail, each small facet traced and explicated like the clues in a detective story (though there are times when this might be necessary). Dreams can be understood through a kind of synthesis. If one fathoms the metaphor, one grasps the dream. "A skillful man reads his dreams for self-knowledge," said Emerson, "yet not the detail but the quality."

A wonderful example of the metaphoric nature of dreams came from a woman patient of mine who was both masochistic and menopausal. Her dream consisted of a single image: a suitcase that had belonged to her husband sitting on the shelf in her closet. She dreamed she saw this and she awoke very upset. Dreams are made comprehensible, of course, by the associations of the dreamer to the material of the dream, and she said of the suitcase that it was very expensive and all leather, and when her husband first bought it he absolutely loved it and used it all the time. Then it began to get scratched and worn and battered, and a point came at which he did not want to use it anymore and he bought a new one. He threw the old one out, but she could not bear its loss, so she rescued it. The single image of the suitcase contained a recapitulation of this woman's entire marriage: She was the suitcase, originally cherished and valued, gradually showing signs of wear, and eventually tossed out and replaced by the much younger woman for whom her husband had left her; despite this, however, she rescued herself, she went on with her life, although she still felt that she was "on the shelf."

Dreams are the metaphoric expressions of the concerns of our daily lives, highlighted and distilled. As Alexander Pope put it: "You eat in dreams the custard of the day." And the dreams of a masochistic person are filled with images of pursuit and paralysis. She is often being chased, hunted, hounded; people are out to get her. In the face of this threat, she exhibits total impotence; she is unable to move, unable to hear, unable to scream or speak, sometimes unable to see.

For example, a young woman is being abducted by robbers in a car that tears along a road at high speed; they reach an intersection with a red light; the car stops and the young woman feels the excitement of victory as she manages to get out of the car; but the moment she is out, she finds that her legs are paralyzed and she is unable to move; she wakes up in a sweat. Potency, or lack of it, is a key problem for the masochistic person. And virtually all the imagery of her dreams has to do with recognition of this. She is someone who is attempting in her dreams to solve the problem of helplessness: How can I scream? How can I walk? How can I run? How can I escape? How can I handle my life more successfully?

In the following discussion of masochistic dreams, or perhaps, more properly, nightmares, it may seem that the interpretations I present are rather arbitrary. But that is due to the limitations of space. Obviously, I can't give the complete background material on each patient that would serve to clarify each interpretation. So I will focus on the central metaphors of the dreams, those metaphors that illuminate masochistic tendencies, and not attempt to deal with all the complexities of the dreams. Often, as a problem becomes clearer, the dreams that reflect and address that problem become less complex. And often they state in one simple metaphor some complicated things the patient has come to understand. That was true of the suitcase dream as it is of the dreams that follow.

A man dreamed that he entered his place of business and saw three men who appeared to be joined together, frozen into a block. He felt this was dangerous and that they might attack him. He also saw, before awakening frightened, that his daughter was observing the three men. This dream states clearly the problem of a very masochistic man. In business with two brothers who criticize and ridicule him and refuse to let him make his own decisions, he feels locked into them, frozen between them in a powerless position yet open to attack by them. His daughter's observing only intensifies the situation as she is also contemptuous of him and often "fresh" and abusive to him.

The next dream suggests in a single image both the patient's problem and her struggle to cope with it. She dreamed that she stood at the Dutch doors of a stable. The top half of the doors was open, and on the other side she could see a lion. She was terrified. In her hand she held a bowl of Jell-O, which she attempted to offer to the lion. As it raised its head above the door, she woke up feeling extremely anxious. Reporting this dream to me, she said, "You certainly can't mollify a lion by offering him Jell-O. Lions are out to devour meat; lions are out to make a kill." She was talking about her husband, who liked to ride horseback and was symbolized in this instance by the lion behind the stable door. The woman experienced her husband as a frightening figure; she had never been able to deal with him adequately. The best she could do was to offer him Jell-O when obviously something more substantial was called for. Talking further about her associations, the woman said, "Lions are dangerous. I felt this one was, too. But male lions are so regal and beautiful that it's always been hard for me to believe how dangerous they are. Still, I wouldn't like to find out." These associations illuminate the conflict at the heart of the sado-masochistic marriage in which the husband is brutal and the wife attempts to go along in conciliatory style: The wife believes her husband is dangerous, but she also finds him compelling, even magnificent in some ways, and she finds it hard to believe how cruel he really is.

A typical masochistic dream metaphor is a woman finding herself nude before a group of people. A patient of mine who was a concert artist dreamed that she had all sorts of difficulties getting to the hall on the night of a concert. She finally arrived, came out on stage, and realized she had no clothes on. This terrified her and she woke up in a sweat. Her nudity expressed several things: the fear that she would be revealed at her worst, her feelings of being seen through, her doubts about herself as an artist, and a general feeling of humiliation that was an ongoing aspect of her life.

Common also, as I said earlier, are images of paralysis or some other sort of impairment that keep the dreamer from being able to function or to assist herself in a threatening situation. One of the starkest of these was a dream of a masochistic patient in which she saw a woman standing alone in an empty room. The woman was paralyzed and could not move. The bleak metaphor speaks powerfully of the absolute sense of incapacity and inadequacy that engulfed this woman and of the feeling of alienation that was a consequence of her masochistic style.

Another masochistic woman dreamed that as she and her husband were entering a restaurant to have dinner, a gang of thieves burst in, robbed the patrons, and took the woman and her husband along with them, demanding to go to their home. Once there, the thieves began looting the house, and when she threatened to call the police, they just laughed at her and said they had cut the lines. Finally, however, she managed to get outside and planned to find a phone and call the police but found that she was paralyzed and could not move. Here the paralysis theme is accompanied by two others that frequently turn up in the dreams of masochistic people: being menaced or pursued by evil people and calling on the authorities for help. The woman in this dream never completes a call to the police, but the idea of doing so looms large. Authority figures, good and bad, appear prominently in masochistic dreams. Also notice that the dream started with the woman seeking sustenance—going to a restaurant for food. This speaks of her emotional hunger that was not satisfied in her marriage.

Another common masochistic dream, related directly to low self-esteem, focuses on making a connection with an important public personalty and deriving strength from the association. Some years ago, a patient of mine dreamed repeatedly of establishing relationships with one or another member of the Kennedy family, an expression of the wish to share in some of the luster and power that attaches to the Kennedy name. This same patient dreamed she was ingesting the flesh of a renowned opera star, a metaphoric statement of her desire to become (literally, and cannibalistically in this instance, by incorporating the diva's body within her own) someone with stature, creative gifts, and power.

A male patient dreamed he was standing in line, waiting to talk to the mayor of New York City, Ed Koch. All the others taking their turn seemed to be at ease and to have no problem talking with the mayor. But this man realized he would have nothing to say, and so he stepped out of line, feeling very disappointed with himself. In the dream he thought, "What is this? Everybody else can talk to this guy. Why can't I?" That he was unable to approach even the seemingly very accessible mayor is indicative of how completely helpless he feels to express himself, as well as how inadequate and worthless.

The dreams of masochistic people, even when they don't center on easily recognizable metaphors such as pursuit, paralysis, nudity in a crowd, or connecting with someone famous, certainly exhibit those aspects of the masochistic personality that have by now become familiar to the reader: fear of other people, a sense of being misused by them, self-destructiveness, a perception of the world as a dangerous place, an inability to stand up for oneself.

A sense of fear of the power of others comes through strongly in the dream of a male patient who saw himself being driven by a chauffeur in a limousine to an exclusive house outside of the city. He was in the car with "other children," he said. When they arrived at their destination, he got out of the car but then realized that he had left behind his coat and some other things he had brought with him. When he finally had those items in hand, he looked toward the front door of the house and realized that the man standing there was waiting for him to give the name of the person he had come to see. He couldn't remember the name. Throughout the dream, this man feels and behaves like one of the children he feels himself to be. When he gets out of the car, he forgets to take his things with him. Confronted with the authority in the doorway, he forgets the name of the person he has come to see. His sense of helplessness paralyzes his brain and he is unable to conduct himself as an adult.

A woman who experienced other people as dangerous reported a dream that resembled an adventure movie. She and some other people were being held prisoner by a group of Nazis in an encampment alongside a river containing a large and frightening alligator. She wondered how she would escape but took no steps to effect that end. Finally, she and her brother were rescued by helicopter. The feeling throughout the dream was that she was surrounded by danger but completely unable to contend with it. Her only hope was to get away, which she did, but through no effort of her own. Another time this same woman dreamed she was in a vacation spot in the Caribbean, waiting at the airport to go home. Suddenly, a military coup occurred and she was detained, held for a long time in one place and questioned by someone who said he came from the police and who she feared might torture her. Ultimately, she was allowed to go, but here again she found herself in the hands of dangerous authority figures.

Another quite masochistic woman dreamed that she and a man were swimming just off a deserted beach when she saw a shark in the water nearby. They quickly swam to a rock, but before the man could pull her up on the rock, the shark bit off her leg below the knee. The man decided it would be best if they stayed on the rock until morning, although she wondered if she might bleed to death. The shark symbolizes this woman's fear of other people, her sense that they are dangerous and can do terrible damage. Even so, she submits to the man's judgment although she believes it may put her life in jeopardy. (Of course, his judgment, whomever he stood for, may have been right, since swimming with a bleeding stump would hardly be safe in shark-infested waters).

This woman also had frequent chase dreams in which she was pursued by either cops or robbers—both authorities, both dangerous—or she dreamed of terrible car accidents with mutilated bodies sprawled all over the scene of the accident. In these dreams, her sense of danger and of being vulnerable to damage and her anger at her own helplessness in the face of others' power come through over and over again.

Then there was a young woman who dreamed she was engaged to a young man who sent her a ring through the mail. At first the ring seemed pretty, but then she began to find it ugly. Just as she was going to meet him for lunch, a friend of hers commented on what a weird person he was, and when they met, she suddenly saw him as sloppy and disheveled, with obviously dirty hair and fingernails. She felt embarrassed to be seen with him, but she did not have the nerve to tell him that she didn't want to marry him, and she awoke feeling very anxious. The central point of this dream is that she saw this unappealing, distasteful man as the sort she would marry because that fit her image of herself as being unattractive and without value.

A young professional woman who is a patient of mine dreamed that she was to attend a conference in her field. When she arrived at the entrance to the room where the conference was being held, she was told she could not be admitted. She didn't ask why but simply walked away and decided to go to the ladies' room. There she waited in line, but when her turn came a woman appeared and said it was not her turn, that she (the woman) had been there first. She accepted the woman's assertion and continued to wait. Aside from her obvious and masochistic inability to stand up for herself, you will recognize that two types of masochistic communication are reflected in her dream: fear to question and the closely related acceptance of the other's premise. This woman was a legitimate participant in the conference, but when she was turned away, she didn't question why, she simply capitulated. Once again in the ladies' room, though she knew it to be her turn, she accepted the other woman's premise that she should go first rather than questioning it or taking an opposite stand.

The masochistic message of spilling is revealed in the dream of a woman who saw herself undergoing surgery for the removal of part of her body. She did not know why this surgery was being performed, but while she was under the anesthetic, she talked volubly. When she awakened in her dream, she found many people standing around who had been listening to her, and she was embarrassed because she felt they were laughing at her and critical of her. The most important feature of this dream is that the woman felt her talking was out of her control and that it left her vulnerable to damage from others. Feelings of helplessness also come through in the metaphor of anesthesia and in the sense of being acted upon by others, carved up by others, without even knowing why.

Helplessness before others was also revealed by a woman who dreamed she was getting dressed to go on a date. Her closet was filled with clothes, but she felt she looked awful in each outfit she tried on. Finally, she settled on something as her date was about to arrive, but he never appeared. This dream reflects the woman's general anxiety, symbolized by the repeated changing of clothes, and her sense that she is vulnerable to being hurt by others and must try to ward off criticism by wearing "the perfect outfit."

Yet another dream displaying feelings of helplessness and being ill-treated by others came from a woman who dreamed she was taking a holiday with three other women, sharing a cabin. The women began to fight with her and told her to leave. When she refused, they tried to push her out. Then they insisted she ought to pay for the entire vacation. They asked to borrow money from her. She said she would not lend it to them but handed over the money nevertheless. This woman made small attempts to stand up for herself, token efforts, but she was powerless to stop the attacks of the others, and ultimately she capitulated to them.

Masochism, ignored or untreated, tends to get worse as the defensive style continues to reinforce itself and the sum of suffering grows. One woman's dream reflected this sense of progressive difficulty. She and a friend attended a tennis class, and the gymnasium was filled with hundreds of people, making her fearful that the pro would not be able to pick her out of the crowd. Members of the class lined up to serve, but just before it was her turn, the pro blew the whistle and said they should all go outdoors. Everyone began to run from the gym, but she couldn't find her way out. When she finally did, she found herself running in a tunnel that gradually inclined uphill, making the going increasingly tough. When she reached the end of the tunnel, she found it was blocked and she could not get out. She awakened in an anxious state.

Many things come through in this dream: the woman's fear

that she is invisible, that there is nothing distinctive about her to make her stand out in a crowd; her sense that she doesn't get her fair share of things, that she never gets to take her turn; feelings of powerlessness and inadequacy, of being unable to do what other people do easily. But the overall atmosphere of the dream is most important, the atmosphere of unending struggle, constantly confronting obstacles, stymied at every turn, and traveling an increasingly arduous and dangerous path that leads nowhere.

This same woman had grave doubts not only about herself but about me as well, as was revealed in a dream in which we had decided she would spend the day with me and go wherever I went. She looked forward to this as a comforting prospect, but then, quite suddenly, I appeared to her as a ten-year-old with pigtails, and *I* was following *her* around. This woman was questioning whether help was available to her. Obviously, I was of no use if I was a child. Her need to be totally dependent in order to survive and her fear that perhaps I wasn't the omniscient figure she fantasized I was, but a child like herself, was very threatening.

In the following dream of a masochistic woman, she was both killer and victim. She was on her way to a shopping center where she had heard there was a sale. Arriving at the parking lot, she saw it was strewn with dead bodies and flowing with blood. Although she was frightened, she pressed on with her shopping, entering the supermarket and grabbing hold of as much as she could carry. Suddenly, she realized her children were home alone and in possible danger, so she rushed home and was relieved to find them alive. This woman saw herself surrounded by death and destruction, an expression of her raging anger about her life predicament. She felt in a sense that she was dead. But, nevertheless, she went on with her life, by rote, as it were, trying to grab what satisfactions she could. Only her children were capable of penetrating the negative, destructive wall around her and exciting in her genuine love and concern. Her dream indicates this woman's awareness of her own destructiveness and its effect on her life, but it also indicates a kind of resignation about it, except insofar as her children are concerned.

A patient of mine is an extremely bright young woman, only a few years out of college but already in a good job with a very decent salary. Extremely attractive as well, she nevertheless has had few relationships with men, as she finds it difficult to reach out to other people and make herself accessible in any way. She had always planned to return to school for her M.B.A. and this year applied to and was accepted at six of seven of the country's best graduate schools. At the same time, she was offered a job at a higher level with a large salary increase. But because she is, unfortunately, quite masochistic, having these two excellent options left her feeling not elation but despair. Her sessions were flooded by tears; she felt her life was a disaster. A dream she reported to me was very expressive of her masochistic problems.

She was going on vacation on an ocean liner, but the day she was due to leave she delayed going home to pack and, after she finally did so and set off for the ship, she realized she had forgotten certain things and had to return home. Then she rushed to the dock only to see the boat pulling away. She called out, but no one heard her. So she jumped into the water and began to swim after the boat, seeming to gain on it for a while but then falling behind. She sank under the water and, looking down, saw herself lying on the bottom, drowned. In the second part of the dream, she was on the boat, which was filled with lots of young men and women. But rather than spending time with them, she was busying herself with organizational tasks, seeing that the chairs were placed right, that everyone had the proper stateroom, and so on.

The delay in the first part of the dream is a metaphor for this young woman's fear of life: She avoids, puts off, misses connections; she uses tangential, circumstantial actions (as well as speech) to keep herself from engaging with life. Then, filled with regret and remorse, she struggles to reverse her course, but it is too late; she has delayed too long. In the second half of the dream, which is an additional effort to solve the problem posed in the first segment, she places herself on the boat. Once there, however, her fear of others overcomes her again, and she is unable to involve herslf with the other people abroad. She is unable to be playful, to be accessible, to join in. She practices avoidance while endeavoring to disguise it with an overlay of busyness. One can assume several roles in the course of a dream and do things that seem irrational but that obviously serve an important purpose in the dream itself. This young woman was able to see herself drowned and then resurrected and on the boat.

The dream of an older patient of mine also featured self-destructive lateness as a key element. A paraprofessional who was approaching menopause, she saw in the first part of her dream a group of cheerleaders milling around on a football field, not properly dressed because they had not had time to put on their uniforms before the game began. In the second part of the dream she was to deliver a paper to her institution, but she arrived late. Standing outside was a group of dreary women, crying, suffering, looking dopey, a few of them drinking. The dreamer debated whether she should join them or go in to give her talk. Then she awoke with considerable anxiety.

When we began to discuss the dream, I said this seemed to make a statement about the American woman, but I wondered if I was imposing some of my notions on the interpretation. It shows a woman beginning life by having to look good and act out a vacuous role (after all, in a football game the players are doing what counts, not the cheerleaders) and ending up without men in an insipid group of women, trying to anesthetize herself. "That's exactly it," my patient exclaimed. "I was a cheerleader, and I spent, or rather wasted, a great deal of time in college trying to achieve some recognition that way. But a cheerleader isn't recognized as an individual, only as part of a group. And I'm afraid because I'm always late with whatever I do that I'll end up being of one of those drippy women. I have no confidence in what I do, no enthusiasm. I'm afraid it will only lead to failure and to being one of the castoffs."

Finally, I turn to the dream of a patient who was very aware of her masochistic problems but had yet to overcome them. This woman's mother had been a powerful and damaging force in her life since childhood, sometimes overprotective, other times brutal. My patient dreamed she was in a car with her mother who insisted on driving. "Let me drive, Mother," the woman kept saying. "You can't see." But her mother refused to stop and change seats, and at one point she veered from the left lane of the road over to the right and crashed into another car. The mother was thrown onto the road, which was strewn with crystal, and the mother's leg was broken off. When the woman looked up the stump of her mother's leg, she could see that it was hollow, as if her mother were a papier-mâché dummy. In a rage, and even though she knew it might hurt, the woman pulled her mother up from the pavement and said, "Why don't you ever listen to me? Do you see what's happened?"

This mother never let her daughter develop autonomy: She never let her drive. When the woman tells her mother that she cannot see, it reflects the reality of the mother's aging, as well as the fact that as the woman has become more mature she has developed a greater awareness than her mother. That she sees her mother as hollow, and no longer the powerful and threatening person she has always seemed is progress for this woman. Still, she continues to submit to her mother, and there is a suggestion that this causes great rage in her. When she yanks her mother off the ground, knowing it will hurt, and says, "Why don't you ever listen to me?" she is really saying that she is grown-up now and still not free of her mother's hold.

The day she had this dream, the woman had made a necklace for herself, combining the black and white crystals of two old necklaces. The broken crystal scattered on the road suggests that while she was able to remake the old necklaces into something new and pleasing, she was not capable of an equally successful effort in her life. Her masochistic sense of futility comes through in this image. It is as though she is saying: What is the use of making an effort if it is destroyed by my mother's refusal to let me take charge of my own life or to acknowledge that I am now the one who sees clearly.

"What is meant by reality?" Virginia Woolf wrote. "It . . . is what remains over when the skin of the day has been cast into the hedge. That is what is left of past time and our loves and hates." Although Woolf is speaking here of reality, I have always thought this passage was relevant to dreams as well. For they are what is left when the skin of the day is cast into the hedge, not emanations from an alien and mysterious place but essential pieces of our selves, our *innermost* reality.

13

Body Images

Several years ago, I worked with a young woman who was studying acting and beginning to get jobs in the theater. When I noticed she was getting thin, I questioned her about it and she gave me appropriate answers, most of them having to do with her career. I suggested, however, that it was now time to return to normal eating, her diet having been an obvious success. Shortly after this, when I saw that the weight loss was continuing and that she was beginning to look like a concentration camp victim, I told her so. She responded, "But I look *fat*."

This distorted body image is one of the most telling features of anorexia nervosa, a condition that is estimated to afflict over 300,000 people (mostly young women) in the United States. Anorexia was recognized as a disease a hundred years ago: it was considered an hysterical condition in which loss of appetite, constipation, amenorrhea (absence of the menses), weight loss, and restless activity prevailed, but its incidence was believed rare. Now it is widespread, which is perhaps not surprising in light of the enormous societal emphasis on thinness that exists today.

Our culture is plagued by a preoccupation with dieting, the tip of the iceberg that is composed of the compulsive quest for youth, a narcissistic concern with appearance, the dictum that women must be as slender as scarecrows to look fashionable in clothes, and the rejection of things "female" in an increasingly homosexual society. We are obsessed with what we are and are not eating, so much so that it is not unusual to hear even the slimmest of women waxing apologetic over nibbling on a cookie or eating a piece of chocolate. It has been suggested recently that anorexia nervosa might better be called a "fat phobia" or a "phobic fear of fat." That seems apt to me. The fear of being fat exists throughout the culture to an extraordinary degree. And in some people it takes on pathological, or phobic, proportions.

In her book *The Obession: Reflections on the Tyranny of Slenderness*, Kim Chernin writes movingly of the effect cultural forces have on women's feelings about their bodies. "The body holds meaning," she declares. "A woman wishing to make her breasts and thighs and hips smaller . . . may be expressing the fact that she feels uncomfortable being female in this culture. A woman . . . wishing to control her hungers . . . may be expressing the fact that she has been taught to regard . . . her passions and appetites as dangerous, requiring . . . careful monitoring. A woman obsessed with the reduction of her flesh may be revealing the fact that she is alienated from a natural source of female power and has not been allowed to develop a reverential feeling for her body."

Geneen Roth supports Chernin's notion that the culture puts pressure on women to reject their bodies. "I had only to look around me to see that desirable women my age were slinkly slim," she writes in *Feeding the Hungry Heart: The Experience of Compulsive Eating*. "All the Farrah mascara media maids who proclaimed that we must look like them to be attractive are bony. Their lean bodies are like powerless mockeries of the male physique. The models look male-weak instead of female-strong."

Obesity, which represents the swing of the pendulum to the other extreme, is also on the rise. And the obese person, like the anorexic, suffers from distorted body-image perception. In both instances, the sense of body image is delusional and represents a break with reality. I looked at my anorexic patient and saw someone who resembled a prisoner in a concentration camp. She looked at herself and denied that she was too thin; in fact, she did not think she was thin enough. The anorexic, no matter how thin she gets, always sees herself fat. Obese people, on the other hand, deny the reality of their size by trying to hide their heaviness. As one patient who was at least seventy-five pounds overweight put it to me: "When I look in the mirror, I only look at my face and it looks to me the way it always did. I see it as thin." Maintaining the delusion is difficult for the obese, however, and they hide their bodies in whatever way they can. They may drape themselves in clothing that is designed to conceal their contours. They are often reluctant to be photographed, knowing there is truth in the maxim; "The camera never lies." Some refuse to look in mirrors altogether.

Along with a skewed body image goes a distorted sense of body functions. The anorexic takes a few bites of food and feels full. The obese person, no matter how much she has eaten, always has room for more. Magical thinking often accompanies body delusion, especially in the anorexic. "If I am thin enough," she might think, "someone will love me." Or, "If I am thin enough, people will respect me." And anorexics and obese people have something else in common: Both believe that their thin self is their "real" self.

These eating disorders are really two facets of a single problem, flip sides of the same coin. They are primitive manifestations of masochism, expressions of self-hate and self-punishment that have crystallized around the issue of eating. The anorexic constantly punishes herself by avoiding food, often using laxatives to an excessive degree, and driving herself to keep up a level of frenetic activity that her lack of nourishment makes extremely taxing. The obese person punishes herself by constantly forcing more food into her body than it can tolerate, like a goose being force-fed for pâté de foie gras, a custom that was outlawed, by the way, because it represented such cruelty to the animal. Both the anorexic and the obese person may also suffer from bulimia, the binge-and-purge cycle of gorging on food and then forcing vomiting. And sometimes the two extremes of anorexia and obesity merge in a single person who veers from one to the other.

Such a young woman was the patient who began treatment with me immediately after moving to New York but only stayed a brief time before deciding to leave the city and return home. When she first came to see me, she was huge. Two years later, she returned to New York and began treatment again. This time I was startled to open the door to a painfully thin, sickly looking young woman. Observing my expression, which I apparently had not concealed successfully, she said, "I know it's a surprise, but don't I look good?" She looked neither good nor like a likely candidate for a photographer's model, a career she intended to pursue. She had obviously engaged in some magical thinking, believing that mere thinness qualified her for such a job.

The societal obession with food and eating is itself masochistic. For today, even as people are eating, they punish themselves by analyzing their intake relentlessly, discussing weight gain and loss ad nauseum, denying themselves certain foods, feeling guilt-ridden if that denial fails and they, God forbid, give in. Rhoda Koenig wrote an article for *New York* magazine several years ago called "Living to Eat," that caught the essence of this obsession: "Though mother had always said it was bad manners to talk about your health problems at the table, at times seventies lunchtime chatter about proteins and carbohydrates and how 'Japanese is very Pritikin' made you think you had wandered into a nutritionists' convention." The increase in eating disorders occurs at a time of great nutritional sophistication and against the background of plenty our affluent society produces. We might be more inclined to savor the irony inherent in this if the disorders were not so desperately destructive. Both anorexia and obesity are life-threatening conditions.

Hilde Bruch, a psychiatrist famous for her work on eating disorders, stresses that hunger is not only a reflection of *physiological* nutritional depletion but also a *psychological* experience. In relation to this, she emphasizes the importance of the early mother-child interaction in the feeding process. The mother, Bruch notes, may not be able to distinguish whether or not the infant's cry is for food, but she may offer or force food on her child regardless. She may also reward the child for being "good" (that is, passive) with food.

The whole separation-individuation process that occurs, or fails to occur, between mother and child is acted out primarily in relation to food. And anorexia and obesity, two extremes of bodily masochism, are further enactments of this early experience. A mother may overfeed an infant or, in the case of a more overtly destructive mother (the same mother who, for instance, might batter her child), she may starve it. A mother may offer her infant what Harry Stack Sullivan called the bad, poisonous nipple. By that he meant that the mothering activities, especially feeding, are tainted by the mother's sense of anxiety, anger, or hate in relation to her child, or a combination of all three. A mother may attempt to maintain control over her child by either forcing or denying food. She may insist on certain kinds of eating, demanding a clean plate, for example, or requiring that a child sit at the table until a particular hated food is eaten. The former could lay the groundwork for obesity; the latter might elicit the angry defiance that leads to anorexia. This defiance serves the defensive purpose that is typical of masochism. Ruth Jean Eisenbud, writing about anorexia, notes how the anorexic somatizes her defiance by moving from *I won't eat* (a defiant statement) to *I can't eat* (a somatic manifestation). In both anorexia and obesity, the child punishes herself, however, using an instrument it is impossible for the mother to lay her hands on—the gastrointestinal tract.

Chernin also observes that the early experience between mother and child has a profound effect on how a woman comes to view her body. She suggests that women who try to cut down on their size and shape are driven by the desire to erase the memory of the primordial mother who ruled over childhood. Being slender spares them from looking maternally plump and thus reminding themselves of the helplessness of their own infancy.

Because "poisonous" circumstances have surrounded the experience of eating, the anorexic has unconscious fantasies that all food is poison. The anorexic is trapped between the need to eat to sustain life and her paranoid projection about food's toxic nature. Her dogged refusal to eat is more than just a compulsive pursuit of thinness. It also represents a phobic avoidance of poison.

The obese girl or woman, on the other hand, may need continually to retain food, as it represents to her a connection with the mother. Food serves as an umbilical cord without which she feels she will die. In such instances an unresolved symbiosis exists between mother and child. Obesity can also result, however, from a pattern of defiance to the mother. Perhaps the mother has forced food on the child or used food as a reward, only to cut back as she sees the child gaining weight. Obesity may be the child's way of stating that she refuses to have limits imposed.

This struggle between mother and child, with food as the battleground, begins in early infancy and increasingly becomes internalized and acted out solely within the individual. The anorexic is struggling against feelings of being enslaved and exploited and unable to lead her own life. She is struggling for *control*. Her compulsive perfectionism drives her to torture herself into starvation in order to be respected. She has no middle ground: She is either perfect or utterly worthless and completely vulnerable. The obese person is fighting to *hang on to* her parent, orally incorporating food-as-mother. This connection carries with it a sense of being a "good girl," of being loved and protected. In either instance, the involvement with food and eating is single-minded; it represents the only real "relationship" in the person's life. And the outcome of the battle may be the ultimate masochistic act of self-destruction, for both anorexia and obesity constitute ongoing passive suicidal activities.

Sometimes the urge toward suicide is more active than that embodied in under- or overeating—acts that after a time seem to involve no volition whatsoever. I think, for instance, of an obese young patient of mine who had as fixed and intense a symbiosis with her mother as I have ever seen. The mother, divorced for years from the patient's father, was saccharine in the extreme. The young woman was not especially attractive except for glorious hip-length red-gold hair, but she was bright and had a good sense of humor, qualities that accounted for her sizable group of acquaintances. She repeatedly regaled me with tales of her daily, lengthy stuggles in the bathroom, trying to force her body to relinquish the food she had compulsively crammed into it when she was not in the bathroom. As our work together went on, she did begin to make progress, developing some new interests, having a few tentative dates, and beginning to separate from her mother. At one point, however, as the necessity for this separation became increasingly apparent, she began to threaten suicide and was hospitalized. I could not help feeling when I visited her that her Mona Lisa–like smile signaled that she felt victorious. She avoided my attempts to discuss this, however, and shortly afterward her mother dismissed me.

Another masochistic element that accompanies these eating disorders is sexual deprivation. The anorexic, frequently amenorrheic as a result of starvation, generally suffers the loss of, or fails to develop, any sexual interest. The obese girl is less likely to be amenorrheic; when she is, it is more often for psychological rather than physiological reasons. She too, however, has diminished sexual interest.

Unquestionably, the pressure to be thin is on the rise in our culture. I have occasionally observed acquaintances of mine who are dedicated to being thin eating with a speed and intensity that indicate they are starving when they sit down to a meal. Bruch feels this emphasis on thinness and the concomitant hostility toward weight as something shameful or evil have had a powerfully destructive effect. I believe such attitudes have contributed to obesity's becoming a serious health problem. The obese person experiences society and its attitudes as a stand-in for mother who is saying, "Thou shalt not eat." Then she feels even more deprived and defiantly eats more. These attitudes push anorexics to starve themselves in the belief that thinness is all, the answer to life, its own reward. When this cultural climate combines with a personal history that causes someone compulsively to reenact the rudimentary struggle of her early infancy involving her gastrointestinal tract, the result can be the most primitive and self-punishing form of masochism there is.

Roth chillingly conveys the persistent, repetitive, punitive nature of the eating disorders in the following passage, a masochistic *cri de coeur* if ever I heard one: "I made myself vomit, using the practiced muscles of my stomach. Why do I do this to myself? Why do I stuff myself with self-hatred and shame, knowing I can never in this way get rid of the ugly anger and paranoia I'm filling myself with. Why can't I control myself? Why do I hate myself? I cried as I reached into the refrigerator and began eating compulsively again."

Anorexia and obesity represent masochistic retreats. People who suffer from these conditions turn from dealing with interpersonal relations to dealing with bodily, or somatic, functions. In this way, the disorders resemble other phobias that are also self-punishing and masochistic. A woman who suffers, for instance, from agoraphobia puts herself in a kind of self-constructed prison when she refuses to leave her home. Her fear is of open spaces, but this is a symbolic replacement of the real nature of her fear—which is that if she is out in the open, she is more likely to be confronted with people and to have to deal with them.

Another sort of somatic expression of masochism was evident in the behavior of a woman who came to consult me about the difficulty she was having in her marriage. Throughout the session, as she talked and cried, she dug the tips of her fingers into her leg or into the arm of the chair. At the end of the hour, she said to me; "You know, I often have skin problems with my fingertips, and I've consulted any number of dermatologists and gotten all sorts of cream, but nothing seems to do any good." This woman, who did not dare to get angry, took all her aggression out on herself, perpetually traumatizing her fingertips. When she sought help for this, and did not receive any, she heaped even more punishment on herself by wallowing in feelings of grievance and martyrdom.

Some years ago, somatic self-rejection was expressed in the extraordinary number of American women who had hysterectomies. These often needless operations constituted a kind of symbolic castration. Viewed psychologically, one could say that these women, at a very deep level, rejected themselves as women and/or rejected motherhood because of its feminine connotations. Today, the focus of this masochistic lack of self-acceptance is on the breast.

Throughout the centuries, breasts have been sexually interesting to men. In times past, they often have been emphasized by fashion, sometimes to the point of near exposure. In our own recent history, Marilyn Monroe epitomized the ultimate sex object, and a large part of the image she projected was based on her full breasts. That was the standard for what was sexually attractive. More recently still, that standard has been redefined by the unisex influence. As the emphasis on thinness has grown, breasts have been minimized. A patient of mine who had been a prostitute and later became a madam of a brothel, told me that in the past, men considered breasts an important part of a woman's attractiveness when selecting a partner. Today, she said, they focus on the derriere, another indication of cultural homosexuality.

Whatever the prevailing standard, women are constantly presented with images of how their breasts should look, a matter that is for the most part beyond their control. The breast is an organ that has its own genetic inheritance with regard to shape and form. Certain external events may have an effect on this (extreme obesity, extreme thinness, nursing an infant), but basically the size of a woman's breasts is genetically determined. That does not deter masochistic women from torturing themselves about their breasts, however. They complain that they are too big, too small, misshapen, ill-placed.

A patient of mine constantly agonizd over the fact that she did not have what she called "half-grapefruit" breasts, a term I have heard more than once since she introduced me to it. These are breasts that have a very wide attachment, resulting in their being rounded but not too full, gentle extensions of the body's contour that do not protrude too much. This woman had a lovely face, a seemingly attractive body, and a husband who was satisfied with her breasts as they were. But all that counted for nothing. Her narcissism and masochism were such that she constantly judged her breasts as inferior—especially after her regular visits to a health club where she compared her body to other women's. Another patient of mine, also attractive and also married to a man who had not complained about her body, insisted that she did not feel like a woman because her breasts were not large enough. She asked me repeatedly for the name of a plastic surgeon, and initially I demurred, urging her to discuss the matter further before she rushed into anything. Finally, I saw that she

was determined, and rather than have her go to someone unknown, I gave the name of a reputable plastic surgeon. She had
silicone implants in her breasts—and feels better for being able to
meet a social concept of attractiveness!

Sadly, a new torment connected with the breast has arisen as
the incidence of breast cancer has increased. Now, not only is the
breast an unsatisfactory object that fails to match the prescribed
stereotypical idea, it is also a threat. And women are constantly
made aware of the threat, of the danger their breasts may represent, by the self-examination that doctors advise. This worry
about breast cancer is often used masochistically.

I believe, and recent research supports me, that when organs
are not used for their proper physiological purpose, they are likely
to develop malignancies. Many women avoid nursing their children because they are fearful of spoiling their breasts. The irony
is that failing to nurse may increase their chances of developing
breast tumors.

The matter of breast cancer poses a terrible dilemma for
women. Constant self-examination, I suspect, may lend itself to a
masochistic emphasis on misery and potential suffering. On the
other hand, waiting for an annual examination by the doctor increases the risk that a malignancy may go undetected for some
time. I recognize that it may be controversial, but my inclination
is to advise women who do not tend to develop cysts in their
glands to avoid self-examination and leave the search to their
gynecologists whom they see once or twice a year. By doing this,
they can at least avoid the incessant worry that they may discover
a malignancy. I am not suggesting that there are any easy solutions in this troublesome area, and perhaps the most important
thing is for each woman to do what is least distressing for her.

I had occasion recently to view some anthropological films of
a New Guinea tribe in which female breasts were on full display.
The breasts of many of the older women had taken on the appearance of drained-out, empty sacks after years of nursing infants, while the young, nubile girls had full, rounded breasts. But
it struck me that the men did not seem especially aware of the
difference in these two types of breasts, nor did the older women

appear to feel inferior or self-conscious because of the shape of their breasts. I could not help but reflect on the contrast with our own culture, its narcissistic preoccupation with the minutiae of body shape and its demand that virtually every woman in every stage of life conform to movie-star standards.

14

Masochism in Literature and Film

Virginia Woolf's story "The New Dress" offers us a truly remarkable portrait of the masochistic woman. Mabel Waring is thrilled to be invited to Clarissa Dalloway's party, but the invitation throws her into a turmoil about what she will wear. She settles on a choice that is within her means, one that is "original," if not fashionable. But from the moment she arrives at the party, she is awash in an agony of self-doubt, self-consciousness, and self-abasement. Her masochistic grandiosity tells her that everyone is concerned with, and making fun of, her new dress. When the cloakroom attendant simply does her job and attempts to be helpful, Mabel suspects she is rendering a judgment on Mabel's appearance. Then a guest she knows says, "It's perfectly charming," and Mabel detects a satirical pucker of her lips. Inundated by her lifelong feelings of worthlessness, she begins projecting these feelings onto others. They are all judging her mercilessly and maliciously; they are all false and deceitful.

But it is Mabel herself, of course, who feels that she is hideous and whose behavior is inauthentic. She sees herself set against the other guests as though the party were a competition: She is hopelessly dowdy and inept; they are all elegant and suave. She feels like a fly trapped in a saucer of milk with its wings stuck together. How should a male guest respond when Mabel says, "I feel like some dowdy, decrepit, horribly dingy old fly"? This bizarre remark (as inappropriate as that of the woman in Salzburg who told me she was "holding up the wall"), the product of

Mabel's enormous self-preoccupation, is hardly engaging and could only drive her listener away. And what if someone else had paid her a compliment? Would she have accepted it at face value? Of course not. She would have thought it a lie. Always anticipating attack, she has slapped herself on the cheek, punished herself, before anyone else has a chance to do so.

Mabel is masochism incarnate; few examples of such women in literature are as insightful, sensitive, or comprehensive. But if Mabel stands alone as an artfully and perceptively drawn portrait, she has a great deal of company when one considers her as the representative of a type. Literature is filled with suffering women.

Literary images of women tend to fit into one of four broad categories: (1) the woman who succumbs to the limits of the constricting cocoon in which society wraps her, the nice, good, and very often masochistic woman; (2) the woman who attempts to withstand these pressures to conform and has to pay a price for her resistance; (3) the woman who attempts to live vicariously since she is not permitted to live freely on her own; (4) the exception to the rule, the autonomous woman who displays self-assertiveness and courage and is not punished for them.

Josephine A. Ruggiero of Providence College believes that most women in literature serve essentially as conveniences for the resolution of masculine dilemmas. The virtuous woman is good and chaste and identified with the positive aspects of a man's life. The sensuous woman is bad, sexually experienced, and identified with the negative aspects. And at the core of the sentimental stereotype of women, says Ruggiero, is the view of woman as primarily emotional, helpless, and incompetent; at the core, in other words, is the image of the masochistic woman who has no power of her own and cannot solve anything for herself.

In a fascinating study of the French novel, Kathryn J. Crecelius notes the predominant pattern of the masculine lives portrayed. The heroes grow up, develop character, learn about the world, and finally achieve a place in society with attendant fame and fortune. The pattern of feminine development stands in stark contrast to this. The women in these novels are not happy or fulfilled. Even in novels of the last twenty years, Crecelius says, it is unusual to find a woman who leads a life that is satisfying but does not entail an enormous sacrifice of either her heart or her spirit. Because these women (or their creators) feel they cannot survive losing what happiness they already have, they are cut off in the flower of their youth.

Suffering Women: Feminine Masochism in Novels by American Women by Rosemary Morris deals with the work of Ellen Glasgow, Willa Cather, Edith Wharton, Gertrude Stein, and Mary Johnstone and studies all the novels of these authors that have a woman as a central character. "Horney believed, as do I," the author says at the outset, "that masochism in women is not an inevitable result of the female anatomy or physiological constitution. Rather it is a coping mechanism used by some women when the development of adequate aggressiveness has been discouraged."

Suffering was the central theme of life for Glasgow, Morris notes, and she "emphasized women who suffered or women who formed stoic defenses against anger." Cather, she continues, "a boyish woman, tended to show identification with two types of characters, the strong, capable women like herself, and with male characters who looked at certain women with romantic adoration." All the authors, Morris says, depicted some women who fit Horney's description of masochism and others who were strong, independent, and assertive. But only Johnstone "consistently identified with women and in her novels emphasized women with their own attitudes of purposeful activity and capability."

Lady into Fox, a stunning allegorical tale by David Garnett, shows the literal transformation of a woman into a victim. Sylvia Fox Teabrick, member of an old English family, fell madly in love with and married her husband after a short courtship. He was given to fox hunting; she had once seen a hunt as a child and when the fox was blooded, she vomited in disgust. Nevertheless, when the husband hears of a hunt, he persuades her to join him. As they near the place where the hunt is being held, Teabrick quickens his pace, while his wife hangs back. Holding her hand, he continues to drag her along, but suddenly, and violently, she snatches away her hand and cries out, causing him to turn around. "And there where his wife had been a moment before," Garnett writes, "was a small fox of a very bright red. It looked at him beseechingly, advanced toward him a pace or two, and he saw at once that his wife was looking at him from the animal's eyes." Now the wife is the victim, the object of the hunt, the creature who depends on her husband for her very life.

You will recognize here some elements of the sado-masochistic marriage: the brief courtship during which the masochistic woman deludes herself that ruthlessness and un-communicativeness are strength, the husband calling the tune while the wife submits—as defenseless prey.

One of the most familiar sado-masochistic marriages in litera-ture is, of course, that of Nora and Torvald in Ibsen's A *Doll's House*. Nora is dependent, passive, incompetent, masochistic; Torvald is charming to everyone else but coldly vicious to his wife. Nora, however, unlike Sylvia Teabrick, finds the courage to leave as life becomes unbearably painful. She takes the first step toward emerging from her masochism. But Nora operates at a great disadvantage even as she moves in the direction of au-tonomy. For she, like Emma Bovary, was not reared to be au-thentic. She has had no experience dealing with real problems; she has never learned to contend with them in an active and thoughtful way. Ruth Crego Benson points out, in *Women in Tolstoy*, that the ambivalence Tolstoy exhibited toward women in his own life carried over into his fiction. In the Russian intellec-tual life of the time, feminism was a real issue that was actively debated, part of the whole movement toward social reform. The consequences of anatomy, the nature of woman, the destiny of marriage, the possibility of true equality between the sexes—all these questions were in the forefront of the social consciousness of the day. And Tolstoy weighed in unequivocally on the an-tifeminist side. He bitterly resented feminist ideas and, Benson notes, was uncharacteristically superficial in considering them.

Tolstoy's notion of the ideal marriage was that the wife was, in effect, created by her husband in response to his teaching and instruction and, as a result, wholly identified with his interests and well-being. The husband, in turn, should provide the wife with a safe setting for her continued dependence and, Tolstoy believed, counter with stern discipline her need to control her own life. (Tolstoy's implacable hostility toward women was evident in a remark he made in his diary: "Women do not use words to express their thoughts but to attain their goals.")

In *War and Peace*, Natasha, after her first acquaintance with André as a suitor, says to her mother, "Only I'm afraid with him. I'm always afraid with him. What does that mean?" Whatever Tolstoy's intentions, he caught in these lines something very common for women: the beginning of their romantic life, their sexual life, signals the end of security and the end of the possibility of being authentic. When a woman is denied her sociological identity in Tolstoy, Benson says, she suffers the loss of her personal identity as well. The two are intimately related. *Anna Karenina* shows how a woman is molded by society, and Anna commits suicide at the end because, stripped of her identity, she has nothing left to live for.

It is impossible to examine the images of women in literature and not be struck by the difference in the treatment of men and women who have done essentially the same thing. Medea, who murdered her own children, is the mythic figure who stands for all that is horrible in women. The degree of passion, rage, and sense of abandonment that led her to act out her feelings is not really understood or taken into account. But Hercules, who committed incest and pedophilia and was thought to have massacred his entire family, is always presented as a symbol of strength and eternal youth. The atrocities he committed are ignored in the telling of his myth; Medea's barbarity is the centerpiece of hers.

In *The Scarlet Letter*, Hawthorne shows us the contrasting attitudes toward men and women who break society's code. Hester Prynne was treated with inordinate cruelty, her suffering was dreadful. Dimmesdale, a coward who did not speak up, suffered no external punishment at all. But this is not the usual tale of the suffering woman. Dimmesdale is the passive weakling in the story, Hester the admirable figure who has the strength to endure her pain. She withstands all the abuse heaped on her, and

Hawthorne even manages, with his extraordinary gift of perception, to fashion a reward for her: Hester, because she is alone, is everything to her child; her motherhood is as complete and satisfying as it could possibly be.

Literature can be, and has been, used by men to keep women in their place. It can be, and has been, used by women to write of their sufferings, to write of the ways in which they have tried to use their intellect, that forbidden element. It has also been used, though more rarely, to show that a woman can be a courageous protagonist just as surely as a man can.

A superlative example of a courageous woman who refused to be restricted by society is at the center of Jane Austen's *Pride and Prejudice*—Elizabeth Bennett, of course, who refuses to embrace the silliness that is her mother's forte or to marry just any man in order to be married. You will remember Mr. Collins, the pompous clergyman who decides that Elizabeth would make an appropriate wife for him. When she first refuses his proposal, he misunderstands because it is inconceivable to him that any woman would refuse him (a masculine notion not uncommon even in our own times). He seems to view her as the guest at a Chinese banquet who is expected to demur several times before accepting a delicacy the host offers, and her refusals spur him on to such windy confidences as, "I am sure you will add greatly to my future happiness." When Elizabeth remains adamant, Collins conveys to her his awareness that "an elegant female must refuse several times." "Please. Please," Elizabeth replies. "I am not an elegant female, but a rational woman." How delicious!

Shakespeare's women are extraordinary: They experience their share of pain, but there is not a true masochist among them. Cordelia suffers but she is authentic, nonmasochistic. When speaking would challenge her integrity, she remains silent, and only a woman who has attained a sense of identity could exhibit this kind of self-containment. On the other hand, when integrity demands that she assert herself, Cordelia speaks up. Gertrude also suffers, but the defensive style is absent from her behavior. Even Desdemona, though victimized, is not masochistic.

Kate in *The Taming of the Shrew* is an example of the degree to which wives were considered pieces of property in Shakespeare's day. But she does not accept her fate with docility, and she hardly fits the stereotype of the sweet, demure, compliant woman. When she is finally transformed into the model wife through torture and what could almost be considered a form of brainwashing, it is in a sense a victory for her as well as a capitulation. She learns the lessons of power well and comes to see that she will make her mark and achieve her status as the wife of a wealthy man, a bargain many women make. By doing this she revenges herself upon her father by proving him wrong, causing him to wonder if the huge dowry he offered was really necessary.

In *The Merry Wives of Windsor*, the women are aware of their limitations, but they are almost masculine in the way they play Falstaff for a sucker. Theirs is not behavior that fits the female stereotype.

All of George Bernard Shaw's women reflect different facets of the feminine personality; they have shortcomings, but they are far from masochistic. On the contrary, Shaw's women are flesh-and-blood creations endeavoring to maintain authenticity in the midst of struggle. Shaw, despite misogynist tendencies of his own, wrote heroines much more often than he did heroes, intelligent, active women capable of taking a hand in their own destinies, even though those destinies were necessarily circumscribed by the restrictions of the society in which they lived.

In a conversation with her daughter in *Mrs. Warren's Profession*, Mrs. Warren says that naturally she would rather have gone to college or been a lady than to have been a prostitute, but those were not options for her. "Respectable" poverty was, however, the kind she saw other women enduring: working in a factory twelve hours a day for a pittance and eventually dying of lead poisoning, or marrying a government laborer and keeping his house and taking care of three children with virtually no money, even less when he takes to drink. She vividly describes the degradation of such grinding hardship and then asks why she should not have made the choice she did. Vivie, her daughter, presses Mrs. Warren to make sure her mother would not advise her to choose the "respectable" course. "Of course not," Mrs. Warren replies indignantly. "What sort of mother do you take me for! How could you keep your self-respect in such starvation and slavery? And what's a woman worth—what's life worth, without self-respect? . . . The only way for a woman to provide for herself decently is for her to be good to some man who can afford to be good to her. If she's of his own station in life, let him marry her. If not, she can't expect it, and it wouldn't be for her own happiness. . . . If people arrange the world that way for women, there's no good pretending that it's arranged the other way." This is a clear-eyed, hardheaded assessment of societal conditions and, given them, Mrs. Warren did indeed make a choice that allowed her to keep her self-respect.

Candida is a different sort of woman, but she is equally forthright. When Marchbanks says, "May I say wicked things to you?" Candida is neither frightened nor aloof, and, because she is secure in herself, she is able to display respect for his passion. "No," she replies. "But you may say anything you really and truly feel. Anything at all, no matter what it is. I am not afraid, so long as it is your real self that speaks, and not a mere attitude—a gallant attitude, or a wicked attitude, or even a poetic attitude. I put you on your honor and truth. Now say anything you want to." A masochistic woman would never be capable of such a clear definition of premises. And toward the end of the play, Candida describes to Marchbanks her marriage to parson James Morell. Her clarity about how the world is set up for men and women and about her own place in that scheme is very like Mrs. Warren's. After telling Marchbanks about James's childhood as "the hero of [his] household," Candida says, "You know how strong he is . . . how clever he is—how happy! Ask James's mother and his three sisters what it cost to save James the trouble of doing anything but be strong and clever and happy. Ask me what it costs to be James's mother and three sisters and wife and mother-to-his-children all in one. . . . Ask the tradesmen who want to worry James and spoil his beautiful sermons who it is that puts them off. When there is money to give, he gives it: when there is money to refuse, I refuse it. I build a castle of comfort and indulgence and love for him, and stand sentinel always to keep little vulgar cares out. I make him master here, though he does not know it, and could not tell you a moment ago how it came to be so."

If in most of his plays Shaw recognizes that the best women can do is to live vicariously through the men they choose, there is one—*Saint Joan*—in which he pleads openly for women to be given a part in shaping the affairs of the world. His Joan is not a simple peasant girl who acts in response to visions but an intelligent, masterful young woman who spends time talking to soldiers, is fascinated by stories of combat, and "never [utters] a word that has to do with her being a woman." Shaw also gives St. Joan the last words: "O God, that made this beautiful earth—when will it be ready to receive its saints—how long, Lord, how long?" Women, Shaw might be saying, might even do better than men if they were in charge of things.

In Virginia Woolf's novel *Orlando* she makes a strong case against the restrictions placed on women when, midway through, the hero Orlando becomes a woman. The two are indistinguishable from one another, the woman being every bit as free, lusty, and appealing as the man. Mar, with whom Orlando, the woman, is having a romance, asks: "Are you positive you aren't a man?" Orlando replies: "Can it be possible that you are not a woman?" "Each was surprised at the quickness of the other's sympathy," Woolf writes, "and it was to each a revelation that a woman could be as tolerant and free-spoken as a man—and a man as strange and subtle as a woman." Sex is, or should be, irrelevant, Woolf was saying. Women and men share *all* human traits, abilities, and potentials.

The images of women in films also serve as models, as sources of informal learning, and they both reflect and influence women's ideas of themselves. Molly Haskell's remarkable book *From Reverence to Rape*, a study of films from the 1930s to the 1970s, conveys in its title alone what the attitudes toward women have been during this period. There used to be more independent-minded heroines portrayed than there are today, she points out, adding, however, that even these relatively strong women always suffered from a kind of vulnerability as well. They generally felt guilty about their self-sufficiency, apologetic for daring to lay them-

selves on the line. Today, Haskell says, we have regressed to por-
traying women as either bland young fashion plates or faceless,
anonymous sex objects. Speaking of Garbo, Haskell says: "Her
spirit leaped first and her body, in total exquisite accord, leaped
after." About whom could we say this today? No one, I think.
Today the appeal is almost invariably sexual.

Generally in films, Haskell notes, and particularly in the
"woman's film," "a regular outlet for self-pity," women have been
exhorted to relinquish everything for love, relegated to the home
and to domestic chores, and denied opportunities for heroism.
They have never experienced "a love that relishes separateness,
grows stronger with resistance, and in the maturity of admitting
dependence meets the challenge of being different but equal." On
the contrary, their relationships have been characterized by
passivity, dependence, powerlessness, and inequality. They have
been, in other words, masochistic women.

In *Psychoanalytic Review*, Ralph Luce in some ways paralleled
Haskell's book with an article called "From Hero to Robot: Masculinity in America, Stereotypes and Reality." Luce traces American male stereotypes from the cowboy hero to the military hero,
folksinger hero, wheeler-dealer hero, and finally to today's robot
hero in which superficial appearance is the primary value. This
has evolved, Luce maintains, because of the deified computer
and the exalted astronauts in whom technical skill and detach-
ment of feelings in dangerous situations are the primary values.
Marshall McLuhan called the electronic media an externalized
nervous system, Luce notes, and without a nervous system inside
him man is truly empty and devoid of feeling. Could this be one
of the reasons man seems to need to keep on pushing woman into
an inferior, nonthreatening, masochistic position?

The film *Rebecca* gives us a highly accurate portrait of a
masochist in the young woman played by Joan Fontaine. Companion to a rich, aggressive, nasty widow summering on the Rivi-
era, she lives in fear of the widow's reproaches and constantly
chastises herself as well. "Oh, I'm so clumsy," she says, when she
accidentally knocks over a vase of flowers. "Why can't I ever do
anything right?" she asks herself time and again. The widow con-

tinually assaults the young woman's self-esteem; she in turn readily and repeatedly capitulates to the widow's demands. Once married to the character played by Laurence Olivier, who admits it is her very ineptitude that attracts him (certainly she is no threat), she is extremely vulnerable to criticism and feels herself to be a wretched replacement for Olivier's dead first wife, the Rebecca of the title. Interestingly, the Fontaine character does experience some growth during the course of the film, so that by the end she is more of a person than she had been.

Gaslight's heroine is another classic masochist. She has been raised by a father who hates her, is endlessly cruel to her, makes her feel completely worthless, and does everything he can to prevent her late-adolescent blossoming. She is a perfect set-up for any man who comes along and pays attention to her, and for the repetition compulsion to come into effect. When she marries, in defiance of her father, it is to a man just like him—one who attempts to drive her mad and, finally, to kill her.

The daughter has also been raised by her father in the film *The Heiress*, based on Henry James's *Washington Square*. The mother, in this instance, died in childbirth, a common enough occurrence in the past, and one that often left the surviving husband and father with a terrible sense of residual rage: He had lost the woman he loved, and his child was responsible. It was not surprising perhaps that men tended to project their rage onto the child. In *The Heiress* the father inculcates his daughter with a sense of her own worthlessness, ugliness, and lack of appeal. He makes it clear that no man will ever want her; he sadistically punishes her for her part in his loss of his adored, and perfect, wife. The daughter incorporates his judgments of her and internalizes his hypnotic suggestions so that when she does meet a man who is a fortune hunter, he quickly picks up the masochistic messages that indicate she is a prime candidate for victimization. She is easy prey. She has been *brought up* to be exploited.

The symbiotic tie between mother and daughter is all important in *Separate Tables*. The extremely masochistic daughter has been subjected to damaging treatment from her mother, a wealthy and formerly beautiful woman who would never let anyone—including her daughter—get in her way. She exacts absolute control, and one has only to see the daughter's posture as an adult to know that she has been disparaged and criticized all her life for how she looks, how she speaks, how she behaves. When the mother and daughter are at a seaside resort and the mother sees a friendship beginning to develop between her daughter and a retired army colonel, himself a very damaged creature, she immediately sets out to break it up. The mother's efforts to keep her daughter in a position of masochistic submission to her override all considerations of decency or fairness. She *needs* her victim. And so she arranges to bring into the open the colonel's past conviction for sexual molestation. But she has miscalculated; her masochistic daughter manages this one time to stand up to her mother and to support the colonel instead, taking one step in the direction of liberation.

The character played by Marlene Dietrich in *Witness for the Prosecution* is a woman perfectly capable of standing up for herself, making her own decisions, keeping her own counsel. Calm, self-assured, relying on herself rather than on unsympathetic men, she is presented as a decidedly suspicious figure whose femininity is suspect. And why? Because she acts like a man.

Ingmar Bergman's *Wild Strawberries* is set in a world in which men are the decision makers, the doers, and achievers, the ones who set the standards, the ones who are being served. What becomes of women in a world where they are either objects or servants; where they are raped by men, literally or symbolically, in or out of marriage; where they are deprived of the possibility of their own achievements and forced to bear children they may not want? Bergman shows that they become hateful wives and hateful, retaliatory mothers who, in turn, damage their own children.

Summer Wishes, Winter Dreams suggests the bleak results for a woman who enters marriage out of desperation, in the hope that it will offer a solution to her problems. Billed as the story of a "modern snow queen," that is, a frigid woman, played by Joanne Woodward, it presents some disturbing images of women. Miss Woodward's mother, a type I have heard dubbed "early West End Avenue," is a tasteless, empty-headed, self-absorbed woman who is mummified beneath layers of cosmetics, batting grotesquely false eyelashes. Miss Woodward's daughter, on the other hand, is ugly, aggressive, demanding, and overly sure of herself, a miniature "new woman." And Miss Woodward herself is the loser in the middle: a woman who made a meaningless match with a man she did not love in order to be supported and to have a home; in other words, she is a sexual domestic.

Haskell finds that films suffer from a fundamental inequity when it comes to treating the subject of age. Women are considered over the hill at forty (perhaps the age has even lowered a bit), while men of the same age are judged to be in their prime. This double standard comes through clearly in the ill-fated and misunderstood *Ash Wednesday*, in which the main character, played by Elizabeth Taylor, undergoes complete face and body surgery in order to win back a husband who has become involved with a younger woman. Her husband, the aging but still handsome Henry Fonda, has no need to rejuvenate himself in such an artificial and grotesque fashion. He can gain his new lease on life by connecting with a young woman, and he has found one who is willing to cling to him just as tightly as his wife did thirty years earlier.

While writing this chapter, I happened one night to see on television part of a Hollywood B-movie that startled me by the contrasts it presented to images I had been considering. The movie was lowbrow male-chauvinistic, and yet in two different scenes a woman was shown asserting herself in deft, unequivocal fashion. She is a gorgeous young woman, and when she sets up her beach chair on the sand, a man immediately approaches her with a pick-up ploy: "Having trouble?" he asks. Gazing at him without expression, she replies, "I wasn't." He changes tactics: "It's been a long time," he says. "We've never met," she counters. Seeing some suntan oil alongside her chair, he makes a third try: "Help you with your back?" "No," she answers, "but there *is* something you can do. Call a policeman. There's a man annoying me."

In a later scene, a man asks the same woman what her name is and she tells him it is Margaret. "Do you mind if I call you

Maggie?" he asks, chipping away at the formality that her full name suggests. "I don't like Maggie," she says calmly, settling the issue.

So vivid, and uncommon, were those instances of a woman standing up for herself that I found myself wondering if perhaps a film had to be grade-B in order to show something so subversive.

In *The New Assertive Woman*, Bloom, Coburn, and Pearlman note that for generations femininity has been equated with being accommodating, passive, and nonassertive. And what is the price women have paid for this? The price, they declare, is that women have become anxious, inhibited, and emotionally dishonest.

I would not quarrel with any of these propositions. They are all accurate, as far as they go. But they address symptoms rather than causes. Worry, crying, feeling inauthentic, anxiety, and emotional dishonesty are all symptoms of masochism. *That* is the underlying cause of women's inability to assert themselves. That is the deep and damaging affliction of which all these symptoms are a part.

Worry is the masochistic torturing of oneself with irrational fears and anxieties; because they are irrational, it is not possible for the masochist to separate out those problems that can be solved from those that cannot. She is unable to make that distinction because she feels guilty and wrong about nearly everything. The message the masochist conveys with her tears is that she is pitiful and, therefore, she hopes, safe from attack. Masochistic people are not motivated by their natural, true feelings in interactions with others; *their primary goal is defense*. They are impostors in the sense that they have lost access to their genuine selves. They pretend to like and respect people of whom they are terrified; they regularly accede to people they would rather resist. And the more fraudulent their behavior, the more anxious, uncomfortable, and self-hating they become. It is important to recognize all these feelings and attitudes as part of the masochistic gestalt. For only when you have gone to the heart of a problem, only when you have identified the wellspring that gives it life, can you truly begin to overcome it. Only then can you start to dig your way out from beneath its oppressive weight.

Masochistic processes are both simple and complex, simple in that they can all be seen as defenses against feared others who are perceived as powerful; complex in that they can take on many different forms. Throughout this book I have delineated the myriad guises in which self-hurt can make its appearance. Now the question occurs: What can be done about it? Although

15

Digging Out

The rapid and prolific growth of assertiveness training courses in the wake of the women's movement reflected a recognition that women were unable to speak up for themselves in certain situations. Assertiveness groups addressed ways to deal with these situations and offered a setting in which women could rehearse the behavior they hoped to establish in their lives. Despite the intense focus on assertiveness, however, there seemed to be little or no attention paid to why women suffered from such a severe deficit of self-confidence.

In the last decade much has been written that touches on the underlying causes of women's inability to operate autonomously. The writers speak about stress, anxiety, depression. An article in *Vogue* by Barbara Langstern defined worry as a "pit of the stomach" feeling that something bad might happen, one that is more focused than anxiety but less definite than fear. Langstern offered the classic advice about worry: Separate those problems you can do something about from those over which you have no control. Inherent in this is the classic antidote to worry: Demonstrate that you have the capacity to influence something.

Carol Tavris, a psychologist for whom I have great regard, has written about what she calls "the language of tears" and the effect of crying on the spirit. She has also addressed "the impostor phenomenon." Women harbor negative feelings about themselves, according to Tavris, and fear that they will be found out. Even when they are uncertain that they will be found out about, they suffer from a feeling of being inauthentic.

masochism is far too complicated a problem to address with a "how-to" formula, I do intend this book to be helpful. And help is available if you, the reader, will put forth some effort in conjunction with the guidance I can offer.

Achilles was killed when Paris wounded him in the heel, his one vulnerable spot. Now is the time for you to examine yourself and identify *your* Achilles' heel, or heels, those masochistic weak spots that are threatening to your psychological life and health, those aspects of your personality that leave you vulnerable to self-damage. Ask yourself some searching questions. What have you learned about your own socio-cultural conditioning, early life experience, and upbringing that may have contributed to your developing masochistic tendencies? Did you recognize your own style among the masochistic messages outlined in Chapter 4? Are you able to recognize your own fearfulness in dealing with others? Are you able to acknowledge the low self-esteem that lies behind this? Attempting this kind of self-diagnosis may not be easy, but it will be well worth it if you are interested in overcoming your masochism.

Perhaps you feel you need help identifying your Achilles' heel. If so, a good friend, one you feel is trustworthy, may be able to offer assistance. Ask your friend if she or he has noticed aspects of your behavior that might be troublemaking. Have you seemed fearful, indirect, evasive, overly compliant, and so on? The answers you get can help to confirm your areas of difficulty.

Having determined those areas that are especially troublesome for you, there is another question you must ask yourself: Will self-help be sufficient to overcome your problems or should you seek professional help? Try to assess, as honestly and accurately as you can, the degree of alienation you feel. Do you identify at all with the woman in Salzburg who was "holding up the wall?" Try to evaluate just how fearful you are of those people you see as authorities. Are you, like Mabel Waring in the Virginia Woolf story, obsessed with and consumed by the judgments of others? Try to gauge the extent to which your masochistic problems keep you from living your life as you would like to. If you feel that your masochism constitutes a serious interference, then you must consider consulting a trained professional, either a psychiatrist, a psychiatrist/psychoanalyst like myself, or a psychologist who has been trained as a psychoanalyst. And make sure this person is someone you believe is knowledgeable about the problems of women and feminine psychology. The American Academy of Psychoanalysis, the American Psychiatric Association, the American Psychoanalytic Association, the American Psychological Association, your local psychiatric association, or local medical society may be able to suggest someone to you.

Women today frequently raise the question of whether or not they should undergo treatment with a male therapist. Generally, I would say that considerations of good training, sensitivity, and skill outweigh the matter of gender in choosing a therapist, most especially when the person being treated is seriously disturbed. On the other hand, certain gender-related nuances of behavior may be more comprehensible if one has grown up with them oneself. And men and women, as I have observed, grow up in very different worlds. Two vignettes come to mind in connection with this question.

The first involves a woman who entered treatment in the midst of a divorce action occasioned by her husband's affair with a woman he intended to marry. She was extremely distraught, and her husband agreed to pay for therapy. She found the male psychiatrist to be helpful. Once the divorce came through, however, her standard of living was considerably lower and she was concerned about the fee. Discussing it with a friend she was surprised to learn that her analyst's fee was much higher than that charged by others in the area. She told her doctor that she wanted to continue treatment but that she could not pay the present fee. And then she added, "I hope you can reduce the fee, especially since I've heard it's somewhat high in comparison with other analysts'." Enraged, he said to her, "What an aggressive woman you are!" Alas, he certainly had violated a primary principle of all dedicated doctors: *primum, non nocere* (above all, do no harm).

The second story concerns a patient of mine who, before coming to me, had spent seven years with a male analyst and had gotten progressively sicker. Early in our association, I told her that as she described those years to me I saw the image of a beautiful cathedral whose entire surface, including its brilliant stained glass windows, was covered with an accumulation of filth deposited on it by birds, pollution, and time. Our task, I said, would be to clean it up. The next session she reported to me a dream she had had of a big old house with many rooms, all of them empty. She climbed the stairs and, at the head of them, turned to the left, and there, to her surprise, came upon another room. It was lovely, filled with sunlight streaming through its windows, and in it there was a beautiful old oak desk. This dream, her own confirmation that there was something valuable about her, was the beginning of a difficult but productive collaboration between the two of us.

Women often experience problems that are difficult for male analysts to comprehend. In some instances, they may see the problems as trivial. A therapist must have a kind of prescience, an ear attuned to those subtle aggressions to which women have been subjected for years. This kind of well-developed radar may be more likely in a woman therapist, although there are men who possess it as well. But the masochistic woman who has problems that relate specifically to her femininity would probably fare best with a well-trained and perceptive woman therapist.

Whether you decide to work on your problems by yourself or to seek additional help from a professional, the effort to overcome your masochistic tendencies will require a great deal of work and courage. No psychic pattern yields to change easily or painlessly, and the deep roots of masochism go back to the very earliest days of life. Change takes time; there are no shortcuts on the road to surmounting the stubborn masochistic tendencies that may seem by now to be innate parts of your personality, fixed aspects of your character. When Thomas Edison was asked how he accounted for his remarkably prolific inventiveness, he answered, "One percent inspiration, ninety-nine percent perspiration." The same formula could apply here.

Perhaps you have discovered that you are inclined to lapse into tangential speech, an indication that you are fearful of getting to the point. You seek refuge in indirection because you have little confidence in your own judgments and perceptions. You fear abandonment, so you bind your listener to you by spinning out a seemingly endless string of words. It takes courage to resolve not to transmit this masochistic message any longer. It takes courage to summon up the determination to try something new. Courage does not mean that you are without fear; it means that you are willing to act in spite of it. And fears, I have come to believe, are often overcome by persistence, as well as by insight into their origins (persistence *and* insight should be an unbeatable combination in attempting to overcome your masochistic fears).

Urge yourself to express yourself directly, unequivocally, even if you are afraid of the response. Resolve that if you are uncertain of the worth of what you are about to say, you will at least keep your mouth shut and say nothing. This is extremely difficult for the masochist, but gradually, as you practice replacing an old, destructive pattern with a new, healthy one, the task will grow easier.

There is simply no doubt that it is always preferable to keep your silence rather than volunteering something that may be hurtful to you. Be aware of active masochistic expressions or actions that are certain to be troublemaking. I think of the mature woman who was visiting her rather overbearing mother with whom she had always had a difficult relationship. When she went to scramble some eggs for her own lunch, she noticed her mother's small frying pan was missing. Immediately she was afraid that she would be accused of having lost or misplaced it. But instead of saying nothing and scrambling her eggs in another pan, she mentioned to her mother that the pan was missing. "Well, I know it *was* there," her mother said, "so you must have misplaced it." Upon being predictably accused, the daughter was upset and began defending herself. Soon she and her mother were engaged in the same destructive parry-and-thrust act they had been doing together for years. Had the daughter said nothing, there would have been no incident.

Masochistic women often need to train themselves to be less prompt in responding to others. Just because someone asks you a question does not mean you are *obligated* to answer instantly. You are *entitled* to think your response through carefully. Try not to concern yourself with what the other person is thinking. Concentrate instead on what it is *you* want to say and wait until your statement is clear before you make it. Then speak as succinctly as possible. You will be, in effect, training yourself to exercise a new style.

Accepting the premises of other people is, as I have said, one of the prime hallmarks of the masochistic personality. Learning to question these premises, learning to substitute your own, is one of the biggest changes that must occur if you are to overcome your masochism. Consider the woman alone on the street who is approached by a stranger asking for a match and who stops to give one to him. She accepts his premise that he wants a match (heaven only knows what he wants) and that it is her obligation to give it to him, a hazardous attitude on her part. How might she turn this around? By responding to his approach with a counter-premise of her own: This may be a dangerous situation; I'm not going to risk my life for a match, or anything else; I have no obligation to stop and respond to him; I'm going to walk on—or run—instead.

Presented with someone else's premise, ask yourself if it is correct. If an accusation is involved, ask yourself if you are blameworthy or not. Gradually, as you move away from automatic acceptance, as you begin to question the way things are presented to you and whether or not they are valid, you will also begin to assert your own point of view. It will become easier to say no, I don't agree with that; no, that's unacceptable to me.

A young patient of mine had all her life been the focus of critical attacks by both parents. Nothing she could do pleased them; they constantly found fault with her. It was no surprise that her behavior was quite masochistic. But in treatment, she finally gained a grasp of her problems and was eager to begin putting knowledge into action. A voice student, she was making great strides with a new teacher. Although her parents had been critical of her music in the past, she determined that she would no longer suffer their fault-finding in silence, that she would beat them to the punch (not even let them get their premises on the record). At a family gathering, she sang to generally warm applause, and as soon as she finished, she turned to her parents and said, "Well, does this teacher do a bad job, too?" Her parents were speechless.

Another young woman also had spent a great deal of time examining her relationship with her mother and trying to understand the part she herself played in its destructive nature. She, too, was used to her mother's negative views of nearly everything she did but determined to change her responses. In love with a man she planned to marry, she knew her mother would not approve, so they were married in another town and she didn't tell her mother until the ceremony was over. "I have some good news," she said in a phone call afterward. "You have a new son-in-law." "I don't want anything to do with him," her mother replied. "That's too bad," the bride said, "because we hoped you'd be able to help us celebrate." In the course of the phone call, her mother came around considerably, and did in fact end up celebrating with the newlyweds. This was due in no small part to the positive way her daughter presented the news.

I recently watched a man being interviewed on television and, as is often the case, the interviewer took up an inordinate amount of time with his wordy questions and frequently interrupted the guest to paraphrase and interpret his answers. At one point the guest said quietly, "You're putting words in my mouth. I'd like to finish what I started to say." With these two short sentences, uttered pleasantly, the guest managed to challenge every one of the interviewer's premises—that he could express the guest's will, that his interpretation was the correct one, that he could behave in any way he wanted. The guest's behavior, his quiet assertion of his own rights, exemplified the essence of autonomy.

Perhaps during your self-examination you discerned that you have a tendency to inflict physical harm on yourself (running into things, cutting yourself with a knife, burning your fingers on a match, etc.) or by breaking or losing possessions. These are outward hurtful manifestations of an unexpressed anger within. Try to think back and examine what you may have been angry about when these "accidents" occurred. Try to discover why you were afraid to express the anger or to take appropriate action to dispel it. And when you next feel angry, try to be aware of it and acknowledge it at least to yourself. The more you are aware of things going on within you, the more choice you have in how to respond.

Ambiguity, as I have noted, is especially difficult for the masochistic person, and her tendency is to convert an unclear situation into a destructive, hurtful one. Feeling threatened, someone with masochistic tendencies would rather leap to a negative conclusion than to hover fearfully in uncertain territory. At least then the matter is settled and she need not live with her fantasies about the terrible things that might happen. But part of digging your way out of your masochistic suffering is to try to tolerate ambiguity. When something happens that causes you to feel wounded, question your interpretation of the incident. Is it correct? Might there be an alternative explanation? Have you rushed to place a negative construction on it and, in the process, perhaps overlooked something positive? Do you have to feel threatened by this incident? Very often positive things exist in the masochistic person's life, but she is incapable of acknowledging them, of giving them the same weight she assigns to negative occurrences. Busy defending herself against what is hurtful, and busy adding to the store of damaging interchanges, she is unable to see the positive aspects of her exchange with other people. They get lost in the negative shuffle.

Geraldine, a very masochistic patient of mine, had been out of the country for several years but now was reestablishing herself here. A friend she had not seen for some time invited her to spend the day with her and planned to pick her up by car. When she was a bit late, Geraldine got on the phone with an airline to arrange reservations for a trip she was planning. She was attempting to distract herself from the fear that the friend might not come and from the thought that she didn't value Geraldine enough to be on time. When the friend did arrive, Geraldine kept her waiting for some time, which annoyed the friend.

This was a very masochistic beginning to the encounter, and the day they spent together was not all that comfortable. Geraldine felt ambivalent about the friend and felt the friend was not all that fond of her. However, the friend invited Geraldine to spend an upcoming holiday weekend with her in the country. Despite the fact she had no definite plans, Geraldine declined and said she had already made arrangements for the weekend. Telling me about this, she reported that she was aware of a sense of victory when she was able to turn down her friend. But what an empty and destructive victory this was. Geraldine's relationship with her friend, as with other people in her life, was a power struggle, and she needed to feel that she could come out on top, that she could win out. This is sometimes the other side of the coin of feelings of worthlessness. The masochistic person pays insufficient attention to *what* it is she is winning; she just needs to feel that she can triumph, that she can be better than, that she is in control, no matter what the price to her.

Notable also in the interchange between these two women is the fact that at no time did Geraldine feel there was anything she could do to influence positively what happened between them. Because of her sense of helplessness and passivity, it never occurred to her that she could somehow contribute to making their time pleasant or to cutting down the distance that existed between them. As we talked further and she described their lunchtime conversation, she began to see that perhaps her interpretation of things was not quite accurate. It seemed from some complimentary remarks the friend made that, in fact, she thought highly of Geraldine and liked her very much. But this had been utterly lost on Geraldine until we unearthed it in a session after the fact. She had been so absorbed in her masochistic need to defend herself and one-up her friend that all the salutary aspects of their meeting had gone unremarked.

I described Geraldine's "victory" over her friend as an empty and self-destructive one. In contrast to this, I think of the feeling of victory that occurs when one begins to overcome one's masochism, when one puts into practice a new, autonomous response in place of an old, defensive one. That victory is a self-enhancing, self-sustaining one. And just as masochistic behavior generates more suffering and thus perpetuates itself, so a feeling

of success breeds more of the same. You will begin to notice that
your tolerance for discomfort decreases. You do not put up with
things the way you used to.

A patient of mine bought a pair of shoes one day when she
was in a hurry, and when she got home and put them on, she
discovered they were too tight. Still mired in her masochism, she
was fearful of confronting the salesman and could not take them
back. He would, she was convinced, accuse her of having worn
them or, at the very least, tell her she should have known they
were the wrong size when she bought them. So she decided that
she had to wear the shoes even though they hurt her feet, a
masochistic punishment if ever there was one. Had this same incident occurred a year or so later when she had begun to overcome her masochistic tendencies, I have no doubt that she would
have behaved quite differently. First, she might have attempted
to return the shoes. If the store had not taken them back, she
might have tried to correct the problem by having them stretched.
If that did not work, she probably would have been able, due to
her increased self-esteem and self-respect, to acknowledge that she
had made a mistake and then simply to give the shoes to a friend
with smaller feet.

The masochistic woman has wedged herself into a narrow behavioral mold that causes her a great deal of pain and suffering,
just as a pair of too-tight shoes hurts the feet. In contrast, the
woman who is beginning to dig out of her masochism and practice assertive, autonomous behavior feels the kind of comfort and
ease that come with wearing a pair of shoes that fit just right.

Margaret arrived at a concert just as it was about to begin.
There were no assigned seats, but she noticed in the first row of
the balcony two empty places next to each other that had coats
on them. "Is this seat taken?" she asked the man sitting next to
one of the seats. "No, it's not," he replied, "but neither is the
other one, and I want to leave my coat here." "I don't want to get
involved in a battle about who will move a coat," Margaret said,
"so would you please just move yours since that seat is closer to
me." The man became quite angry, but Margaret quietly asked
him to stop and then the concert began and put an end to the

dispute. Although the incident was unpleasant, Margaret was pleased with her responses. In the past, she said, she would have fled at the first sight of the man's annoyance.

Margaret also told me of another incident that occurred at the lunch counter of a restaurant. She was in rather a hurry, and as she sat down, she signaled the waitress that she was ready to order. "Just a minute," the waitress said, turning her attention to a man who had come in after Margaret. After chatting with him for a time, she began to move away, but Margaret stopped her by saying firmly, "Waitress, come here please. Is this man's time more valuable than mine?" "He knew what he wanted," the waitress replied weakly. "So do I," said Margaret and gave her order. In both these instances, Margaret noted that she was particularly pleased she did not feel guilty when she asserted herself.

Margaret did not bring either of these situations on herself, but in the past, in passive masochistic fashion, she would have absorbed the slights and felt damaged by them. You may believe it is useless to protest every discourtesy you encounter. On the other hand, every injury you sustain reduces your sense of well-being and self-esteem.

A friend of mine in line at the food counter at Bloomingdale's had taken a number and was waiting her turn but stepped forward to get a better look at the fine assortment of cheeses. "You have to take a number, you know," the woman next to her snapped. "Yes, I have one," she replied. "Well, what are you elbowing ahead of me for?" her antagonist said nastily. "I just moved forward to get a closer look," said my friend. "I'm waiting my turn. It has nothing to do with you." Despite this, the unpleasantness continued, so my friend moved away. When her turn finally came, the clerk snapped at her as well, as if the attitude of the other woman were contagious. Refusing to be a passive masochistic victim of this unexpected and unwarranted rudeness, my friend asked if there was any reason for the clerk's unpleasantness and requested that he be more courteous. His manner changed, and she made her purchases in a much more agreeable atmosphere.

I witnessed another example of the refusal to be a passive victim while riding one day on the Third Avenue bus. A tall, somewhat surly looking young woman was sitting with her legs stretched out into the aisle. When a woman who was obviously well into her seventies approached, the young woman saw her but did not move her legs, and the older woman tripped and nearly fell to the floor of the bus, catching herself at the last moment. She looked over at the young woman who gazed back with a smirk and murmured, "I'm sorry." While the insincerity of this "apology" was evident, a masochistic person would have accepted it or, even worse, have said, "Oh, no, *I'm* sorry." Not this older woman. "What do you mean you're sorry?" she said forcefully. "What the devil were you doing with your feet out like that? You didn't even make any effort to move them. You damn well *ought* to be sorry!"

I am recommending assertion, not defiance, as one of the tools to help dig out of the masochistic morass. Often masochistc women have a great deal of secret anger and defiance, and they may veer from being overly compliant to being overly defiant. Neither extreme will serve to get them out of the masochistic position, however. Both are indications that the woman is still locked in a power struggle. Her behavior at either end of the spectrum is defensive.

Sometimes an incident is trivial, not worth the energy you would have to expend to address it, and you may decide that letting it go will not hurt your self-esteem. Other times, self-assertion may be imprudent or even dangerous. A friend of mine got on the subway and found it was crowded, but there was a section where several people were spread out, and she asked them collectively if they would mind moving over so that she could sit down. A large woman at the end of the row said, "I will not." "That's not fair," said my friend. "There's room for someone else to sit here and I don't want to stand." The large woman responded with a stream of invective. "Look," my friend insisted. "I have a right to a seat that I paid for where there is room. Please move over." Though there was still little effort to accommodate her, she shoved herself between two people, and gradually others shifted over to make room. Telling me about this afterward, she said that she felt everything she had done was appropriate, but that as she looked around the car and saw not one sympathetic face, she realized her stance might have been foolhardy in this situation. I had to agree.

When you experience one success in putting into practice new, nonmasochistic behavior, it leads to a second and then a third, in a domino effect. A new sense of self-worth helps you dig away at the tenacious foundations of the anticipatory defense system. All masochistic defenses are compulsive, that is, they recur repeatedly in order to avoid anxiety about expected attack and hurt. And anyone imprisoned in compulsive behavior necessarily suffers from rigidity and restriction. But when you begin to break through, there is an expanded sense of living and a new feeling of authenticity.

When you conduct your self-examination, I suggest that you keep a special kind of diary, writing down the ways in which you are aware of expressing your masochism. And as you continue the work of digging out, continue the habit of keeping notes. It takes only a few minutes and if there is not time when they occur, jot things down in the evening. Write down those occurrences that have been unpleasant or hurtful. At the end of a week or so, look over your notes and see if you can discern certain masochistic expressions or actions that turn up repeatedly. What do these reveal about you that you need to work on? Keeping a running log as you attempt to put new patterns into practice can help you to focus on the most troublesome areas and also to keep you abreast of your progress. It is also productive to keep a ledger on the credit side of your interactions. Note down those things you have said or done that you are particularly pleased with. See how they reflect improvements. This will raise your self-esteem and also show in what ways you have changed and suggest how you can continue to do so.

Another aid I would recommend to anyone having difficulty overcoming masochism is autohypnosis. The roots of masochism lie in good measure in the negative hypnotic imprints of early experience. Self-hypnosis, in conjunction with the other steps I have mentioned, may help to reverse the effects of those damaging imprints. The essential factor in self-hypnosis is to establish a kind of cue that will help you overcome a particular problem. Many people run groups that teach self-hypnosis, and you may want to explore that possibility. Or you can teach yourself by the following method, which is basically physical relaxation coupled with focused concentration.

The first step is to "write" a script. Fantasize a scene in which there are only positive elements. This would be different for everyone, of course, but for the purposes of illustration, let's say you are walking in the country. You feel the warmth of the sun, you note the way its rays sliver off the surface of the pond, you take in the lush, vibrant green of the trees around you and the colors of the wildflowers you pass. It is a truly glorious day, and you feel good just being a part of it. Then, let's say an attractive man approaches and says to you, "Isn't it a lovely day?" Try to think what response you might give that would allow you to continue feeling good. Construct for yourself a picture of how you would respond if you were happy, relaxed, comfortable, and enjoying a beautiful day.

Having written your script, practice sitting in a relaxed way in a comfortable chair, and each time you raise a finger in front of you and look at it, conjure up the image of the beautiful day and the pleasant encounter. Do this once a day, preferably at night. Allow yourself to experience the positive image, the good feelings, the sense that no one is criticizing you, and everything is all right. Gradually, with repetition (and that is crucial to make this work effectively), you will be able to sit back comfortably, raise your finger, and the pleasant feeling will be automatic. You are imposing new ideas on yourself—ideas of your own worth, your own acceptability, your own competence, and of your joy in life.

Now begin to address items you have written down in your notebook. Select a painful issue, an expression of your masochism that crops up regularly. Induce the hypnosis and, while you are in this positive frame of mind, think how you could behave in this situation. The response that comes to you from the midst of your good feeling will be very different from a response that is generated when you are feeling full of anxiety, self-hate, and guilt.

Another way to accomplish the self-hypnosis while sitting in a comfortable and relaxed fashion is to imagine two television screens in front of you. On one you project and see yourself acting the way you would ordinarily act out of fear, on the other, project the way you would behave if you were in harmony with yourself and not feeling threatened. Turn off the screen in which you act fearfully, and concentrate on the one showing how you act when feeling good about yourself.

Overcoming your masochistic tendencies is a demanding and challenging process that takes work, courage, and time. You will probably become discouraged on occasion, particularly when you find how obstinate these tendencies are. But if you persevere, the effort will be one of the most rewarding you will ever undertake.

Patricia Ball and Elizabeth Wyman, writing about battered wives in *Victimology*, proposed a list of entitlements that I believe can serve as a sort of bill of rights for masochistic women who are attempting to dig out of the masochistic defense system that has imprisoned them. These rights are listed below, and I suggest them as a framework for the effort of digging out.

Allow yourself:

1. to be angry
2. not to be abused
3. to change situations
4. to be free of *fear* of abuse
5. to *expect* assistance from policy and social agencies [or, I would add, from a trained, sensitive therapist, if you so desire]
6. to share your feelings
7. to want better communications
8. to leave a battering environment [any place where you are abused]
9. some privacy

10. to express thoughts and feelings [or, just as important, to keep them to yourself]

11. to develop your talents and abilities

12. to be less than perfect

13. to prosecute an abusive spouse [or to respond appropriately to anyone who injures you]

16

Masochism
on the Job

In the chapter about dreams, I described a young woman faced with a choice between attending one of the country's best graduate schools or accepting a high-level job offer with a substantial salary, enviable options but ones that caused her masochistic tendencies to burst into full bloom, leaving her distraught. She was beset by fears. She had made plans to enter school in the fall before the job offer occurred and feared reversing her decision. She was afraid, simultaneously, that she was not really qualified for the job and that she would be bored by it. She was afraid that as she came under closer scrutiny for the job that the offer would be revoked. She was afraid that if she took the job and delayed returning to school, her parents would be critical of her decision. She was afraid that the schools to which she had applied would not accept her in the future because she had turned them down. Each session we went over these fears as tears streamed down her cheeks.

Away from my office, meanwhile, she hurried from friend to friend, asking what they would do if they were in her place. At one point, she called her father, who had never been especially well disposed toward her, and asked him what she should do. Hearing that the job would pay her well over $50,000 his first remark was, "Boy, that's quite a salary." But he was no more helpful to her than anyone else had been. When I pointed out that the salary was probably higher than any he had ever received, and what a shock it must have been to hear that his pretty, "silly" little daughter (as he had always conceived of her) was thought to be worth such a substantial sum, she laughed and agreed.

We worked hard to discover the roots of her fears, of her sense of inadequacy. Her belief that other people would somehow have more valid answers for her than she could find for herself (she also noted that her repeated questioning of other people revealed her self-preoccupation and how annoyed people became with it). And we uncovered a piece of her early experience that accounted, at least in part, for her extreme disturbance.

Her mother's criticism of her had seldom been direct, and, as a result, it was difficult to detect. Her method had been constantly to compare Marjorie, my patient, to others, and always to Marjorie's detriment. "If Nancy were in this situation," her mother would say, "she would do thus and so." "Peggy would never do that." "Mrs. Andrews said *her* daughter would be doing this or that." And so on. This sort of subtle attack in which comparison is used to disparage the child is often more difficult to deal with than a direct onslaught. For one thing, it is harder to recognize. Marjorie did not realize what was causing her difficulty. It was as though she were shadow boxing rather than fighting a real opponent.

Despite these insights, Marjorie didn't really make much progress toward resolving her dilemma. One day in my office, extremely distressed and tearful, she began to rock back and forth, murmuring over and over, "What will happen to me? What will happen to me?" This reminded me of an experience of my own, and I recounted it to her. Once on a trip to Leningrad, I stayed behind at St. Isaac's cathedral after the group I was traveling with had gone on. I wanted some time alone with the lapis lazuli and malachite interior of that magnificent structure. When I eventually boarded the bus to return to my hotel, I suddenly realized I wasn't certain of its name, I didn't know at what street I should get off, and I didn't speak any Russian, so was in no position to make inquiries. Getting more and more upset, I clasped my hands in front of me and found myself saying aloud, "What will I do? What will I do?" Nearly everyone on the bus, it turned out, understood English, and a soldier helped me off at the proper stop and escorted me to my hotel.

Hearing this, Marjorie made an interesting and astute observation. "I said 'What will happen to me?'" she said. "It's so passive. But you said, 'What will I *do*?' You were searching for a solution—but I've been sitting and worrying about what would happen to me without my doing anything."

Marjorie's recognition of this was an indication that she had begun to overcome her masochistic problems. But I cite her story as an illustration of how damaging masochistic tendencies can be to a woman's professional life. Her behavior, if unexamined and unchecked, would almost certainly undermine, and perhaps even obliterate, the accomplishments that her gifts and her intelligence made possible.

The career woman must fight her masochism in both her personal life and in the competitive atmosphere of her professional world. In the latter, which turns on the axis of power—who has it, who does not—the stakes are especially high. The salary she will be paid, how far and fast she advances, the degree of respect she receives from colleagues—all these depend on how a woman comports herself. What she says and does takes on special significance. The "mistakes" a masochistic woman makes in her professional life, that is, those instances where she behaves in an unassertive, nonautonomous manner, will have far-reaching effects. Masochistic defenses, the masochistic communication style, are damaging whenever and wherever they occur. But when a career woman's professional conduct is shaped by these, the results can be devastating.

"If anything goes wrong, I immediately think it has to do with me. I spend a lot of energy trying to see how to avoid trouble, and I can't because it's unpredictable. I seem to be looking for the opportunity to make myself anxious. Sometimes I get all upset about things that don't even happen. Any change is threatening to me. Yesterday something happened that reminded me of my mother—or rather how I used to feel with her. My boss wasn't enthusiastic about a project I had finished. I immediately thought I would lose my job. Here I just got a promotion and an increase in salary, I knew he was upset about something personal, and yet I reacted as if it was my fault. I feel as if whatever I do, it's not enough."

It is not difficult to see the troublemaking potential of this young woman's outlook. Her passive grandiosity—dictating that she always puts herself at center stage—is unmistakable. She directs a great deal of energy toward activating anticipatory defenses, even though she recognizes that they are rarely effective. Rather than expressing *herself*, she tries to second-guess authority figures upon whom she has superimposed the images of powerful figures from childhood. She is inflexible and relentlessly critical of herself. She leaps to negative conclusions even in the face of evidence to the contrary. These masochistic tendencies are bound to interfere severely with her ability to function productively in her professional life.

To return for a moment to the tennis analogy, I would not describe her as having a very strong game. She probably wouldn't exhibit an effective return of serve, good reflexes at the net, or strong groundstrokes. She would be more likely to hit out blindly, miss the ball altogether, and then apologize profusely for her error. And all this because she is afraid of her opponent and is rendered ineffectual by that fear.

After some time in therapy, this young woman was doing much better but still had not left her masochism behind altogether. She started her own business, with partners, and one day in my office became aware that she explained her decisions to her partners in considerable detail, eliciting their opinions about them, while they informed her of their decisions after the fact. Describing her feelings of anger at this, she suddenly clapped her hand to her head and said, "I see what it is! I don't have to explain at all. But I do it to ward them off. I should make these decisions and act on them, just as they do. But I've been trying to avoid criticism, so I'm still acting as I did in the past but on a higher level." Obviously, it is gratifying to both therapist and patient when a sudden and important insight like this appears.

Considerations of power are paramount in business and career life, and power is the masochistic person's area of greatest vulnerability: she is quick both to attribute it to others and to disclaim it herself. This being so, the career woman with definite masochistic tendencies really ought to consider seeking the additional support and perception that professional help can offer.

But if you're going it alone, the first step toward overcoming problems is to focus on how your general masochistic tendencies are reflected in your business or professional life. What guises are your defenses most likely to take on in a career context? Only when you've identified and understood them can you go on to develop those special skills and strategies you will need to make your way ahead in business or a profession.

Even though it may not come naturally to you, expect respect. Try not to approach others fearfully but with confidence in what you have to say. And do not assume that what you have to say is any less vital or accurate or true than what someone else contributes.

Questioning someone else's premise is as important on your job as it is in your personal life. The other person's premise may not necessarily be wrong, but it is important that you examine it and decide whether or not you agree with it before you respond. Forgoing an immediate reply, taking the time to think something through, is extremely difficult for the masochistic woman. Because she anticipates attack, her instinct is to respond immediately in order to ward it off. She doesn't dare to wait and stay in that gray zone of ambiguity where her fate is undetermined. It has been said that "the certainty of misery tends to be preferred over the misery of uncertainty." And that aphorism could very well serve as the masochist's credo. But in career life, you must learn to take the time necessary to formulate an appropriate response. And it is up to you to do whatever is necessary to get that time for yourself. It might even mean saying to your boss, "I don't want to speak to you about this until the end of the day because I am working on something else now." Even the boss can be asked to adjust to realities.

One of Janet's partners, a man based in another city, was extremely competent in sales but knew very little about the creative side of their business in which Janet was involved. Nevertheless, whenever anything went wrong, he would call her up and launch into a harangue. "What's the matter with you?" he would ask. "You women just aren't to be trusted. You always slip up and make problems for me." At first, Janet responded to this by justifying herself, attempting to answer his specific complaints, and, by doing so, implicitly accepting his premise that she was at fault. Her early experience had conditioned her to expect censure even when she had done nothing wrong; she was an expert at assuming blame. But then she began to realize the part she played in permitting this kind of exchange to continue.

The next time her difficult partner was in town, she asked him to meet her for a drink. "I don't think you're really aware," she said to him, "of how hard I work, how much time I put in, and just how demanding the creative part of the business is. I'm as responsible as I can be, just as I'm sure you are at your end. And I don't want to receive phone calls that go on about women not being trustworthy. You're really defeating our purpose, which is to produce and sell goods and to do it well. When you tear me down, you're interfering with my ability to do my part, so I suggest you stop it." "You're absolutely right," he replied. "I know I get very difficult at times, and I'll try to be more careful about that in the future."

In finally speaking up and challenging her partner's premise, Janet defined the issue as she saw it and put the focus where it belonged: His behavior was counterproductive to the business. When she was able to point out that in fact the problem was *his* tendency to project blame onto others, the situation changed.

A woman with her own business took in a male partner who, with her masochistic collusion, was soon treating her as if she were his employee. One way she participated in this was to make remarks like, "I'm leaving a little bit early tonight because I have to get a manicure." The moment she volunteered that, he responded by twitting her. "I'm surprised you get any work done," he would say. "Obviously, you're more concerned with your fingernails than you are with the business." She gave him the opening; he took it. Gradually, however, she came to realize how she elicited such responses from him and began to change her behavior. She recognized that she was not accountable to him; she had no obligation to tell him where she was going when she left the office. It was, after all, her business. The only thing that mattered was that she be reachable if something important came up. "I'm leaving now," she began saying instead. "After five o'clock you can find me at such-and-such a number, if necessary."

Closely allied to challenging the other person's premise in a confrontation is the matter of timing. It is important to know that you can choose the proper time and place for a difficult encounter. You can decide when to act, and when not to.

Beva, a resident physician, was astonished and disturbed when an attending physician turned on her and said she was not a good resident. It was true that something had gone wrong that day but, in general, she was a capable and diligent doctor. She said nothing at the time and, in fact, retired as soon as possible to the ladies' room to cry (the right idea, because it's best to keep crying out of sight). This one negative comment made Beva feel she had been totally condemned. She spent a great deal of time working on this in treatment and did a lot of thinking about it on her own. She came to realize that this same attending doctor frequently made chauvinist remarks to her that bordered on a kind of sexual harassment. She began to understand both his position and her own more clearly.

Some months after the original incident, a similar remark was made to her. "Doctor," she replied this time, "would you mind giving me an outline of the things that lead you to say I'm not a good resident?" "Well," he said, "look at what happened today." "How about some other examples?" His silence indicated that he couldn't think of any. "Look," she said, "I've been on duty for sixty hours straight without a chance to sleep, and I've reached the point where it's very difficult for me to think. I may not have done the best possible in this instance, but that has nothing to do with the fact that I'm a woman. It has to do with the fact that I'm human and that there is a limit to one's endurance. Fortunately, nothing untoward happened. In the future, I'll thank you not to make unpleasant remarks to me. They don't help anyone." The doctor, to Beva's surprise, agreed with her, and their encounter ended on a positive note.

There may be times, of course, when you are caught by surprise and forced into an unexpected confrontation. Keep cool and remember that you are entitled to take time to think before replying. Try to decide if anything needs to be said or if silence might serve you best. If you decide to speak, ask the other person a clarifying question that will put him on the spot and temporarily take the heat off you. If you can use humor, do so—it's a great tension-reliever. Whatever the issue, present your side of it as clearly and simply as possible, and try to stand your ground.

Masochistic women must be careful not to fall back on knee-jerk excuses of gender or age when they encounter criticism in the work enviroment. Either of these factors may create trouble for you, but it is not helpful to rush to the conclusion that sex or age bias are at the root of all your difficulties. It is not helpful for a woman to begin a new job, for example, operating on the assumption that all the men in the company are against her. A them-against-us attitude will end up creating more problems than it solves. A woman who is not inclined to look for poor treatment, on the other hand, who is able to be generous in her judgments of her fellow employees, probably increases the odds that she will be accorded equitable treatment. When difficulty arises, try to stick to the issue at hand and deal with it on its own merits.

You may remember that TV anchorwoman Christine Craft charged that she was dropped by a Kansas City television station because she was "too old, unattractive, and not deferential enough to men." A jury awarded her $500,000 in damages. Despite a judge's setting aside this verdict and ordering a new trial, it seems obvious to me that Craft was *not* suffering from gender paranoia and that her difficulties did indeed stem from the fact that she was a woman who refused to meet certain male standards of appearance and conduct—and who rejected the idea of being old at thirty-seven.

In general, it serves a woman well to avoid controversy and keep larger goals in sight. A good way to bypass a clash over something unimportant is simply not to hear it. Ignore the provocative remark, the unjust implication, the inaccurate assessment. Don't get angry and sink into name-calling. This never settles an issue; it is only inflammatory. Choose to focus on the solution to a problem rather than on the "luxury" of venting emotion, for that is a luxury that may cost you dearly. Being reckless or defiant in an exchange with someone in a position of power is not self-assertive. It is destructive.

Tact does not come easily to masochistic people. Their energies are primarily directed toward the operation of their anticipatory defense system. Their self-preoccupation is enormous. Their narrow and intense focus on their own pain and their own problems often renders them incapable of concern for the feelings and sensibilities of other people. But in professional life, a gift for diplomacy is a great asset. Watch someone who is able to exercise diplomacy successfully. Use the energy you would ordinarily expend anguishing over your own mistakes to observe how tact works. It helps to shift the focus away from yourself and what is wrong with you and onto what is good and positive about someone else.

Maria is a researcher who works with a prominent scientist given to making rather oppressive demands on her, frequently, for example, asking her to attend to some minor busywork while she is in the midst of an experiment. The affirmative way she has learned to handle his intrusions is extremely effective. "Of course," she answers him, "I'll do it as soon as I finish this experiment." This response acknowledges his power by indicating that his request is reasonable and that she is willing to satisfy it. But, it also makes clear that her work is significant. Most important, it accomplishes both these things in a positive way that does not force a confrontation.

Masochistic dependence and an inability to trust one's own feelings and judgments can turn decision-making into prolonged agony. Masochists are fearful of making unilateral decisions and tend to seek support to bolster themselves. In one's career however, especially at higher levels, it is necessary to make judgments and settle problems on your own. As you begin to move toward autonomy and away from your masochistic defenses, as you learn to think things through alone and to create your own premises, you will be much better equipped to *act* independently. Margaret Thatcher, I am sure, consulted her ministers on the Falklands crisis, but she alone could, and did, make the decision to defend the islands. And she stood her ground in the face of criticism.

Learning to recognize and overcome your masochistic problems in the context of your work is half the battle. The other half lies in developing certain skills and strategies that can be crucial to professional success. Let me make some suggestions.

Try the truth. Suppose a masochistic woman is confronted with this dilemma: She is likely to put her foot in her mouth when she speaks up, but commitment to a career demands that she volunteer information. Opportunities for active masochism abound. My advice in this regard is to try the truth. Masochistic people learn early in life to sidestep it—evasions, half-truths, inchoate communications become their stock in trade. They can be quite unused to honest, direct expressions of information. The truth, if presented in a matter-of-fact way, is often much less troublemaking than the evasions you think will help you avoid trouble.

The effect of language. Language has been used for centuries as a subtle but deadly weapon with which to attack women. It is often used to denigrate them, confuse them, dupe them, and keep them in what men have deemed to be their place. Professional women must learn to recognize these attacks, however they are disguised, and to respond to them. They must learn to delve beneath the surface of the linguistic hypocrisy that is often characteristic of communications between men and women. They must learn to detect offenses and not let them go by unanswered. For each time an insult passes unremarked, it only leads to more of the same. Failure to respond to linguistic attacks constitutes a tacit acceptance of them.

The simplest form of linguistic attack occurs by attaching trivializing appellations to women. The most common of these is "dear." Anyone addressing you this way in a professional situation intends disrespect, you may be certain. The very use of the word is a denial of your professionalism, whether it comes from someone's secretary, an answering service, a client, or a colleague. I believe it often reflects the growing hostility that many men feel toward women as they are becoming more assertive and successful. Rather than absorbing this sort of assault and letting yourself feel damaged by it, try to respond to it, without anger, perhaps even with humor. Judge Shirley Levitan counterattacked in a most graceful and effective way when the lawyer who was trying the case before her addressed her as "dearie." "Correction," said the judge, "your Honor, dearie." (Of course, she was the one in power, which made it easier to be witty.)

A young physician reported that a doctor on the staff of the hospital where she was a resident frequently called her "honey." Eventually she was able to respond to this by saying, "Dr. So-and-so, I think it would be more helpful to me if you called me doctor. I'm just getting used to it at this stage in my professional life." She didn't attack him but enlisted his help and support instead.

Occasions may arise when it is difficult to respond to a linguistic attack. Perhaps the person addressing you is someone who holds great power: You are the newest member of a law firm and he is the senior partner. If the situation is such that it seems most prudent for you to accept "dear" or "young lady" without comment, be aware that you need not feel damaged by the slight, or obligated to absorb similar disparagement from the next person who comes along.

Another young doctor, a surgeon, was on her way to emergency room duty and passed the scene of an automobile accident. She stopped to help and was caring for the injured person when a second car stopped and a man rushed up and pushed her aside. "Stand back, lady," he said, "I know first aid." This happened to Dr. Jeanne Petrek, the first woman ever to receive a full-time faculty appointment in the Emory University Medical School Department of Surgery.

Another woman surgeon, Christine Haycock, recent President of the American Medical Woman's Association, accompanied by her husband, was driving a car with MD license plates. When a policeman stopped Dr. Haycock for speeding, he said to her husband, "Listen, doc, don't let your wife drive so fast." The conditioning that causes men never even to consider that a woman might be a doctor in these instances is the same conditioning that causes men to belittle women even when they achieve positions of status and power.

A microbehavioral study in 1955 by Margaret Mead and Helen

Wolfenstein concluded that an individual experiences between three thousand and five thousand transactions during the course of a day. I would estimate that for a woman probably five hundred of these are linguistic attacks generated by interpersonal exchanges, newspapers, television, magazines, etc. Fed into that remarkable computer, the human brain, what effect must these assaults have on a woman's sense of feminine identity and self-esteem? This kind of onslaught on another species would raise alarm. We would cry that it could not be expected to withstand such environmental pollution or encroachment on its territory, or slaughter of its young. We would designate it an endangered species. But when women are the object of such attacks, we barely notice. It just seems like business as usual.

A few years ago, I was to chair a conference at the annual meeting of the American Psychiatric Association, and part of my responsibility was to obtain and read beforehand all the papers to be presented. The conference was set for Monday, but on Saturday I still had not received a paper from one colleague. Then at *noon* on Saturday he called me. "Did I wake you?" he asked, a remark I think it unlikely he would have made to a male colleague. "Listen, honey," he went on, "I just couldn't get the paper done, but I'll have it at the meeting." I imagined the sort of judgments he would heap on a woman who was so late in delivering a manuscript. And I noted the "honey." "My dear Dr. So-and-so," I said to him, deliberately striking a tone of mild condescension by the counter use of the term of endearment, "since you're speaking to me in my office, I am hardly likely to have been asleep. As for the paper, it's unfortunate that you haven't been able to comply with rules everyone else was able to meet. It better be a good paper . . . and I'm sure it will be." I added this final remark to soften somewhat the tone of my admonition to him. After all, I had no desire to create an enemy. My interest was simply to rebut his derogation of me.

A compliment can often hide a linguisitic attack. In connection with the annual APA meetings, I had participated in a discussion on closed-circuit television. Afterward a colleague approached me and said: "Natalie, you looked great, just great."

"What did you think of what I had to say?" I asked. "I'm not interested in what I looked like." He obviously could not remember what I had said and was stunned that I had not graciously accepted his compliment. What more could any woman ask than to be told that she looked good? The professional woman, I cannot stress strongly enough, must ask a great deal more than that. She must ask that her work, not her appearance, be the focus of interchanges with colleagues.

Some years ago, I began paying attention to the jokes and stories that lecturers in academia used to "warm up" their audiences, and I was astonished at the number that were at the expense of women. These attacks are not readily discerned as such, veiled as they are by cleverness and humor; women may be just as likely as men to laugh at them.

When Professor Martin Roth, an expert on depression from England (he has since been knighted), spoke at the New York Academy of Medicine, he opened his lecture with this story. A group at Oxford was putting on a play about ancient Greece but found itself stymied by the setting, a Mycenean hut. Nobody knew what one looked like. The department of antiquities had two professors, one male, one female, and the drama group approached the male professor first and asked for his advice. "I can't tell you what a Mycenean hut would look like," he said, "because to the best of my knowledge there is no remaining record. But go to Professor Wetherall—you won't be able to *stop* her from telling you."

The following appeared in a newsletter called *The Executive Woman*, and it conveys superbly, I think, how the linguistic treatment of men and women differs.

How to Tell a Businessman from a Businesswoman

A businessman is aggressive; a businesswoman is pushy.

He is careful about details; she's picky.

He loses his temper because he's so involved with his job; she's bitchy.

He's depressed (or hung over), so everyone tiptoes past his office; she's moody, so it must be her time of the month.

He follows through; she doesn't know when to quit.
He's firm; she's stubborn.
He makes wise judgments; she reveals her prejudices.
He is a man of the world; she's been around.
He isn't afraid to say what he thinks; she's opinionated.
He exercises authority; she's tyrannical.
He's discreet; she's secretive.
He's a stern taskmaster; she's difficult to work for.

Sexual harassment. This is more common than is generally realized. It ranges from the bargain proffered by the boss, overtly or covertly—you have sex with me and I'll look after you—to the sexual innuendo of many male chauvinist remarks. Whatever temporary advantage the masochistic woman may think she gains by sleeping with her boss or by laughing at his chauvinist jokes will be canceled out by the price she pays: further loss of self-esteem. Sexual harassment should be seen for what it is: part of the power struggle between men and women. Nothing serves one better in a power struggle than the possession of self-respect.

Many women shy away from responding to sexual innuendo because they fear they will be branded "libbers." I certainly can think of much worse things to be called. In fact, I am proud to be known as someone who stands for the liberation of women. But suppose a man throws that label at you, and you are not comfortable with all its connotations. Perhaps he says, "You're not one of those women's lib types, are you?" "Why do you ask?" you could say, throwing it back to him, changing the venue, remaining noncommittal yourself. If he says, "Well, they're all man-haters," you might answer, "It would be just as foolish to hate all men as it would be to dislike all women because they want equality. Actually, I like men very much. But it's also true, since no one's perfect, that there have been times when men have been very uncaring and unfair to me."

What if an employer makes a direct sexual approach to you? "Look," you could tell him, "I know you can find any number of women who would be happy to oblige you, and all they would want is a nice evening out, not a job. But I'm interested in the job, and I know I can do competent work for you. Please let's have a real business relationship. Give me a chance to show you what I can do."

A case of sexual harassment a few years ago in the Italian government can serve as a cautionary tale to career women everywhere. Aprile de Puoti, a journalist, was expected to become the first woman to serve as spokesperson for the Ministry of Labor, a particularly gratifying prize to her, as the upper echelons of the Italian bureaucracy are almost entirely male. However, she was not chosen, and she believed she was denied the job because she rejected the sexual advances of Labor Minister Vincenzo Scotti. De Puoti appealed to a higher authority, Prime Minister Giulio Andreotti, in the hope that he might override Scotti and see that she got the job. Andreotti refused to intervene, however, and added insult to injury by making the outrageous statement that de Puoti should recognize that he was not in a position to "control the hormonal discomfort of [his] cabinet minister."

This was a traditional male response, implying that the problem was in de Puoti, not in the Labor Minister, and also implying that her very legitimate discomfort was of no concern. (This same principle lies behind Arab women being garbed in the chador, the thesis being that if women are not entirely covered, men will be aroused and, ispo facto, need to act out their arousal. Therefore, *women* must bear the burden and discomfort of controlling men's temptation.)

Applying for a job. Many masochistic tendencies come into play here. My overall advice is to remember the tennis match: take the serve and *return* it. Ask questions and volunteer as little as possible. Your prospective employer already has your resumé, so he knows what you have done. Your aim should be to extract from him the maximum amount of information about the job. When you must answer a question, be sure you pick the most factual answer: "I *did* thus and so and *achieved* this and that," rather than prefacing your answers with "I believe" or "I feel." Keep your answers brief and don't volunteer anything extraneous—unless it is to cite some special achievement or distinction.

The matter of salary is often difficult for women to handle because they tend to underestimate what they are worth. Force vourself to tack on an additional amount to the figure you think is acceptable.

Once women are settled in a job, they are often afraid to ask for advancement or, if they do, they are not prepared to present a well-documented case for the change. They tend to say simply that they want the new job or need the additional salary rather than factually noting the accomplishments that lead them to think they are qualified for a promotion or to receive more money. Let me give an example, however, of a young woman who handled the question of advancement in a positive way, even though she had been masochistic most of her life. Recently divorced, Florence managed to get her M.B.A. while looking after her two young children and soon thereafter took a job that didn't pay very well but seemed to have promise. After only three months, it was apparent that she was gifted in her field and her immediate boss was pleased by her work. But because she was new to the job, she was very poorly paid. In the past, Florence would have accepted the situation as it was, telling herself she had no right to make waves as she had just joined the company. But she decided instead that her new life called for new behavior.

She pointed out to her boss that because she had been eager to get into the company she had taken a job with inadequate compensation, especially in light of the fact that she had a family to support. She realized she had only been there three months, Florence said, but the quality of her work suggested that she was worth a great deal more than her present salary. Her boss readily acknowledged that her performance had been outstanding and that she was underpaid. He was not in a position to pay her more now, he said; however, in a few months, the business was going to be reorganized, and his plan was to create a new job for her that would carry with it a higher salary as well as a new title.

Florence thought this over carefully. Had she been assertive enough? Should she accept what her boss said and wait to see what transpired when the changes occurred? In light of his generally positive response to her, she decided that it was worth taking a chance on waiting. She had approached this situation in autonomous fashion: She called her views and her needs to her boss's attention, she heard his response and weighed it, then she agreed to wait—a wise choice. She got both her increased salary and new job when the company reorganization went through.

Being noticed. When I was a first-year resident in psychiatry, my notion was that if I did the best I could and worked hard, I would be recognized and rewarded. Nothing could be further from the truth, I quickly learned. It is up to a woman to call attention to her work, something men seem able to do almost automatically. A woman who is shackled by masochistic fear will find this difficult, for it involves speaking up for herself. But be assured that if you don't do it, it's very likely that no one else will. When it's appropriate, put some effort into a little honest self-promotion.

What not to talk about at work. Women have been conditioned into overtalking as a kind of social style. Masochistic women in particular have a strong bent in that direction. Spilling, as I have said, frequently leads them into disclosing self-damaging information. My advice is to leave all personal matters at home. Talking about your outside concerns really can't do you any good in the office; it may do you harm. Conversations can be overheard; you can easily be misquoted. When I step into my office each day and shut the door, the rest of my world ceases to exist, and my focus is exclusively on the work I am there to do. Women who want to be successful need to learn to shut certain doors during work hours.

Networking. Much has been written about the necessity of making contacts with other women in your field, and I mention it here just to underline its importance.

Finding a mentor. This also has been much discussed but deserves mention. Having someone in your field who shows you the ropes and keeps you informed is an invaluable asset. Having someone important take an interest in you enhances your self-esteem. You need not wait for someone to choose you: Reach out and be helpful to someone you would like to learn from.

Time out for yourself. Although this category has nothing to do with professional relations per se, it may be the most important of all, especially for those women who are working at double or triple jobs: career, wife, mother. If you work very hard to address all these responsibilities, you may feel you're too busy to set aside time for yourself. But this time is crucial, even if it amounts to no more than an hour or two a week. You need to feel that you can give to yourself, as well as to those around you. You need to feel that you are not always on call, ready to respond to other people's demands. Women have very different ideas of how to spend such time: reading a novel, going to a health club, meeting a friend, attending a concert, cooking alone in the kitchen, sitting on a park bench and thinking. Whatever it is, schedule time for it and insist on using that time just to please yourself.

The feelings that animate the masochistic system of anticipatory defenses are those of fear, submissiveness, and powerlessness. Their roots are in early childhood, where the child's first experience of power relations is poisoned by the treatment she receives from significant others. These significant others very quickly become powerful others, feared and dangerous figures who take up seemingly permanent residence in the masochistic psyche, kept alive by the masochist's compulsive superimposition of them upon nearly everyone she encounters. She populates her world with powerful others and then suffers at their hands. Diseased power relations—the fear of power in others, the inability to exercise it oneself—lie at the heart of masochism.

Jean Baker Miller, feminist psychiatrist and psychoanalyst, in a paper titled "Women and Power," writes eloquently and insightfully about the problems women have handling power. And she gives some vivid examples drawn from the professional arena. When she attended a meeting of sales workers, Dr. Miller observed sharp differences between the conduct of male and female salespeople. A woman getting up to report on her successful record would say: "I really don't know how it happened. I guess I was lucky this period." Or: "This must just have been a good month." A man would describe his performance this way: "First I analyzed components and figured out the trends in buying. Then I analyzed consumer groups. And I worked very hard, putting in overtime three-fourths of the month."

Dr. Miller also describes a woman who was explaining a project she had initiated. The work seemed to be very solid and the project was going well. "I think I'm really on to something here," the woman said, then quickly added, "but everybody probably knows this anyway." Dr. Miller points out in these instances the women's work was just as effective as the men's, but their style was to put themselves down in spite of it. In the latter example, one can see the woman struggling to be autonomous, to recognize her accomplishment and take credit for it, and then one sees how her fear intervenes and causes her to cancel out her positive achievement. It is as though she had written something on a blackboard, clearly and boldly, and then picked up an eraser and wiped it away.

The dictionary, Dr. Miller notes, defines power as "the faculty of doing or performing anything; force; strength, energy; ability; influence; dominion or authority over others." Her own definition, which stresses creative power, is "the capacity to produce a change, that is, to move anything from point A to point B." Generally in our culture, the myth has been maintained that women should not have power of any sizable dimension, nor do they really need it. Since they are viewed as nurturers, it has been considered natural, and fitting, that they use such power as they possess in the service of others, fostering the growth of others, what Dr. Miller terms "using their power to empower others." But women, too, have a *right* to develop, and they must learn to use power in ways that are gratifying to themselves.

Selfishness, I would say, is putting one's own needs first at all times, a quite different matter from putting oneself first when it is important to do so and the situation calls for it. But when women focus on developing their own interests, they are invariably labeled selfish, and this is something they fear greatly. Dr. Miller, elaborating on the notion of power and selfishness, tells of a worker in the health field who sought help because she was very depressed. Her depression originated not when things were going badly for her but when she began to recognize her full potential. She began to see that there were ways she could use herself creatively, that she could effectuate change, that she could do more interesting work and receive higher pay, that she could become more "selfish." It was at this point that fear blocked her, and self-criticism and self-blame produced her depression. The superwomen of today, those professional women who feel compelled to take care of everything themselves—work, husband, home, children—are extremely fearful of being called selfish. They work hard to prove that they are not, and they pay a high price for it.

We are all aware of the kind of labels men have been inclined to attach to women who seek to develop themselves, who use their power not to empower others but to get ahead themselves. And many of these labels (perhaps epithets would be more accurate) make "selfish" sound mild. Women have been given the message that the use of power is disruptive. The weight of centuries, present cultural forces, and their own conditioning all tell them this. Women have come to fear that using their abilities and powers for themselves is *dangerous*. If they strive to achieve, they will be judged unworthy, be unloved, and, ultimately, be abandoned. Unwilling to face such a risk, they flee from power rather than claim it.

At this point in history, the power struggle between women and men is well recognized, and it is a very real one. But perhaps even more crucial is the less overt, but decidedly pernicious, power struggle between women and women. In the past, women used their power to foster the growth of others; they were the powers behind the throne. If they worked for the advancement of their husbands, certain advantages came to them in terms of social position, economic wealth, and so on. Some women today continue to operate as powers behind the throne and do not want to give up what they see as the advantages of their present position in order to function as independent, autonomous people. They fear they may not succeed as well on their own as they do by channeling their energies and ambitions through their husbands. Other women are eager to discard the constrictions and limitations of old role definitions and gender stereotypes and to assume power in their own right. Women are a house divided. And that fact, more than any other, militates against the eradication of masochism in women. For until women can agree on the strategies necessary for them to achieve autonomy, power and its use will remain a serious and damaging problem. Deprived of outlets for the development of their own power, women will continue to fear power in others, to turn their anger and resentment back on themselves, and to cope with the world through the development of masochistic defenses.

One of Shakespeare's sonnets begins, "Let me not to the marriage of true minds admit impediments." It is a love poem, but its opening line embodies the guiding principle I wish all women could embrace together: that they strive to adopt an honest, loyal, helpful attitude toward one another and endeavor to see one another's points of view. With this kind of union among women, autonomy and authenticity would be free to develop and grow—and the suffering and self-destruction of masochism could be left behind.

17

Reaching Autonomy

When Freud sought a model for the problems of adolescent maturation, he turned to Sophocles' drama of Oedipus, interpreting this phase of life as a time when the boy wants to kill his father and marry his mother, the passive prize awarded the victor. This focus on the male figure, virtually ignoring the other half of the human race, was a reflection of what his disciple Ernest Jones called Freud's unduly "phallocentric" view of humanity. In my search for a model for the autonomous woman, I also discovered what I was looking for in Sophocles' Theban plays about Oedipus and his family. Antigone, Oedipus' daughter and my model, did not fit at all with Freud's view of women or generally with women of Freud's time. She was self-reliant rather than dependent, active rather than passive, a young woman motivated by high ethical purpose rather than narcissistic self-involvement, a young woman willing to think for herself and take risks rather than blindly assenting to the established order of things.

In *Antigone*, the last of the three Theban plays, Eteocles and Polyneices, Oedipus' sons, kill each other in battle. Creon, who has taken over as king of Thebes, decrees that Polyneices, having fought against his own city, must be denied burial and left on the battlefield to rot. "He must be left unwept, unsepulchered—a vulture's prize," his sister Antigone observes, adding, "And anyone who *disobeys* will pay no trifling penalty, but die by stoning in the city walls."

Antigone, however, is concerned with the indignity of her

brother's body being unburied, the insult to his memory, and the threat to his afterlife. She decides to bury Polyneices in defiance of Creon's edict, a decision that is not impulsive but carefully considered, a decision that she knows may have grave consequences. When she appeals to her sister Ismene for help, Ismene, who is truly "Freud's woman," resorts to the dodge that "traditional" women have continued to use for centuries: "[We must] remind ourselves that we are women, and as such not made to fight with men. For might is right, and makes us bow to things like this, and worse. . . . I bend before authority. It does not do to meddle." ("And worse" suggests rape and assault, horrors which women rarely had the strength to resist and which led them to feel that deference to men was their only protection.) Ismene recognizes and accepts her own subjugation.

Not so Antigone. It is said of her: "Submission is a thing she never learned." Antigone is *not* resigned to things as they are. She is willing to grapple with the established order, to risk taking a stand based on ethical commitment. She sees her action as doing the gods' bidding; she calls herself "sinner of a holy sin." Her act has a spiritual as well as an ethical component, and it is life-affirming even though it may end in her death. "I go to bury him," she says. "How sweet to die in such pursuit! To rest loved by him whom I have loved. . . . I shall not abandon him."

Antigone's defiance of Creon's command is an act of autonomy and independence that constitutes a mature self-realization. She does not defy Creon out of self-centered murderous rage, such as Oedipus displayed in slaying his father. She exhibits, on the contrary, altruism and lack of self-concern. Her defiance is an act of love. "It is not my nature to join in hating, but in loving," she says.

Electra in Aeschylus' *Oresteia* furnishes an interesting contrast to Antigone and one that encompasses some characteristics of masochism. (Fortunately, Freud did not select her as a universal example of femininity, although you may recognize in Electra elements of his metapsychology of women.) She was a father-worshipper and, like Ismene, a woman unable to think for herself. She would not dare to challenge the existing order or to make a difficult decision on her own. She is not capable of acting autonomously. Facing the funeral of her father, Agamemnon, she says: "Bondswomen . . . give me your advice. . . . What words contrive to please my father's ear? . . . Shall I use the customary prayer . . . or pour [oil] in silence without ceremony? . . . I beg you to advise me. . . . Do not be afraid to unfold your thoughts to me." Agamemnon was the be-all and end-all of her existence, and yet this allegedly loving daughter does not know how to worship at his grave and turns to others for direction. The process of hero-worship has left her empty of substance, without identity or self-knowledge. She is passive; she is nothing. She does what the worshipped person tells her to do, and if he is not there, she turns to substitutes for instruction.

Antigone, on the other hand, is a person in her own right. Facing life's dilemmas, she doesn't need to cast about for someone to direct her. She knows what her ethical standards are, and she acts in accord with them. Is it masochistic that she undertakes an action that may result in her death? I think not. Antigone doesn't act out of fear and the need to defend herself. She is guided by love, and her action is assertive, not defensive.

Haemon, Creon's son and Antigone's betrothed, loves and respects her for the very qualities that lead her to make her difficult decision. His values are closely allied to hers; his persona is as strong a contrast to the intemperate youthful Oedipus as Antigone is to Electra. Threatened by his father, Haemon declares his love: "You know, my father, how I prize your happiness. For sons and fathers crown each other's glory with each other's fame." And he continues, speaking to his father as an equal: "Then, don't entrench yourself in your opinion, as if everyone else were wrong. The kind of man who always thinks that he is right, that his opinions, pronouncements, are the final words, when once exposed shows nothing there. But a wise man has much to learn without a loss of dignity." Haemon, too, would join in loving, not hating.

Antigone is not the average woman. But she is what the average woman might become: a person of autonomy and high principle, not narcissistically self-involved, not defensively suffering, but willing to take risks to live authentically. When Freud asked his famous question, "What do women want? Dear God, what do women want?" he would have had to look no further than Antigone to find his answer.

It is hardly necessary, of course, to go as far back as ancient Greece to find instances of women leading their lives with autonomy. Eleanor Roosevelt was such a woman, one who, I feel certain, had masochistic problems of her own to overcome but who learned to respond to life's challenges with autonomy. There surely was a great deal of pain in her life. She lost her mother at an early age; her adored father was an alcoholic. When she married her handsome cousin Franklin, they went to live with his mother, a controlling, imperious woman who could only have exacerbated Eleanor's feelings of being a plain and insecure young woman in an elegant and assured family. When Franklin became ill with polio, Eleanor's role as server and need-supplier was emphasized. When his political life took him away a great deal, she must have been lonely. And his long affair with Lucy Mercer had to have caused her terrible suffering.

Yet as life forced these painful circumstances upon her, it also presented her with the role of President's wife, and she used that as an opportunity. She did not accept the premise that a First Lady should simply look nice and serve as hostess at official gatherings. When her role as wife and mother began to recede, she used the role of First Lady to speak out on behalf of the disadvantaged of this country and elsewhere. She saw that they were plentiful and needed a spokesperson; her life's experience caused her to identify with them. She traveled widely in her efforts to help people, and, during the war, she was often in dangerous circumstances.

Mrs. Roosevelt was ridiculed by many Americans because of her shrill speaking voice. She was unable to move comfortably in the world, secure in the knowledge that she was an attractive woman. Nevertheless, she went out on her own, speaking up publicly for those who had no voice. Later on in her life, she continued to speak out in her capacity as the United States representative to the United Nations. Despite the price to her personally, she did what she believed was right. This took a great deal of courage, and it was through an exercise of courage that Eleanor Roosevelt became an autonomous person. Her life, as it evolved, was very reminiscent of Antigone's. It contained autonomy, high principle, and risks. Notable for their absence were narcissistic self-involvement and defensive suffering.

It may surprise some that I would choose Jacqueline Kennedy Onassis as another First Lady who exhibited self-assertive, autonomous behavior when she encountered new directions in her life. Once in residence in the White House, she saw that it was in deplorable condition and undertook to restore it in a manner that was tasteful, elegant, and historically accurate. This task was quite different from the one Eleanor Roosevelt chose for herself, but it reflected an independent and authentic course of action just as surely as Mrs. Roosevelt's did.

I also discerned an admirable and distinctly autonomous bent in the caring way that Mrs. Onassis raised her children. It was obvious that where they were concerned, she had clear priorities and abided by them. I once read a story that was critical of her for ducking out on a luncheon because she wanted to see a film before deciding if it was suitable for her children. I think she should have been applauded for showing such concern. She is also to be admired for her efforts to keep her children out of the limelight and to protect them from media exploitation. The criticism directed at her for her interest in clothes and money has been particularly vicious, perhaps due to envy After all, don't most women share such interests? That Mrs. Onassis had been able to indulge these interests more than the average woman is due to her life circumstances, and I think it is ungenerous to judge her harshly for those. She seems to me a woman who has been certain of what was important to her, and she has successfully built her life around those values.

One has only to read one particular story about Dr. Rosalind Yalow, the Nobel Prize–winning scientist, to know that she is without question an autonomous woman. In the story, which appeared in the *New York Times*, Dr. Yalow was recalling the difficulties her husband encountered when he took his doctoral exams. One of his examiners challenged Aaron Yalow's answer, told him he was wrong, and he worried that he might have been. "I took my doctorate exam in September," Dr. Yalow then said, "and the guy was stupid enough to try the same thing on me. And my answer was, 'Goldhaber and Hye taught it to me *this* way, and if there's anything wrong, you better talk to them about it.' " (The 1983 Nobel Prize–winner in medicine, Dr. Barbara McClintock, echoed this when noting that her research had been considered unacceptable for a time. "That was all right," Dr. McClintock said. "When you know you're right, you don't care.") Dr. Yalow's statement was an audacious one—bold and fearless. In that intimidating situation, I can think of few women *or* men who would have dared to respond as Dr. Yalow did. Obviously, she was extremely confident of her abilities in her field, and, coupled with that, she had the courage to insist on what she knew. The day after the story appeared, several of my patients mentioned it to me. They were impressed and inspired, as was I, to hear of a woman conducting herself with such authority. They also recognized that it would have been impossible for them to behave this way.

Dr. Yalow's action reminded me of the young Beethoven's when, at the beginning of his career, he went to study with Haydn. Haydn was then a revered figure, one of the premier composers of his age. When Haydn did not accept some of Beethoven's beliefs about musical theory, Beethoven refused to study with him any longer.

The shameless old lady in the film of the same name, based on a Günter Grass novel, developed the capacity for autonomy after she became a widow late in life. She began to believe that she was entitled to be free and to pursue those elemental pleasures that interested her, such as buying a few new kitchen utensils or having her hair washed by a young woman hairdresser with whom she becomes friendly. This occurs on a very simple level, but that does not make it any less autonomous. This woman, despite her advanced age, has discovered that she can define her own life rather than living the one imposed on her by the male-dominated Italian society. When her grown sons attempt to force her back into her old behavior, she stands up to them.

Rosina Lhevinne, the renowned piano teacher, might seem to be an example of autonomy abandoned, rather than achieved. Just days after marrying the great pianist Josef Lhevinne, she gave up playing the piano in concert although she was herself at the beginning of a promising career. Years later she explained, "I always thought there would be a certain rivalry, which would be absurd, because I didn't put myself on the same plane with him." Mr. Lhevinne, apparently, did not applaud her decision. When she would talk about her "little hands and little feet," he would correct her and say, "Nothing of the sort—regular hands and regular feet." Nevertheless, she stuck to her decision and always deferred to her husband's talent. At one point in their married life, they were invited to play a concert together. Afterward a friend told Mme. Lhevinne she was really the better of the two. "No!" she shouted, and insisted she would never play in public again.

But within these self-imposed strictures, Mme. Lhevinne did achieve a kind of autonomy in her career as teacher and developer of some of this century's finest pianists. She was nurturing the talent of others, but in doing this superbly she made a place for herself as someone other than just the wife of Josef Lhevinne, establishing for herself a life filled with all kinds of satisfactions.

Gloria Steinem could certainly be considered an autonomous woman. She recognized early how disenfranchised and subservient women were, how difficult it was for them to act with autonomy. But speaking for herself she said, "If you're willing to pay a price for it, you can do anything you want to do. And the price is worth it." And Barbara Honegger acted with autonomy when she resigned from the Justice Department after calling the Reagan Administration's efforts to eliminate sex discrimination a "sham." She is certainly an Antigone. She was willing to give up her job in order to speak out on a matter of principle and to do what she could to help women, despite the risks involved.

Most men do not need to struggle to achieve autonomy in the same way women do. It more or less goes with the territory of being male. And there is another quality men frequently possess that, I regret to say, I have virtually never seen in a woman. This is a kind of expansiveness or geniality that, I suspect, comes from having lived a successful life in an unrestricted, unhampered fashion. One definition of genial is "favorable for life, growth, or comfort." Men often grow up in conditions that could be defined thus, women rarely, as Virginia Woolf asserted in *A Room of One's Own*. There are many men who have felt, as the expression goes, that the world is their oyster. Very few women experience this sense of privilege. The world has not been eager to develop autonomy in women, to support and nurture their talents and abilities, to spend money or time to create conditions that will foster benign and joyous growth—and expansiveness—in them. And it shows.

I remember when Paul Robeson first appeared on the scene he possessed this expansive quality. Although he was black, his prodigious gifts as football hero, singer, and actor had gained him wide acceptance, and he obviously reveled in this. Robeson never set himself apart from other blacks, however, and he attempted to use his own good fortune for the benefit of his race, believing that acceptance for *all* blacks was possible. When he saw this was not so, and when people began to vilify him for his efforts on behalf of his race, when the red-baiters accused him of being a communist, he began to lose his wonderful expansiveness.

Being a woman in the world can have this same shriveling effect. Lack of power and lack of support erode what is magnanimous in a person. To possess this expansive quality, you must have had the following advantages: loving, caring parents who were delighted to have you from the moment of birth (males surely hold an advantage here); an environment that supports your growth; and a world that accepts you at the height of your creative abilities. The chances of a woman having all these things is indeed slim.

I have often thought that Golda Meir may have come close to enjoying such conditions in the course of her life. For her to have become the woman she was, she must have been welcomed, accepted, and loved by her parents. She never bore what could almost be thought of as the liability of physical beauty; undistracted, men simply responded to her competence. Her success may have come about in large measure because people virtually ignored the fact that she was a woman. Mercifully free of the sort of narcissism one sees in so many of today's political leaders, indifferent to the accoutrements of power, she had one overriding priority: to see Israel established and flourishing as an independent state. In her single-minded devotion to this one goal, she almost grew up like a man, she was virtually accepted as a man, she became Prime Minister of Israel as though she were a man.

Autonomy can appear in many guises, just as masochism can. But always, whether it shows itself in a political figure, a president's wife, or an elderly Italian widow, its cornerstone is authenticity, being true to oneself.

The Big Country, a huge, brawling, marvelous western film always sticks in my mind as a powerful illustration of this principle. Gregory Peck, who plays the hero, is a man from the East who has met and fallen in love with the daughter of a rancher, and they have decided to marry. When he goes West to meet her family, her father welcomes him warmly, but the foreman of the ranch, who had his own designs on the daughter, becomes an instant enemy who never passes up an opportunity to attack Peck. The brothers who own a neighboring ranch are cohorts of the foreman and one day they rope Peck and drag him through the dusty open spaces of the ranch. The father is incensed and vows to help Peck seek revenge. But when Peck demurs and says he does not think it is worth a big fight, the father brands him a coward, and it is clear that the daughter is beginning to make the same judgment.

There is on the ranch an ornery horse that no one has ever been able to ride successfully, and the foreman challenges Peck to ride him. No, Peck says, knowing what the foreman intends, but perhaps another time, maybe next week. The daughter becomes more and more disgusted by Peck's refusal to exhibit a macho style. During the week, Peck spends every night attempting to ride the horse, being bucked off and clambering back on, gentling the horse, finally teaching him who is master. He also during this period walks away from a brawl with the foreman, saying he does not believe in fighting. But the next time the foreman challenges him to ride the horse, he does so, and with authority, to everyone's amazement. The horse is gentle as a lamb. The daughter's interest in him is revived, of course, but he spurns her because their values are so different.

This film speaks of both the strategies of autonomy and its essence. It says that you can choose the time, the place, and the premises for any confrontation. You need not rise to the bait just because it is there. You need not be forced into "proving" yourself on someone else's terms. You can have your own definition of what a man, or a woman, is. And that definition is forged from those qualities in you that are authentic, those principles that are primary.

Aristotle's remark on dissent seems appropriate here: "Anybody can become angry—that is easy; but to be angry with the right person, and to the right degree, and at the right time, and for the right purpose, and in the right way—that is not within everybody's power and is not easy."

Autonomy is shaped by the determination to think for yourself. It is a freedom from tyranny, outer or inner; freedom from the tyranny of fear of exclusion or mistreatment; freedom from compulsion. The autonomous woman is not bound by the acquiescent, servile, secretly hating but outwardly conforming behavior patterns that result from capitulation to the prevailing cultural notions of what a woman should be. She is neither defiant nor imprisoned by defenses against a pervasive anxiety or by the anger, vindictiveness, self-contempt, and self-hatred that forced submission so often generates. The autonomous woman asserts herself as she *must*, not fearful of male power, not primarily concerned with male judgment. Her image of who she is and how she must live has been interiorized; it rests securely within her, safe from outside attack.

In the early years of this century the poet Rainer Maria Rilke described, in *Letters to a Young Poet*, a magnificent vision of the future of woman that might serve as a beacon for those women who are today seeking to move toward autonomy:

> The girl and woman, in their new, their own unfolding, will but in passing be imitators of masculine ways, good and

bad. . . . [The] humanity of woman, borne its full time in suffering and humiliation, will come to light when she will have
stripped off the conventions of femininity in the mutations of
her outward status, and those men who do not yet feel it approaching today will be surprised and struck by it. Some day
. . . there will be girls and women whose name . . . will be
something in itself, something that makes one think, not of
any complement or limit, but only of life and existence: the
feminine human being.

Bibliography

Abrahamsen, David. *The Murdering Mind*. New York: Harper & Row, 1973.

Aquinas, St. Thomas. Articles on the Production of Woman. *Summa Theologica*. New York: McGraw-Hill, 1964.

Ball, Patricia G., and Elizabeth Wyman. "Battered Wives and Powerlessness: What Can Counsellors Do?" *Victimology* 1977–78: 2:545–553.

Barbara Dominick A. "Masochism in Love and Sex." *American Journal of Psychoanalysis* 1973: 33:73–79.

Bard, Morton, and Dawn Sangrey. *The Crime Victim's Book*. New York: Basic Books, 1979.

Benson, Ruth C. *Women in Tolstoy*. Chicago: University of Illinois Press, 1973.

Bernard, Jessie. *The Female World*. New York: Free Press, 1981.

Bickel, Alexander M. *The Morality of Consent*. New Haven: Yale University Press, 1975.

Bieber, Irving. "Sadism and Masochism." *American Handbook of Psychiatry Vol. III*. Edited by S. Arieti. 2nd Edition. New York: Basic Books, 1974.

Bowlby, John. "Nature of the Child's Tie to His Mother." *International Journal of Psychoanalysis* 1958: 39:35–373.

———. "Separation Anxiety." *International Journal of Psychoanalysis* 1960. 41:89–113.

Bruch, Hilde. *Eating Disorders*. New York: Basic Books, 1973.

Chernin, Kim. *The Obsession: Reflections on the Tyranny of Slenderness*. New York: Harper & Row, 1981.

Crecelius, Kathryn J. "Do You Want to Grow Up like Her?" Lecture given at the Annual Meeting of the Society of Women Engineers, 1979.

Dalton, Debra, and James Kantner. "Aggression in Battered and Non-battered Women as Reflected in the Hand Test." *Psychological Reports* 1983: 53:703–709.

Dinesen, Isak. "Sorrow-Acre." *Women in Fiction Vol. 2.* Edited by S. Cahill. New York: New American Library, 1978.

Eidelberg, Ludwig. "Zur Metapsychologie des Masichismus." *International Journal of Psychoanalysis* 1935: 15:245–251.

Einstein, Albert. *The Born-Einstein Letters,* London: Macmillan, 1971.

Eisenbud, Ruth Jean. "Masochism Revisited." *Psychoanalytic Review* 1967: 54:561–582.

Erikson, Erik. *Childhood and Society.* New York: W.W. Norton, 1950.

Fine, Reuben. *The Hate Affair.* Lecture given at Symposium on Sadomasochistic Relationships, April 7, 1979, New York City.

Francoeur, Robert T. *Eve's New Rib.* New York: Harcourt Brace Jovanovich, 1972.

Freud, Sigmund, "A Child Is Being Beaten." (1919). *Collected Papers, Vol. II.* New York: Basic Books, 1959.

———. "The Economic Problem of Masochism." *Collected Papers, Vol. II.* New York: Basic Books, 1959.

Fromm, Erich. *The Anatomy of Human Destructiveness.* New York: Holt, Rinehart & Winston, 1973.

Garnett, David. *Lady into Fox.* New York: W.W. Norton, 1966.

Gelles, R. J. *The Violent Home.* Beverly Hills: Sage Publications, 1972.

Green, Maurice R. Review of *Understanding Sexual Attacks* by D. J. West, C. Roy, and F. L. Nichol. *Bulletin of the American Academy of Psychiatry and Law* 1982: 3:224.

Harlow, Harry F. "Primary Affectional Patterns in Primates." *American Journal of Orthopsychiatry* 1960: 30:676–684.

Haskell, Molly. *From Reverence to Rape.* New York: Holt, Rinehart & Winston, 1974.

Horney, Karen. "The Problem of Feminine Masochism." *Feminine Psychology.* Edited by H. Kelman. New York: W.W. Norton, 1967.

Krafft-Ebing, Richard von. *Psychopathia Sexualis* (translated from the 12th German edition by F. S. Klaf). New York: Stein & Day, 1965.

Langstern, Barbara. "Worries: What They Say about You." *Vogue*, December 1982.

Lessing, Doris. "To Room Ninteen." *A Man and Two Women and Other Stories*. New York: Simon & Schuster. 1958.

Levy, David M. "Maternal Overprotection." *Psychiatry* 1938: 1:564; 1939: 2:563.

Luce, Ralph. "From Hero to Robot: Masculinity in America, Stereotypes and Reality." *Psychoanalytic Review* 1967: 54:608–630.

Merriam, Eve. *The Double Bed (From the Feminine Side)*. New York: Marzani and Munsell, 1958.

Michaud, S. G., and H. Aynesworth. *The Only Living Witness*. New York: Simon & Schuster, 1983.

Mill, John Stuart. *On the Subjection of Women*. 1869; reprint, New York, Fawcett, 1972.

Miller, Jean Baker. "Women and Power." *Work in Progress*. Wellesley College Press 1982:82–01.

Morris, Rosemary. *Suffering Women: Feminine Masochism in Novels by American Women*. Ann Arbor: University of Michigan Press, 1975.

O'Connor, Frank. "Fish for Friday." *New Yorker*, June 18, 1955.

Pepitone-Rockwell, Fran. "Counseling Women to Be Less Vulnerable to Rape." *Medical Aspects of Human Sexuality*, January 1980.

Phelps, Stanlee, and Nancy Austin. *The Assertive Woman*. San Luis Obispo, Calif.: Impact Publishers, 1975.

Press, Shirley. "No One Wants Girls Except . . . " Letter to the *Journal of the American Medical Association* 1983: 249:2305.

Rilke, Ranier Maria. *Letters to a Young Poet*. New York: W.W. Norton, 1954.

Rioch, J. McK. "The Transference Phenomenon in Psychoanalytic Therapy." *Psychiatry* 1943: 6:174.

Rosenbaum, Mai-Britt. "Gender-specific Problems in the Treatment of Young Women." *American Journal of Psychoanalysis* 1977: 37:215–223.

Rosenman, Stanley. "Inner Promotings of the Victimizer as Illustrated in the *Psychodynamics of Anti-Semitism*." Lecture given at Symposium on Sado-masochistic Relationships, April 8, 1979.

Rossiter, Margaret H. *Women Scientists in America: Struggles and Strategies up to 1940*. Baltimore: John Hopkins University Press, 1982.

Roth, Geneen. *Feeding the Hungry Heart: The Experience of Compulsive Eating*. Indianapolis: Bobbs-Merrill, 1982.

Ruggiero, Josephine, and L. C. Weston. "Sex-role Characterization of Women in Modern Gothic Novels." *Pacific Social Review* 1977.

Sack, R. L. and W. Miller. "Masochism: A Clinical and Theoretical Overview." *Psychiatry* 1975: 38:244–257.

Scully, Diane, and Joseph Morella. "Why Men Rape." *Virginia Commonwealth University Magazine* 1983: 12:2.

Seidenberg, Robert. *Corporate Wives—Corporate Casualties?* New York: AMACON, 1973.

Selkin, J. "Don't Take It Lying Down." *Psychology Today*, January 1975.

Shainess, Natalie. "Psychological Aspects of Wife-Battering." *Battered Women*. Edited by Maria Roy. New York: Van Nostrand Reinhold, 1977.

———. "Psychological Significance of Rape." *New York State Journal of Medicine* 1976: 76:2044–2049.

———. "Vulnerability to Violence: Masochism as Process." *American Journal of Psychotherapy* 1979: 33:174–190.

Shulman, Irving. *Jackie: The Exploitation of a First Lady*. New York: Trident Press, 1970.

Spitz, Rene A., and W. Godfrey Cobliner. *The First Year of Life*. New York: International Universities Press, 1965.

Stolorow, Robert D. "The Narcissistic Function of Masochism and Sadism." *International Journal of Psychoanalysis* 1975: 56:441–447.

Sullivan, Harry Stack. *The Collected Papers of Harry Stack Sullivan*. Edited by H. S. Perry and M. Gawel. New York: W.W. Norton, 1953.

Tavris, Carol. "The Imposter Phenomenon." *Vogue*, December 1982.

Thompson, Clara. "Penis Envy in Women." *Psychiatry* 1943: 6:123–131.

Ullman, Montague. "The Social Roots of the Dream." *American Journal of Psychoanalysis* 1960: 22:180–196.

Walker, Lenore. "Battered Woman and Learned Helplessness." *Victimology* 1978: 2:525.

Wallerstein, J. S. and J. B. Kelly. "Effects of Parental Divorce." *American Journal of Orthopsychology* 1976: 42:20.

Weakland, John W. "The 'Double Bind' Hypothesis of Schizophrenia and Three Party Interaction." *The Etiology of Schizophrenia*. Edited by D. Jackson. New York: Basic Books, 1960.

Woolf, Virginia. "The New Dress." *A Haunted House and Other Stories.* New York: Harcourt Brace Jovanovich, 1944.

———. *Orlando.* New York: New American Library, 1960.

Zemlich, M. J. and R. I. Watson. "Maternal Attitudes of Acceptance and Rejection during or after Pregnancy." *American Journal of Orthopsychiatry* 1953: 23:570.

Index